A Woman's Will

A Woman's Will

The Changing Lives of British Women, Told through the Things They Have Left Behind

Viki Holton

AMBERLEY

First published 2023

Amberley Publishing
The Hill, Stroud
Gloucestershire, GL5 4EP

www.amberley-books.com

Copyright © Viki Holton, 2023

The right of Viki Holton to be identified as the Author of this work has been asserted in accordance with the Copyright, Designs and Patents Act 1988.

ISBN 978 1 4456 9243 2 (hardback)
ISBN 978 1 4456 9244 9 (ebook)

All rights reserved. No part of this book may be reprinted or reproduced or utilised in any form or by any electronic, mechanical or other means, now known or hereafter invented, including photocopying and recording, or in any information storage or retrieval system, without the permission in writing from the Publishers.

British Library Cataloguing in Publication Data.
A catalogue record for this book is available from the British Library.

1 2 3 4 5 6 7 8 9 10

Typesetting by SJmagic DESIGN SERVICES, India.
Printed in the UK.

CONTENTS

Introduction: Anne Trigg and the Body Snatchers   7

1 In the Beginning with the Anglo-Saxons and Slaves   14
2 Wives, Widows and a Thief Called Cutpurse Moll   29
3 Witches Historic and Modern   44
4 The Extreme Danger of Dying in Childbirth   52
5 Fewer Wills and Far Less to Leave   65
6 A Green Parrot, Two Grandsons and Sutton Hoo   80
7 A Castle in Norfolk and Feather Beds   94
8 Jane Austen and the Regency Era   104
9 Actors and Miss Burdett-Coutts, the Wealthiest
   Woman in England   116
10 *The Tale of Peter Rabbit* and the National Trust;
   Votes for Women   129
11 Emily Tinne's Wardrobe and Emily Green, a Servant   141
12 1,000 Years of Women's Lives and Women's Wills   151
13 Other Wills: Molly the Bruiser, Chasing Butterflies
   and Harvard University   196

What You May Not Know about Wills	222
Glossary of Common Terms Used in Wills	224
Appendix 1: The Woman Who Stole Our King! Wallis, Duchess of Windsor and Her Jewels	229
Appendix 2: Northampton Wills: Women's Voices from the Fifteenth Century	241
Appendix 3: The Will of Lady Margaret Beaufort	247
Notes	253
Bibliography	269
Index	284

Introduction

ANNE TRIGG AND THE BODY SNATCHERS

In 1769, Anne Trigg of Stevenage asked in her will that her age not be disclosed. It was certainly an unusual request, though some women in modern times are similarly reluctant to reveal their age. However, another request was probably unique: she left 40 shillings to pay for her uncle Henry to be buried, even though he had died more than forty years before in 1724. Afraid that his body would be dug up by graverobbers, Henry had asked in his will for his coffin to be stored in a loft rather than buried in a graveyard. This story was once so well remembered in Stevenage that a blue plaque marks the site where Henry Trigg's coffin was safely kept.

But more about this later.

Whether famous, infamous or just like us, the stories of the wives, mothers, sisters, mistresses, aunts, daughters and grandmothers long ago are often hard to find in standard texts. Indeed, this book began as a way to hear women's voices from earlier times.

Books, diamonds, recipes, mourning rings, tapestries, wedding veils, silver spoons, feather beds, cattle and sheep – not to mention 'my best red petticoat' and 'my worst petticoat' – are all mentioned as bequests in women's wills. There are gifts of money for the poor, and in particularly wealthy cases a chantry or an almshouse. Clothes – 'my best beaver hatt' – are left to female friends and relatives, along with gifts for the local church plus so many small, sentimental gifts to remember the person who has died.

Few women feature in the history books, and by looking at women's wills we can glimpse something of the lives they led, and their hopes and sorrows, to appreciate some of the constraints and prejudices they encountered. Women undoubtedly played their own part in British society through every age, in every town and village.

The 'ideal' woman in almost every earlier age was virtuous and modest, dutiful and obedient, first to her parents and then to her husband – her 'lord and master'. Beauty and a good dowry were valued far more than intelligence. Women were considered inferior to men in earlier times, as reflected in the title of Antonia Fraser's book about the seventeenth century, *The Weaker Vessel*.[1] This Bible quote highlights the general belief of those times that women were less capable than men.

Women's past power and influence is mostly invisible. Few inherited aristocratic titles or family estates as invariably these passed from father to eldest son in a system known as primogeniture, excluding younger sons and all daughters. When there was no son, inheritance was 'entailed', meaning it was directed to the nearest male relative. This can be seen in Jane Austen's *Pride and Prejudice*, in which the pompous cousin Mr Collins is set to inherit the family estate of Longbourn while the five daughters must hope instead to find rich husbands.

Chequers, now the Prime Minister's country residence, passed between families due to marriage or inheritance, as did Marble Hill and Wrest Park (from aunt to nephew) and Waddesdon Manor (from Rothschild aunt to great-nephew), marking them out as just a few of the important country houses linked to women. Another is the seventeenth-century manor house Weston Hall, which until recently belonged to the Sitwell family; bequests between mother and daughter, or aunt and niece, meant it passed across six generations of the female line.

The earliest female wills are surprisingly old, belonging to the Anglo-Saxon era, predating the Norman Conquest of 1066. Most were written by wealthy widows who owned a good deal of property and had a great deal to bequeath. While Anglo-Saxon men and women were both likely to leave land and money to the Church, in their other bequests we find distinct differences reflecting their respective spheres of life.

Weapons were an important part of life for the Anglo-Saxon man. England was by necessity a warrior kingdom, with frequent battles and Viking raids. Excavations at Croft Gardens in Cambridge have revealed sixty early Saxon graves including grave goods, short blades, bronze brooches and bead necklaces. Even young boys might be buried with a spear and a sword.[2] Some men included weapons such as javelins and swords in their bequests.

Women, however, were more likely to include in their wills domestic items such as clothes, wall hangings and chair covers.[3] The pride they took in their embroidered tapestries, homespun sheets, napkins and towels is clear in every age right through to the nineteenth century when large-scale manufacturing took away the importance of such items. Even the term for a single woman, spinster, comes from the fact that young, single women in medieval and early modern households often did the spinning. (It was only in Georgian times that spinster became a derogatory term for old maids, a caricature of a woman too ugly to marry.) A woman in early Saxon times might be buried with small weights from a weaving loom or spinning whorls, or with the 'keys' for the household.

A number of wealthy lady patrons in medieval times founded some of the earliest colleges at Oxford and Cambridge. By the time of the Dissolution of the Monasteries in the sixteenth century they were centres of learning, but initially their purpose was purely religious. These were places for priests to pray for the souls of the founder, their family and their friends – sometimes a will stipulated 'for all Christians'. Such prayers were essential to ensure the deceased could travel through purgatory and reach heaven more speedily. The colleges also educated priests.

With the Dissolution came the new Protestant faith. The Catholic prayers for the dead officially ceased, and so the primary role of the colleges became the education of men. Gradually, the colleges emerged as the type of institutions of learning familiar today – but only for male students.

Aristocratic, wealthy, influential and deeply religious women played a crucial but largely forgotten part in founding medieval colleges at Oxford and Cambridge. They could not have imagined that their colleges for prayer would be transformed into our modern university colleges of education. Oxford has Balliol College, co-founded in 1263 by John Balliol's widow Dervorguilla of Galloway, and The Queen's College, established in 1341 in honour of Philippa of Hainault, wife of Edward III. Cambridge, meanwhile, boasts Pembroke (founded in 1347 by Marie de St Pol), Clare (re-founded in 1338 by Lady Elizabeth de Clare), Queens' (founded in 1448 by Margaret of Anjou), Christ's College and St John's (re-founded in 1505 and founded in 1511 respectively by Lady Margaret Beaufort) and Sidney Sussex (founded in 1596 by Frances Sidney).

Another type of lady patron appears in modern times, helping the National Trust in its earliest and most difficult years. The trust was created in 1895, and at the time there was considerable doubt it would survive. It needed generous people to lead the way, and one of these was Mrs Fanny Talbot (d. 1917), who in 1895 gave the National Trust its first piece of land. Close to her home, it was roughly 4 acres at Barmouth in Gwynedd, Wales. Known as Dinas Oleu, or Fortress of Light, the hilltop plot has a remarkable view of the surrounding countryside.

Even as late as the 1950s, when Sybil, Lady Bedingfeld (d. 1985) gave Oxburgh Hall to the National Trust, few people knew about its work. There were fewer than 8,000 members (these days there are more than 5 million). Lady Sybil was determined to save the fifteenth-century moated hall which had been the home of the Bedingfelds since 1482. Thanks to her powers of persuasion, the family raised the £5,000 needed to buy it back and then handed it to the trust. It came within a whisker of being lost; when purchased it was being prepared for demolition by a timber merchant who calculated only the financial value of what stood before him rather than appreciating any of its beauty or historic importance. While Oxburgh Hall was spared, many other country houses during the early part of the twentieth century did see their woodlands cut down for timber.

Men also gave generously to the National Trust, but a number of women's bequests made all the difference, among them the Lake District farms given by Beatrix Potter and 70 acres of land at Box Hill owned by pioneer photographer Miss Agnes Warburg. It is also worth noting that many of these women were part of a new generation: wealthier, more independent, and owning property in a way they did not in earlier times. Some were childless, too, allowing them to consider bequests outside of the family.

Helena Cooper was similarly motivated in giving her father's traditional 1920s farm of 160 acres. Obriss Farm in Kent, given to the Landmark Trust, was one of the last of its kind before intensive farming swept away all that had gone before. The Landmark Trust, though a minnow by comparison, is like the National Trust in its mission to save important buildings which otherwise might be lost.

In the early 1980s, the Landmark Trust was fortunate to receive Elton House, a Georgian townhouse close to Bath Abbey, from Miss Philippa Savery (d. 1996), who had spent years patiently acquiring the leases of various sub-flats before returning the house to its former glory. Her antique shop on the ground floor was immensely popular with locals. She also played a key role in the battle to save the town's historic architecture during the 1970s, opposing powerful developers who wanted to replace Bath's Georgian splendour with modern buildings.

There also are the bequests of women travellers. Gertrude Bell (1868–1926) found her calling in the Middle East. She was as widely respected as Lawrence of Arabia for her influence and expertise in the region's politics in the early 1900s. Her passion for archaeology was equally strong, prompting her to leave the considerable sum of £6,000 to the British Museum to fund a school of archaeology in Iraq, which was duly created in 1932. For context, Stonehenge (and 30 acres around it) was sold at auction for £6,600 in 1915.

Another woman sharing that same spirit of adventure was Marianne North (1830–1890), an artistic genius who travelled the world painting flora and fauna. She gave over 800 glorious paintings to Kew Gardens, also funding a delightful gallery to house them on condition that the paintings were shown together and not altered. Kew was a fitting location, as it was here during visits with her father that she first became interested in studying flowers and fauna. The gallery was opened in July 1882 and there it remains, a glorious monument to an inspired painter with a brilliant affinity for nature.

Marianne North never married, staying home first as a dutiful daughter to look after her mother and then her adored father. Only at the age of forty did her painting and travelling seriously begin. With a guide and letters of introduction to influential people, over the next fourteen years she visited fifteen countries and six continents. Along the way she created an innovative style of painting flowers in their natural habitat, as earlier conventions had shown flowers apart from their habitat.

This book is a selective account of women's bequests across the ages. It is not a transcription of wills but instead uses bequests and wills to illustrate women's lives in earlier times. Along with magnificent gifts to the nation like the Sutton Hoo treasure, there are countless smaller keepsakes and family heirlooms such as a pretty turquoise ring once owned by Jane Austen, and these are just as precious in their way, and sometimes gifts to the man they loved. One example comes from 1631, during the reign of

Charles I. When Mary Vickers of Duston in Northamptonshire died, William Collis, the man she hoped to marry, was by her side. Mary left everything to him, writing, 'My love is still unto him better than ever it was.'[4]

Let us return to Henry Trigg.

Determined that his body would not be dug up, Henry left his money to his brother on condition that his coffin was stored, 'decently laid there, upon a floor in the loft'.

People everywhere were terrified of these body snatchers who came at night into the churchyards digging up fresh bodies to sell for dissection, even using wooden shovels to muffle the sound of digging. Matters became so bad – as in Edinburgh where the infamous Burke and Hare also murdered and stole bodies – that iron railings were placed around some graves, heavy stone slabs on others, and watchmen (or watchtowers) employed at graveyards.

Henry's niece Anne had the best of intentions when she requested a decent Christian burial for her uncle, but it never happened and well into the twentieth century his coffin remained in storage at the barn.[5] There are varying accounts as to precisely when, and how, the bones in his coffin disappeared. What is certain is that it was only in the late 1990s, when the building became a National Westminster Bank, that the coffin was taken away.

I

IN THE BEGINNING WITH THE ANGLO-SAXONS AND SLAVES

'And I grant to each of my brothers a wagonload of wood.'

Siflaed's Will[1]

So let's start at the beginning, before '1066 and all that', in Saxon times when Siflaed left valuable wood to her brothers, as well as property to the Church.

Siflaed, Aethelflaed, Aethelgifu, Madselin, Aelfgar, Mantat, Wulfwaru, Leofgifu, Aelfswith and Wynflaed are the names of some of the women who made wills. We are fortunate that, of more than fifty surviving wills from the Anglo-Saxon era, a number are written by women. And while the names sound strange to us, they reflect the heritage of the tribes from Jutland, Denmark and Saxony who settled here.

It is a miracle – in fact a whole series of miracles – that these works on vellum survived a thousand years. Despite the upheavals of the Norman Conquest, the Anarchy (a civil war in the 1100s), the Wars of the Roses, the Dissolution of the Monasteries and the English Civil War, not to mention the twentieth-century Blitz, these wills somehow survived. Hardly any Saxon buildings remain as they were built from wood rather than stone, making these fragile documents even more extraordinary.[2]

Most of these wills belonged to aristocratic widows who owned large estates spread across different counties. These women were not just rich but deeply religious – the Saxons arrived as pagans but over time became pious Christians. By far the most shocking thing about them, however, is that they kept slaves – of which more later.

The Sword and the Spindle

There is evidence of equality between men and women at this time. We find from the wills that women could both inherit and bequeath land, as with two daughters of King Alfred the Great who were bequeathed estates on the Isle of Wight.

The notion of the woman as the wife and lady of the house, who weaves and spins, is a tradition reaching far back into Antiquity; certainly, weaving and spinning date to the early Bronze Age in Britain. Alfred the Great's will in 899 mentions the 'sword side' of the menfolk, while women were the 'spindle side'. A spindle was used to twist fibres from wool and flax into yarn for weaving, which was always considered women's work.

Women's bequests in the Saxon wills include estates and books, horses and gold, headbands and veils, clothes, tapestries, money and jewels given to family, female friends, and servants alongside generous gifts to the Church. Clearly this society both valued and rewarded loyalty, as we see with a woman named Leofgifu, who gave land to her steward Aelfnoth and to stewards of other estates. Sometimes a bride received land of '*morgengifu*' or morning-gift, a Germanic tradition honoured by the husband on the morning after their wedding. The gift was then hers to bequeath as she wished, and was sufficiently important to be mentioned in her will. If a widow remarried within a year of her husband's death, she had to return the *morgengifu* to his family.

A number of the wills from this time include a gift for the king and queen, partly due to allegiance but also to help ensure that the final wishes of the testator (the writer of the will) were carried out. Three copies of a will were made: one for the king, one for the local church, and one for the testator. Often a curse is addressed to anyone who might be tempted to interfere, as in Aethelflaed's will: 'And whatsoever man shall alter this bequest, may be a companion in the torment of hell of Judas who betrayed our Lord.'[3]

A woman named Aethelgifu left horses, shields and spears as well as staghounds to the king, making a traditional gift of allegiance.[4] Even making a will depended on the king's permission as Wulfwaru, around the turn of the tenth century, asks King Aethelred 'of his charity that I may be entitled to make my will'. She gave estates and what is described in the will as her principal residence to her younger daughter, Aelfwaru, and elder son, Wulfmaer, to share 'as justly as they can, that they shall each have their equal shares'. Her eldest daughter, Gode, also received land plus a complete set of women's clothing and two brooches that seem likely to have had more sentimental value than financial worth.

With Needle and Thread

Household goods are often mentioned in the wills and reveal how important such items were in Saxon times. Linen and hand-woven blankets, fine embroidery, seat covers, bedclothes, curtains as well as gowns and clothes all reflect an immense pride in weaving.[5] Anglo-Saxon women were famous across Europe for their exquisite embroidery skills, including fine goldthread work.

Weaving clearly happened on a large scale, as weaving sheds have been discovered at Goltho in Lincolnshire dating from around AD 850. A similar site at Stevenage revealed ring-shaped loom weights made of clay, used to weigh down threads to improve tension and quality. Most Anglo-Saxon sites had sophisticated weaving sheds with a sunken floor, so the community could make their own clothing and household textiles. At one excavation near Thame, Oxfordshire, where a building caught fire and collapsed, some fifty-six loom weights were discovered.[6]

Saxon expert Professor Gale Owen-Crocker concluded that probably most women of the time could weave.[7] Those who were rich would have had clothes made from the finest linens and silks, whereas servants and poorer folk would make do with cheaper materials.

Queen Emma, Twice Queen of England

In 1002, a young woman named Emma (c. 984-1052) came from Normandy to marry King Aethelred. She was the Duke of Normandy's sister, and the marriage was a dynastic one rather than anything romantic. Not yet twenty, she received a new Saxon name, Aelfgifu,[8] and her dower lands included Exeter and Winchester. After her husband's death she married the new king, Cnut, making her twice Queen of England. Two of her sons would rule England, and her daughter Gunhilda became Empress of Germany.

In later life, Emma schemed in a deadly and real-life version of *Game of Thrones*, trying to outwit Edward the Confessor, one of her sons from her first marriage. She held a lot of power as Cnut's wife, and she wielded it in her attempts to ensure her sons by Cnut inherited the throne, rather than her sons by Aethelred. This might merely have been seen as Emma supporting her new family. Ultimately Edward won the power struggle. One of his first acts in 1043 was to confiscate the royal treasure his mother had kept at Winchester, a sure sign that her political influence was over.[8]

Queen Emma's will was lost, but some of her bequests are known. Gotbegot Manor was given to St Swithin's Priory, Winchester, 'tax free and toll free forever'. This plot of land, in the centre of Winchester, survived into Tudor times but was lost with the Dissolution of the Monasteries. The lead was stripped from the roof of the manor house and sold to help fund Henry VIII's army fighting in France.

A Pious Age

Despite all the strife, with battles between the different Saxon kingdoms and then raiding and outright invasion by the Vikings, this was also a glorious age of Christianity. Canterbury Cathedral came first, built in AD 597. St Paul's in London followed in 604 and York was bult in 625, together with countless abbeys, priories, local churches and chapels commissioned by local noblemen and thegns. One of the many pre-Norman bequests to the Church came from Thurgunt, wife of Turkil the Dane. Her will (c. 1055–66) left land at Sawtry (then Saltretha) to Ramsey Abbey for her soul so that she might be buried there.

Countess Judith, Gospel Books Bound in Gold

Not long before the Norman Conquest, in 1051, Judith of Flanders (1030–1094) made a diplomatic marriage to Tostig, brother of Harold Godwinson, later King of England. The couple ruled Northumbria and became generous patrons of the Church, with gifts for Durham Cathedral at St Cuthbert's shrine. They also encouraged the cult of St Oswald, a seventh-century warrior and martyr king of Northumbria.

In 1061, Tostig and Judith went on pilgrimage to Rome with Tostig's younger brother Gyrth and Ealdred, Archbishop of York as part of an embassy to the Pope. During these years Countess Judith commissioned four Gospel Books, manuscripts written in Latin and made by monks at Canterbury, where the finest work was produced. These illustrated and coloured books were expensive and prized possessions of the elite, used to emphasise their wealth, status and piety. When Emperor Charlemagne died in 814, an illuminated manuscript was placed in his grave. Judith's Gospel Books were bound in gold covers (made of silver gilt) and studded with precious gemstones, though possibly the first bindings were plain.

Tostig actually turned on his brother and died fighting as part of Harald Hardrada's invading Norwegian army at the Battle of Stamford Bridge in 1066, just before the Battle of Hastings and the Norman Conquest. Judith had fled into exile with Tostig in Flanders the year before, where she had remained when he went to battle. In 1071, she married Duke Welf of Bavaria. The Gospel Books went with her.

When Judith died around 1094, she was buried at Weingarten Abbey. The abbey received her precious Gospel Books together with a fine library as well as a phial of Christ's blood. There were also relics of St Oswald, which later helped spread his fame as a warrior saint into Scandinavia, Germany and northern Italy. (St Oswald is still revered within England, for example at the church in Oswaldkirk, Yorkshire.)

Weingarten Abbey kept the Gospel Books for over 700 years, but by the eighteenth century they were on the move. First they went to Salzburg, and by 1805 they were in the Netherlands. The following year they could be found in France, before spending over 100 years in England in private collections such as that of William Coke, Earl of Leicester. Then, two of the books were bought by J. P. Morgan, the famous American banker. Today those two books are in the Morgan Library in New York, counted among its most precious items.

Nearly a thousand years after Countess Judith first commissioned the Gospel Books, they returned again to England. Not to Canterbury, where they were made, nor Northumbria, where Judith and Tostig ruled, but close enough. The Gospel Books were briefly on show in London, included among the treasures of the 2018/19 Anglo-Saxon exhibition at the British Library called 'Art, Word, War'.

Wynflaed's Will and Slavery

Sometime around AD 950, a noblewoman called Wynflaed dictated her will to a scribe or clerk.[1] We know little about her save for what can be gleaned from the will. Although kings Eadwig and Edgar the Peaceful had a grandmother called Wynflaed who would have lived around this time, it is unclear if this is the same woman.

Wynflaed's is one of the earliest surviving wills written by an English woman and it provides a vivid picture of a great lady and her household. Her lands as well as various gifts are distributed among friends and family, and servants are mentioned. The Church receives gifts to the nuns at Wilton, a royal convent, and to Shaftesbury in Dorset; both religious foundations would survive until the Reformation in the sixteenth century.

Notably, to return to an earlier topic, the will gives slaves as bequests:

> ... And Wulfflaed is to be freed on condition that she serve Aethelflaed and Eadgifu [her daughter and granddaughter].
> ... And she bequeaths to Eadgifu [her granddaughter] a woman-weaver and a seamstress the one called Eadgifu, the other called Aethelgifu.

The two women given to her granddaughter have valuable skills: weaving and sewing.

Wynflaed owned estates in the south of England, in Berkshire, Dorset and elsewhere, and also a considerable number of slaves. Her properties included Faccombe in Hampshire; Coleshill and Adderbury (Eadburggebrig) in Oxfordshire; Chinnock and Charlton Horethorne in Somerset; and Inglesham and Ebbesbourne Wake in Wiltshire. The Faccombe estate (known later as Netherton) was Wynflaed's marriage gift and bequeathed to her son Eadmaer. Her daughter Aethelflaed also received land. Many places mentioned in the will are familiar still – Wilton and Yeovil, Coleshill and Wantage, Shrivenham and Shaftesbury. Almost all place names are established by this time. Similarly, in Aethelgifu's will,[10] there are the familiar Hertfordshire locations like Offley, Hitchin, Tewin, Stondon, Welwyn, Gaddesden, St Albans, Henlow and Ashwell.

Wynflaed's will now belongs to the British Library. Written on a single sheet of parchment, it is written in Old English; indeed, of the fifty-eight Saxon wills which have survived almost all were written in English rather than Latin. A short extract from the will below illustrates how great the difference is from Old English to our modern tongue:

In the Beginning with the Anglo-Saxons and Slaves

> Wynflaed cyo hu hio wile ymbe paet hio baefo ofer hyre daeg hio becwip into cyrcan hyre ofring ... u 7 hyre beteran ofr`ing-sceat 7 hyre rode 7 into beodern hiwun twa selefrene cuppan 7 hyre to saulsceatte aelcon godes peowe ...

Translated into modern English this means:

> Wynflaed declares how she wishes to dispose of what she possesses, after her death. She bequeathes to the church her offering- ... and the better of her offering-cloths, and her cross; and to the refectory two silver cups for the community; and as a gift for the good of her soul ...[1]

Her grandson receives wild horses while her granddaughter Eadgifu shares the tame horses. Eadgifu also received slaves, two chests, and Wynflaed's best tunic and cloak. There was also a good deal of household linen, no doubt woven by the women of the household. Wynflaed's best bedcurtain is mentioned, plus a linen covering, all the bedclothes, her best dun tunic, a nun's habit, her best holy veil as well as the better of her cloaks:

> ... And she grants to Coelthryth whichever she prefers of her black tunics and her best holy veil and her best headband.

In among these belongings are her books for Aethelflaed, her daughter. Presumably these are religious texts, Gospel Books or prayer books, but we do not know as none are mentioned by title:

> ... And she trusts that she [Aethelflaed] will be mindful of her soul. And there are also tapestries, one which is suitable for her, and the smallest she can give to her women.

The fact that a nun's habit and her 'best holy veil' are bequeathed suggest that a deeply religious life was combined with existence as a noblewoman. A pious, prayerful life of chastity was often also chosen by wealthy (and royal) widows in medieval times. The historian Michael Wood neatly sums up Wynflaed as 'a recognisable English countrywoman: capable, fair-minded, strongly aware of class and status but with a sense of obligation to the less well off – pious and practical'.[9]

For every future generation this would be the 'ideal' Lady of the Manor. Someone with a powerful sense of duty, caring for the people who worked for and invariably depended upon the estate and the kindness of the family who owned it. A lazy, careless woman with no interest in the workers and tenants under her charge would have spelled hardship for the poor.

Set My Slaves Free

These final years of the Anglo-Saxons indicate a considerable degree of piety but at the same time there was a much darker, bleaker world of slavery. Sometimes the wills include requests to free slaves, as in Leofgifu's will[1] and in the following examples:

> And to my tenants their homesteads as their own possessions: and all my men free ... [all my men to be set free]
>
> Will of Siflaed of Marlingford,
> Norfolk, *c*. 990-1066[1]

> And I wish that half my men in every village to be freed for my soul...
>
> Will of Aethelflaed[1]

Releasing slaves, an act known as manumission, was thought to speed the journey of the deceased's soul through purgatory towards heaven. More educated slaves are sometimes mentioned, including Mann the goldsmith and his wife. Three women – Leofrun, Aethelflaed and Aelfwaru – were to sing psalms for their lady Aethelgifu for a year after her death,[10] while slaves within the household included those able to sew and weave. Wynflaed asked her children to release some other slaves:

> ... at Faccombe, Eadhelm and Man and Johanna and Sprow and his wife ... and Gersand and Snel are to be freed.

Slaves were an essential part of the Saxon economy, kept on large estates and by elite households. Some were prisoners of war but in times of famine people would sell themselves – or the whole family – into slavery rather than starve. There were major slave markets in Rome, Dublin and Bristol which indicate it was a well-organised and profitable system; everywhere the Vikings traded, be it Russia or Sicily, such markets existed.

Estimates based on Domesday Book, so from 1086, show that over 10 per cent of the English population was in slavery. Aethelgifu's will mentions a herd of swine to be given to St Albans Abbey, and with it the swineherd himself; the will dates from around the year 980 or 990.[10] However, it was only discovered in 1939 in the archives of the abbey,[11] where she was buried.[12] Such documents were kept by abbeys and churches as proof of their ownership of the lands they had received. Of course, in 1066 all such lands were seized by the Norman conquerors; little was left in Saxon hands.

A Bad Nephew

Aethelgifu's will mentions that her husband's nephew Edwin, son of her lord's sister, took Stondon as it was land given to her by her husband. Presumably he assumed his aunt would gracefully give way. Au contraire! A document witnessed at Hitchin, on oath, was organised to support her claim. The fact that this oath was taken by the reeve Byrnic and by all the chief men of Bedfordshire and Hertfordshire, as well as by their wives, illustrates Aethelgifu's determination.[13] She directly appealed to the king, and after paying the sum of £20 regained Stondon.

Edwin returned it 'against his will', and in her will Aethelgifu left it to Byrhaston, who was to keep it for Edwin on condition that Masses were said annually for her and her husband.

Saintly Matters

Not only were Saxon women deeply religious, they also played a vital role in the establishment of Christianity. This certainly was the view of historian Frank Stenton, though the surviving records do not make it clear;[14] the belief is echoed by Kate Cooper and Barbara Yorke, who studied the role of royal women.[15]

St Hilda (d. 680), who founded a large double abbey at Whitby (with both monks and nuns), was one of the most important women involved with the early Church. She educated five of the earliest bishops.[16] Another woman of consequence was St Cuthburga of Wimborne (d. 727), while Bath Abbey was first a nunnery built on land given by the local king in 757.

Of the coins minted for Cynethryth (d. 798 or later), wife of King Offa of Mercia, few have survived; she is the only Saxon queen (as far as we know) to have coins minted in her name. When widowed she became abbess at Cookham Abbey near Oxford in 796, and excavations in 2021 have confirmed the exact site of the building. Many of the early female saints belonged to the elite and royal families. St Etheldreda (d. 679), founder of Ely Abbey in 673, built on land received as her marriage gift from her first husband. Her grave was an important shrine up until the Dissolution of the Monasteries.

Aethelflaed, Warrior Queen of Mercia

Women in pre-Conquest society appear to have enjoyed greater equality than after 1066. Historian Doris Stenton concluded that Saxon women were more nearly equal to their husbands and brothers than in later Norman times.[17] Aethelflaed (d. 918), eldest child of Alfred the Great, is an example. She ruled Mercia with her husband and then continued alone after he died. Known as the Lady of the Mercians, she led warriors into battle against the Vikings and was on the way to York to accept the defeat of the Vikings when she died.

Warwick and Chester are among several fortified burghs or towns created by Aethelflaed. No other woman would rule in her own right until 1553, when Mary Tudor became queen. Empress Matilda in the twelfth century should have inherited her father's throne but instead there was a bitter civil war with her cousin Stephen, remembered as the Anarchy.

Thirty Oxen and Twenty Cows

Shortly after the Battle of Hastings, a joint will (c. 1066–68) was made by a man named Ulf and his wife, Madselin. Preparing to set off on pilgrimage to Jerusalem, they made provision in case 'I do not come home'. Both owned land in their own right, and they bequeathed it to three local religious houses including Ramsey and Peterborough. In return, prayers for their soul would be said.

Aethelgifu, who died around 990,[18] gave generously to the Church in return for her funeral and burial at St Albans Abbey, leaving gold, thirty oxen and twenty cows. Valuable lands at Munden, Westwick, Longford and Gaddesden (a few miles from St Albans) also went to the abbey. In return, her grave was placed close by the altar. This was the prime spot, the best place for a Christian to be buried.[19]

Honey, Butter and Salt

An earlier will from Kent[20] is by Abba, a reeve, a senior official for the Crown. Dating from 833–839, it records the bequest of land at Chillenden, just a few miles from Canterbury, to his wife Heregyth if they have no children. As a condition for this inheritance he insists that she live in chastity. The will details an annual payment from the Challock estate for Christ Church, Canterbury. This included ale, loaves of bread, lard, cheese, a bullock and a pig, some sheep, six geese, ten hens and thirty tapers (candles). If paid during the winter then it should include three full sesters (approximately 6 lbs) of honey, butter and salt. Livestock and food were critical in these times, when careful storage, preservation and planning was essential if a community was to survive the winter or a bad harvest.[19]

Honey was important as the only source of sweetness. Mead, the usual drink, was simply fermented honey. So valuable was honey that it could be used to pay rent. Refined sugar was only available from Elizabethan times, and even into the 1700s it was a rare luxury, so expensive it was called 'white gold' and kept under lock and key.

Shields, Spears and Gold

The will of Aelfgifu (also known by the Latin name of Elgiva) mentions estates at Linslade and Marsworth given to King Edgar, together with the nearby village of Wing, Buckinghamshire. Wing was probably her main estate, and work on its church was completed at this time. Her estates, spread over five counties, included the manor of Berkhamsted (Berkhampstead in the will) in Hertfordshire. This is the first mention of the town, and the same is true for Chesham (Caesteleshamm in the will), which was bequeathed to the abbey at Abingdon. Today in Chesham there is an Elgiva Theatre named in her honour.

Elgiva's sister-in-law received a headband which she had been 'lent' – an interesting phrase in the circumstances – while her sister was also given all that had been lent to her. We do not know if this was money, jewels or other property.

Some lands were given to the king, along with a drinking cup, shields and spears, perhaps because she also asked him to take the allegiance of her faithful men. Slaves were set free, and generous gifts were for the clergy of Winchester, Bath, Romsey and Abingdon Abbey. Aelfgifu was married to King Eadwig, though the marriage was annulled in 958 on the grounds they were too closely related.

Some accounts claimed Aelfgifu was exiled for a time to Ireland. The land left to her two brothers and a sister was only theirs while they lived; after that it was destined for the Old Minster at Winchester. The translated will (written *c.* 966–975) is set out below.

In the Beginning with the Anglo-Saxons and Slaves

This is Aelfgifu's request of her royal lord [King Edgar]; she prays him for the love of God and for the sake of his royal dignity, that she may be entitled to make her will.

Then she makes known to you, Sire, by your consent what she wishes to give to God's church for you and for your soul. First, she grants to the Old Minster [at Winchester], where she intends her body to be buried, the estate at [Princes] Risborough just as it stands, except that, with your consent, she wishes that at each village every penally enslaved man who was subject to her shall be freed and [she grants] two hundred mancuses* of gold to that minster and her shrine with her relics. And she grants to the New Minster [at Winchester] the estate at Bledlow, and a hundred mancuses of gold; and a paten [a plate which usually went with a chalice] to the Nunnery and the estate at Whaddon to Christ and St Mary at Romsey; and Caesteleshamm [Chesham] to Abingdon [Abbey], and Wickham to Bath [Abbey].

And I grant to my royal lord the estates at Wing, Linslade, Haversham, Hatfield, Marsworth and Gussage [in Dorset]; and two armlets [bracelets], each of a hundred and twenty mancuses, and a drinking-cup and six horses and as many shields and spears. And to the Aetheling the estate at Newnham [in Oxfordshire] and an armlet of thirty mancuses. And to the queen a necklace of a hundred and twenty mancuses and an armlet of thirty mancuses, and a drinking-cup.

And I grant to Bishop Aethelwold [of Winchester] the estate at Taeafersceat and pray him that he will always intercede for my mother and for me. And with my lord's permission I grant the estates at Mongewell and Berkhampstead to Aelfweard and Aethelweard and Aelfwaru in common for their lifetime, and after their death to the Old Minster for my royal lord and for

---

* A gold coin, slimmer and slightly smaller than today's pound coin. Worth about an eighth of a pound, this represented some thirty days' wages for a skilled worker. Fewer than ten such coins have been discovered so far, including one in 2001 found near the River Ivel, Biggleswade.

me. And they are to pay a two-days' food-rent* every year to the two minsters, as long as they possess the estates. And to my sister Aelfwaru I grant all that I have lent her; and to my brother's wife Aethelflaed the headband which I have lent her.

And to each abbot five pounds of pence for the repair of their minster. And, Sire, with your consent, [I wish] that I may entrust the surplus to the Bishop and the Abbot for the repair of the foundation, and for them to distribute for me among poor men according as seems to them most profitable for me in God's sight.

And I beseech my royal lord for the love of God, that he will not desert my men who seek his protection and are worthy of him.

And I grant to Aelfweard a drinking-cup and to Aethelweard [her brothers] an ornamented drinking-horn.††

---

* Food-rent is mentioned in other wills and was rent paid in bread, ale, honey, butter or other foodstuff and livestock instead of money. Regular food supplies were as important, if not more essential for survival, as money.
† Source: Will number 8, Dorothy Whitlock, see note 1, with permission

2

WIVES, WIDOWS AND A THIEF CALLED CUTPURSE MOLL

'Two candlesticks; four saucers.'

Women Founders of Oxford and Cambridge

The 'ideal' woman in earlier centuries was expected to be obedient, virtuous, and able to make a good marriage for her family. An alternative in medieval times was to become a nun, a bride of Christ, and daughters often joined a convent at an early age.[1] The latter class of women still kept their family links, and a study of medieval nunneries carried out by Eileen Power has found that families sometimes left a gift for their local nunnery as a legacy for an aunt, sister or daughter who had found their calling there.[1] Marilyn Oliva's study of medieval Norwich[2] found bequests were equally likely to be made to monasteries as to convents.

Bequests made to religious establishments could sometimes be on a lavish scale, as was the case for Margaret de Courtenay (1325–1391), Countess of Devon. A granddaughter of Edward I with much to leave, she made pious bequests to various religious houses. She also gave the swans (boasted on her family's heraldic emblem) from Topsham to her son.[3] A grand tomb and effigy in Exeter Cathedral beside her husband Hugh, 10th Earl of Devon, has swans at her feet instead of the usual lapdogs seen on a lady's tomb. She is far grander, as the swans emphasise her royal descent and her lineage from the de Bohun family. Another of Edward I's granddaughters, Lady Elizabeth de Clare, re-founded Clare College, Cambridge in 1338.

This chapter looks at wives as well as widows. The closing section considers those brave women in the seventeenth century who risked death in order to defend their faith by hiding Catholic priests from the new Protestant establishment.

Some Wives

Once married, a woman's obedience was due to her husband. Indeed, until the late nineteenth century a wife had few if any legal rights. It was a patriarchal world in which women were considered inferior to men in both society and law. It was only at the end of the 1800s that married women gained the legal right to own property. Until that law changed, it was the husband who was the rightful owner rather than the wife, even if the land came from her family. Nor could a married woman make a will without her husband's approval.

If a man should die before his wife, then the usual division of his property in early centuries meant a third went to his children, another to funeral expenses and legacies, and the final third to the widow. In the medieval City of London it was a third for the widow, a third for the children and the final third to fund prayers for his soul.

However, once a woman became a widow, supposing there was a reasonable income, she might gain more freedom and independence than as a wife. Little wonder then that some women preferred widowhood rather than remarriage. A marriage contract between wealthy families typically outlined the wife's rights if widowed; her dower as a third of her husband's estate would supply a valuable income. As early as the Saxon era we see examples of two copies of a marriage contract, in this case between one Wulfric and a bishop's sister,[4] doubtless to ensure each side fulfilled their end of the bargain.

A bride in any well-off family was expected to bring a dowry to her husband. Property or other valuables were also acceptable, and this principle filtered down the social hierarchy. In 1850, one young bride took eight New Forest pony mares to Setley village in Hampshire. Her great-great-great-grandson still keeps ponies in the New Forest.

In the medieval age, wills are filled with many requests of prayers and Masses for 'my soul'. Women leave a multiplicity of Church gifts including their wedding ring, money with requests for prayers and Masses for the salvation of their soul through to property and valuable jewels. Such patterns can be found elsewhere, as wills from France closely mirror English piety with countless bequests for Masses and prayers for the deceased.[4] Substantial amounts of money were spent on huge requests. For example, Henry VII of England left £250 in his will for 10,000 Masses to be said by the monks at Westminster Abbey for his soul and for that of his wife, Elizabeth of York.

A noble family might establish a grand chantry, like that founded at Wingfield College, Suffolk in 1362 by Lady Alianore de Wingfield as requested in the will of her husband Sir John. Similarly, the almshouses at Ewelme, which survive today, were founded back in the 1430s so that the almsmen in residence would pray for their founders, Geoffrey Chaucer's granddaughter Alice (d. 1475) and her husband William de la Pole, Duke of Suffolk.

Being a chantry priest could be a profitable lifetime's work. Towns everywhere were dominated by the clergy; Northampton,[5] Exeter,[6] Lincoln, York and London were all filled with chapels and churches. In the small Hertfordshire village of Hexton, almost every will from the fourteenth, fifteenth and sixteenth centuries included gifts left for the Church.[5] It was the same everywhere across the land.

In fifteenth-century wills from Ipswich, as many as eighty-two churches are mentioned and many of these were outside of the city.[6] Medieval Norwich, the most important city after London at the time, had fifty-eight parish churches – daily services and confession, saints' days, Mass and fasting days were part of everyday life. Lincoln Cathedral had as many as fifty chantries, necessitating a timetable setting out when prayers would be held at each.

Katherine French in *The Good Women of the Parish*[7] illustrates how closely women were involved with their local parish. They often had favourite female saints, including St Anne, patron saint of childless women. St Margaret of Antioch helped women during childbirth, while shrines to the Virgin Mary were understandably often popular.

Practical bequests to help save the soul of the deceased might include gifts to the poor, to the Church or acts of charity. Margaret, Duchess of Norfolk (d. 1494) made her will in 1490 and asked for two virtuous priests to sing Masses for her soul in the local church for three years. She also wanted 300 priests to say 300 Masses and dirges (a lament for the dead) for her soul. The duchess was buried at Stoke by Nayland in Suffolk and made various local religious bequests in her will at Sudbury, Clare and Colchester. All were within a few miles of her home, and were places she must have known well. Most distant were the Poor Clare nuns at Bruisyard, over 30 miles away.[8]

Where Shall I Be Buried?

Deciding on a burial plot might be complicated if a woman had married more than once. Should they be buried with their current spouse, their first husband, or even a second or third in the middle? From the will of a widow in Rickmansworth, Hertfordshire in 1504/5 by the name of Johan [Joan] Baldewen, we know her preference was to be buried in the churchyard beside her first husband, John Reed.[9]

Another choice for a rich woman might be in the family vault with her parents and ancestors. Some women were rather more independent than we might expect,[9] as with Katherine Green, who died in 1459. She had a fine monument constructed beside the grave of her first husband Ralph Green, who died in 1417. It had been a short marriage of only three years and Katherine ordered an impressive double tomb at St Peter's church in Lowick,

Northamptonshire, where it remains today. Carved in stone, the couple hold hands in a most touching sign of affection,[9] although at the time this was likely intended to symbolise the sacred marriage vow. Katherine's second marriage was to Sir Simon Felbrigg, and her own funeral some forty years later saw her buried in Blackfriars, Norwich, with Sir Simon.

In some instances, family fortunes changed. Lady Margaret Beaufort (1443–1509) made her first will before she was thirty, the year she remarried. At that time, she intended to be buried in Bourne Abbey, Lincolnshire. Arrangements were made in the will, and money allocated, to bring the body of her late husband Edmund Tudor from Carmarthen in Wales over to Bourne, reuniting them in death. But when their son defeated Richard III at the Battle of Bosworth, Margaret suddenly became the king's mother and could plan a far grander burial at nothing less than Westminster Abbey. Hers is one of the most elaborate monuments. Her prayer book and one of her large travelling chests can still be seen in the abbey.

Another widow who much preferred a grand tomb – her husband had asked for a plain one – was Lady Joan Brooke (d. 1437). She survived her husband by nineteen years, and Thorncombe church in Devon still holds their grand and most impressive monumental brass.[9]

A Widow's Destiny

Widows were often the custodians of heirlooms in wealthy families, not only precious jewels but those expensive illuminated manuscripts which would be carefully passed through the generations. The widow would bequeath to the eldest son and heir an illuminated missal or a 'book of hours', a costly item made in much the same way as the Saxon Gospel Books for Countess Judith of Northumbria. With texts and prayers set out for eight separate hours (hence the name), and with added family entries for births and marriages, the book of hours often became a treasured family heirloom. Later, in the fifteenth century, with the arrival of the printing press conventionally printed books were added to such collections. Cambridge University Press, the oldest publisher in the world, printed its first book in 1584: *Two Treatises of the Lord His Holie Supper*.

The Beauchamp/Beaufort Book of Hours which descended to Henry VIII was commissioned in the early 1400s by John Beaufort and his wife Margaret Holland. Then the illuminated manuscript passed to Margaret Beauchamp and her daughter Margaret Beaufort, mother of Henry VII. Family dates were noted in the book, which became Lady Margaret's prayer book, and it also has medicinal recipes including 'medson for the meigrem [medicine for the migraine]'. The Beauchamp/Beaufort Book of Hours remained with the royal family in the Old Royal Library until 1757 when it was given by George II to the newly created British Museum.

In medieval London, Norwich and elsewhere it is clear that a widow might also continue the family business after her husband's death. Indeed, she might already be an equal partner before that time. Matilda Penne continued in the fur trade in the City of London after her husband's demise. Johanna Hill similarly took over a bell foundry together with her husband's apprentices.[9] Some of Johanna Hill's bells have survived in Dorset, Sussex and Suffolk, bearing her mark above that of her husband; it is a diamond-shaped lozenge, the traditional heraldic shape for women in place of a shield.

Occasionally in the wills we catch a glimpse of daughters inheriting items to help them make a living, but it was more common, as Kate Staples[10] found, for the sons to receive such bequests and the daughters to receive a sum of money for their marriage.

In Norwich, Elisabeth Haslewood became a silversmith in 1684, with her own silver mark of EH rather than the AH of her husband Arthur.[11] Elisabeth ran the business for the next twenty years before their son, also Arthur, took over. She died in 1715 aged seventy-one and is buried alongside her husband in St Andrew's, Norwich. Their tombstone survives. Her work is rarely found today, but one of her silver beakers is in the Royal

Collection; it was given to Queen Elizabeth II in 1968 when she came to open the new county hall in Norwich.

A Taste of Honey

In Zennor, Cornwall, a widow by the name of Alice Pellamounter died in 1639. Two of her daughters were married, but three remained unmarried. On their father's death a few years before, each had received a sum of money. Alice's will added to this, leaving four of her five daughters a butt or hive of bees.[12] This was a valuable gift often found in country wills, given the importance of honey before the arrival of sugar.

Smaller bequests from Hertfordshire and Bedfordshire illustrate a wide variety of household items valued by women:

> A brass pan; a quarter of malt; 2 bushels of barley; a couple of steers; a kettle; a bolster; sheep; all manner of implements to my bakhows [bakehouse] and bruhowse [brewhouse]; the best beads; a folding table; the best brass pot; cushions; cooking dishes of pewter and brass; napkins; one pair of blankets; a coverlet [quilt]; 2 candlesticks; four saucers; a pillow; 2 pewter platters; a plain tablecloth and a plain towel; a pot and a pan.

Alys Cooke, a widow of Eaton Bray, wrote the above will and died in 1521. Money for her daughter Agnes, as well as livestock and a few items that would improve any house, are also mentioned:

> ... to daughter Agnes 40s. in money, a cow, a red heifer, four sheep, the best brass pot, the best pan, half testator's napery ware, a cauldron, a coverlet, a bolster, 2 pillows, 2 coffers, 5 platters, a basin, a chafing-dish, four saucers, a candlestick.[1]

Often the godchildren are mentioned, as with the will of the widow Elizabeth Wynch of nearby Luton:

> ... to each god-child 20 pence ...[1]

The sixteenth-century will of Alys Peddar, a widow from Salford, divides various sums of money among different religious foundations:

> ... to mother church at Lincoln, 6d [pence]; to high altar at Salford church half a quarter of barley ... to the church at Holcot 3s 4d; to the church at Cramfelde [Cranfield] 3s 4d; to the church of Mulso 3s 4d; to the church of Broughton 3s 4d; to the church of Medelton Keynes [Milton Keynes] 3s 4d; to the church of Wavendon 3s 4d; to the church of Asplay Gyes [Aspley Guise] 3s 4d; to the fraternity of Fenestratford [Fenny Stratford] 3s 4d; to the fraternity of Our Lady of Newport Pannell [Newport Pagnell] 3s 4d; to the friars of Dunstable 5s; to the friars of Bedford 5s ...[1]

The most generous amounts were for the friars at Dunstable and Bedford, both important local priories. Dunstable Priory was a particular royal favourite where just a few years later in 1533 Archbishop Cranmer announced Henry VIII's divorce from Catherine of Aragon.

Dorothy Wadham, Founder of Wadham College

Few women completed anything on such a grand scale as Dorothy Wadham (*née* Petre, 1535-1618). Her husband Nicholas, who died in 1609, left her as executrix with the immense sum of £19,200 to establish a new Oxford college. Dorothy was already seventy-four when the project began and she oversaw everything, completing an amazing building project that saw her and Nicholas remembered as joint founders of Wadham College.

Little is known about Dorothy's early life, and if not for Wadham College she might have been unknown to history. Her family were a tier or two below the aristocracy, albeit with exceptional connections at court. Dorothy's father, Sir William Petre, had held a significant role as Secretary of State to Henry VIII and his children Edward VI, Mary I and Elizabeth I in turn.

The college would open to students within five years of Nicholas's death. This was a most impressive achievement considering all the challenges involved – not merely constructing the buildings themselves but manoeuvring the tricky political issues of the Stuart world, including claims on the will itself. The Wadham and Petre families were known to have Catholic sympathies, which also created problems, but Dorothy managed to gain the support of James I, who granted Wadham its charter.[13]

To begin with, there was the land to be bought for Wadham College. An architect and master builder had to be appointed. The stonemasons, who came from Somerset, took three days to walk to Oxford. Dorothy was involved in every detail, from choosing the first warden down to overseeing the accounts, writing the college statutes, appointing the servants and the cook. (To be exact, two cooks were considered necessary.)

Then there was the library. The books were so valuable they were to be chained to the desks. Only graduates were allowed to use the library, and one of the Fellows was paid 30 shillings each year to be librarian. One of Dorothy's practical suggestions was for the library to be built above the kitchen so as to keep it warm. Many later generations of students must have blessed their wise founder for providing such a cosy, warm place for studying in a chilly winter. As soon as work commenced, the first students were recruited, many from the West Country; Somerset was Nicholas's home county, and he had always intended the college to be for men of that region.

Dorothy never visited Oxford. Instead, she corresponded through letters written by John Arnold, her servant and man of business. She lived in Devon at the Wadham dower house at Branscombe but remained actively involved, approving the monthly accounts of the college. The total cost – including library fittings and a chapel – came to £11,360. Dorothy added £7,270 of her own money to the endowment.

Originally founded exclusively for male scholars, just like every other early college, Wadham was among the first at Oxford to admit women students (in 1974).

Remember the Poor

Often testators left money to share among the poor; if not, they might specify the distribution of bread, drink or a funeral meal. A few churches still have a bread shelf, among them St Mary's, Warwick, where money was bequeathed to buy bread which could be taken away by the poor at the end of a service. Some amounts mentioned are modest, in pennies or a few pounds.[14]

Another tradition was to distribute food, mourning clothes or money at the funeral itself, though this sometimes degenerated into a mêlée. In 1601, the funeral of Lady Mary Ramsey was held. The widow of the Lord Mayor of London, and known as 'Rich Ramsey', her reputation for charity was widely known. She left £1,000 to the City of London to be distributed for charity and the same amount to Bristol, her hometown. Unsurprisingly, crowds came to Mary's funeral hoping for a generous gift of money and what should have been a solemn funeral descended into a riot. Seventeen people died trying to seize the valuable six-penny dole money.[15]

Almshouses for the poor were set up in almost every town, an ancient tradition from Saxon times. The founder left sufficient money for a building and income to pay for food, fuel and the other necessities of life. Often the inhabitants were asked to pray for their founder. Brian Bailey in *Almshouses* notes that women over the centuries have been men's equals in founding such charities.

One most thoughtful gift to the poor was made by the widow Sophia Beale Bonnell (d. 1841) at Old Windsor. She left £10 'for a dinner every Christmas day to as many poor men and women as that sum will furnish'. Held at the Fox public house each year, it was to be 'roast beef and good plum pudding … each man to have one quart [of beer] and each woman to have one pint', with an extra 10 shillings 'for a good fire in the room when they dine'. This fine Christmas tradition lasted right up into the 1960s. A portrait of the generous Mrs Beale Bonnell hangs in the Fitzwilliam Museum, Cambridge.

Cutpurse Moll

While most women, whatever their social class, led modest, virtuous lives, there are some in every age who did not. Cutpurse Moll is such a woman. She led (and thoroughly enjoyed) a bad, outrageous and most unconventional life. Larger than life, loud and bolder than most, she must have been a firecracker.

Mary Frith (*c.* 1584–1659) was Moll's real name, and she became a thief among other disreputable occupations. Born into a poor family, she lived in London and prospered, wily enough to overcome all the misfortunes poor women usually faced. By the time she wrote her will in 1659, Moll had squirrelled away sufficient money to own a house on Fleet Street close to St Paul's Cathedral and could afford servants.[16]

The epithet 'cutpurse' refers to the way thieves stole or 'cut' a purse from the belt to which it was attached. Moll was famous for wearing men's clothes and smoking a pipe, in an age when smoking was a new-fangled idea suited only for men. She also swore, and was said to be louder than any man.

The Roaring Girl, written in 1611 by Thomas Middleton and Thomas Dekker, is a comedy about Moll. In this play she is portrayed as an honest matchmaker, though in truth she might well have been mixed up in organising prostitution. Moll attended performances of *The Roaring Girl*, even appearing on the stage. A book had been written about her by John Day the year before, but it did not survive; it seems to have been light-hearted as it was entitled *The Madde Prancks of Merry Moll of the Bankside, with her walks in Man's Apparel and to What Purpose.*

The Church considered Moll's behaviour disgraceful. Certainly there was little virtue or modesty about her, but it is hard not to admire her unrepentant ways. She had to live by her wits and rebelled against the strict social conventions governing women's behaviour. And regardless of fines, court appearances and even a public penance enforced by the Church, she thrived.

Cutpurse Moll did conform in one rather unexpected way. In 1614, at the relatively advanced age of thirty, she married Lewknor Markham. Little is known about him and they had no children. A marriage naturally helped create an image of respectability, and some historians believe it was all a sham. But was it? Maybe not entirely. In her will, written a month before her death, Moll begins, 'I Mary Markham, alias, Frith...' She kept his name.

Moll's epitaph, like those plays during her lifetime, are testament to her fame. Written by no less a figure than the poet John Milton, it includes the following:

> For no communion she had,
> Nor sorted with the good or bad;
> That when the world shall be calcin'd [burnt to ashes],
> And the mixd' mass of human kind
> Shall sep'rate by that melting fire,
> She'll stand alone, and none come nigh her.[16]

However scandalous her life might have been, the Church had evidently forgiven Moll as she was respectably buried at St Bride's. And apart from £20 to a kinsman, everything went to her married niece Frances Edmondes, who was also executrix. The bequest for Frances was 'unto her own sole use', a legal phrase Moll included to be sure nothing could be claimed by her husband.

Concerns over husbands getting at the inheritance are evident in every age, as when William Shakespeare left a sum of money to his daughter Judith rather than her unworthy husband. In an eighteenth-century Cornish will, a mother left bequests for her three daughters, saying that each 'shall have and enjoy seperate [sic] and apart from her said Husband'.

Women, Catholic Priests and Treason

The Civil War of the 1640s was a most bitter and bloody affair. There were occasional moments of peace: 'Christmas Common' near Watlington commemorates an event in 1643 when both sides declared a truce so they could go home to enjoy Christmas. For the most part, however, it was a grim business which divided families and ruined many, leading eventually to the execution of Charles I and exile for his followers. Often among the families exiled (or away fighting) the wife was left to run the estate in the place of her sons or husband.

As far as the two sides' views concerned women, the Royalist Cavaliers were more egalitarian, while the Puritan Roundheads of Cromwell's victorious army believed women should be submissive.[17] Both sides had their heroines. Lady Brilliana Harley defended the family castle at Brampton Bryan during the first siege by the Royalists, while Lady Mary Bankes was twice besieged by the Roundheads at Corfe Castle, Dorset. As acknowledgement of such bravery, Mary Bankes was allowed to keep the castle keys, which feature in a later portrait of her. Lady Mary's will did not mention the keys, but they remained at Kingston Lacey as a family heirloom. Other women, including Lady Lucy Percy and Lady Jane Whorwood, spied for Charles I and the Royalist cause. Author Nadine Akkerman calls them 'invisible agents', as their sex allowed them to evade suspicion while carrying letters, secret information or money. Few would suspect a woman.[18]

A Lethal Game of Hide and Seek

In earlier Elizabethan times, with Protestantism in the ascendancy, equally brave women hid Catholic priests. With a government terrified of Catholic plots and assassins, women like Lady Cecily Stonor supported and promoted a secret network of priests, moving them from one safehouse to another.[19] Cleverly concealed hiding places, called priest holes, allowed the fugitive clergymen to go undetected while government forces ransacked the houses of suspected Catholics.

Many leading Catholic families like the Throckmortons at Coughton Court, Warwickshire and the Bedingfelds at Oxburgh Hall, Norfolk had secret priest holes. If a priest was discovered, everyone involved could be executed for treason. It was a most deadly game.

The constant danger to Elizabeth I from Catholic assassins was such that a food taster was employed. There is a delightful story about the queen's summer progress in 1572. Upon arrival at Sandwich, it was discovered that Mistress Gilbart, the mayor's wife and her sisters, together with the wives of the jurats (the town council) had prepared a special feast for the queen. It must have been a glorious, most impressive sight; some 160 dishes were laid out as a banquet in the School House on a table 28 feet long. As a sign of great favour to the ladies, the queen sat down to eat without any dish being sampled by her official food taster – a rare compliment. (Surprisingly, the employment of food tasters still has a place in our modern age. Russian President Vladimir Putin has a food taster, while in the 1940s Margot Wölk was one of fifteen young women recruited to taste Adolf Hitler's food at the Wolf's Lair, his headquarters on the Eastern Front.)

Catholics such as the Stonor family paid triple taxes, lost most of their estates and could only educate their children by sending them abroad as Catholics could not buy land and were forbidden to attend universities; this latter law actually applied until 1871! The Stonors did manage to keep their home, but not their estates. Elizabeth Rookwood (d. 1759) in Suffolk later managed to secure their family estates safe for her son. She was undoubtedly another brave woman, as Christopher Howse commented:

> In the shadowy recusant world, women have often been underestimated. Many women, as in the Rookwood family, went abroad to the Continent and lived as nuns at English convents in Dunkirk or Bruges.[20]

These women were immensely courageous and determined to preserve the Catholic faith. So much so that Antonia Fraser has concluded that the true heroes of the Catholic persecution were neither Guy Fawkes nor his colleagues, who tried to blow up the Houses of Parliament and the royal family, but the women who risked their lives to guard the Catholic faith and hide the priests.[21]

In various subtle ways many people secretly remained Catholic. One example is the Wiltshire will of Jane Forget, a nun before the Reformation. Her livelihood at Wilton Convent disappeared, but she continued to live in the same devout way. She died in 1588, fifty years after the Reformation, leaving all her clothes to the poor. There must surely have been many others who simply went on observing their faith.[22]

In the Tudor era, bequests to the Church and requests for prayers and Masses to save the soul of the deceased quickly disappeared. After a thousand years, the ordered Catholic world of religion and faith, with prayers to get to heaven or avoid purgatory, was gone.

An intriguing religious bookmark from the seventeenth century has survived, a fragile object made from thirteen silk ribbons. Each ribbon has a Latin quotation from an important Catholic text, including a medieval prayer to Jesus. Made in London sometime around 1632, the bookmark was found in an embroidered Protestant Bible, suggesting that it was used to both confuse and conceal. The owner, ostensibly holding the correct book, was outwardly conforming yet stayed true to the old faith by holding this subtle token of their faith.[23]

Religious division continues to cast dark shadows right through to modern times, as in Northern Ireland. Only in 1829 were Catholics legally granted religious freedom, the right to hold public office or stand for Parliament. Indeed, the first Catholic Prime Minister did not arrive until much later, in 1997 with Tony Blair, and even then only after his time leading the country. Some time later, Boris Johnson, elected as Prime Minister in 2019, surprised everyone (his staff at Downing Street included) with a secret Catholic wedding in May 2021.

3

WITCHES HISTORIC AND MODERN

When shall we three meet again in thunder, lightning, or in rain?
Double, double toil and trouble, fire burn and cauldron bubble.
The Three Witches, Macbeth

We have examples of witches who have left wills from both the modern era and the distant past, but perhaps it is best to start close to today, with a modern witch. Born a few years after the First World War, Doreen Valiente (*née* Dominy) lived from 1922 to 1999. Known as 'the mother of modern witchcraft', her obituaries in The Independent and The New York Times are possibly the only ones dedicated to a practitioner of witchcraft.

Doreen began her black magic at the age of thirteen by putting a curse on someone. She taught herself witchcraft, finding many ways to learn, as well as to collect, what she needed to practise magic and join a coven. On one occasion, hearing from her bank manager of a doctor's widow who inherited spell books and magical items, Doreen set off by bus to find out more. The doctor had recently died, and his widow was frightened by the objects left to her. Nonetheless, she wanted them disposed of safely.

During the Second World War, Doreen worked as a translator involved in military intelligence at the top-secret Bletchley Park. Some evidence suggests she continued in this role after the war.

One story claims the Queen Mother (wife of George VI) invited her to tea to chat about witchcraft. Her own flair for publicity, as well as her dedication to magic, made her a notable character and a poster girl for modern witchcraft, often known as Wicca (a Saxon word meaning sorceror).

Doreen Valiente died at the end of the twentieth century aged seventy-seven. All the belongings in her Brighton flat were left to her friend John Belham-Payne so that he might continue her work. John and his wife had recently founded the Centre for Pagan Studies, of which Doreen was patron. Her books about witchcraft and Wicca are still in print and are regarded as important texts.

A commemorative blue plaque was later placed outside the block of flats where Doreen lived, in Tyson Place, and although this did attract some media interest it was a rather low-key affair. The notion of a practising witch was no longer as sensational or shocking as it had been in the 1930s and 1940s when Valiente first learnt her magic. It also seems highly unlikely that she would have been selected as an ideal candidate for work at Bletchley Park if her occult interests had been known.

Keeping Witches Out

In medieval times, rural peasants would keep their doors shut tight on May Day as it was thought that a witch could enter the house if the door was left open. A horseshoe placed upwards above the front or back door of the house also offered protection against a witch. Rarely seen these days, until the 1970s a horseshoe was a popular housewarming gift with its roots in this practice, although the tradition had been smoothed into the less pagan notion of a 'lucky charm'. The tradition in Devon was to plant a rowan tree in a garden as protection against witches, and in Yorkshire rowan trees were celebrated for their use in warding off witches every year on 2 May until Victorian times.

Hiding certain items in the house (up a chimney, by a door or in the attic) – shoes, written charms, witch bottles, even a mummified cat[1] – was thought to dispel witchcraft. More than 100 witch bottles (and pottery flasks) have survived, mostly from the seventeenth century. A mid-nineteenth-century wine bottle was examined on BBC's *Antiques Roadshow* programme by glass expert Andy McConnell. He made the reasonable assumption that it might hold ancient wine and cautiously sipped the contents. Only much later, after the contents were analysed, did he discover it was a witch bottle filled with the traditional anti-witch recipe of nails and urine!

Northampton Museum's Concealed Shoe Index was launched in the 1950s.[2] At first staff had been baffled by the fact that old shoes kept being discovered hidden in old houses, but they eventually realised old shoes (the 'sole' of the shoe having been thought to be mixed with the 'soul' of the innocent person who first wore them) were once believed to repel black magic and witches. The collection now has around 3,000 shoes, with the earliest dating from Tudor times. They have been found at Hampton Court Palace, Ely Cathedral and at cottages as far north as Shetland and all the way down south to the Scilly Isles. Some are simple children's shoes, but in a Warwickshire manor house was discovered a single most elegant, fashionable Francois Pinet silk and leather-heeled French shoe from the nineteenth century.

A Witch Hunt

We still talk about a 'witch hunt' when describing the determined persecution of an individual or a group of people. While a modern witch hunt might imply pursuit by the press through mass media, in earlier times it could literally involve a ruthless hunt with deadly intent. There are countless examples of local mobs on witch hunts conducting trials wherein the accused was 'tested' by various methods including ducking in water; they often died as a result of such ordeals or were hanged afterward.

Superstition and fear of witches often increased in times of difficulty such as war or bad harvests, and it was often neighbours accusing each other. Execution as the punishment for witchcraft became law in 1563 following the Act Against Conjurations, Enchantments and Witchcraft in the reign of Elizabeth I. Of course a convicted witch could bequeath nothing in a will, her estate was forfeit to the crown. The 1563 Act was replaced in 1735, but only repealed in 1951.[3] In fact, Helen Duncan (d. 1956) was tried at the Old Bailey for witchcraft during the Second World War. Some people thought she was a fraud, but others were convinced by her séances. The court found her guilty, sending her to Holloway Prison for nine months, much to the disgust of Prime Minister Winston Churchill.

Killing Fields

During the sixteenth and seventeenth centuries, thousands of women were tried and executed across Europe. This was a barbaric witch hunt so prolonged and on such a vast scale that no one is sure of the exact number. Half the executions and trials took place in Germany,[4] but trials were also held in France, Holland, Italy, Denmark, Poland, Hungary, Slovakia and Switzerland. In Norway at Vardo in 1617 a violent storm sunk fishing boats and forty men drowned. Rather than the weather, locals blamed witches, claiming they had created the storm. Some were tortured to 'confess'. In all, in the biggest witch trial in Scandinavia, eighty women were burned at the stake.

In Scotland, Janet Horne was the last witch executed when she was burned in 1727. In the small town of Dornoch, a stone marks the site of her death. It is estimated that about 2,500 women (as well as some men) were accused of witchcraft and executed in Scotland between 1590 and 1662.[5] At Crook of Devon, a village near Perth, ten women and a man were executed for witchcraft in 1662.

England also held many trials, as in the cases of the Pendle and Samlesbury witches at Lancaster in 1612, but nearly every county held trials. Carrickfergus held a trial in 1711 and Tring in 1751.

One of the most shameful witch hunts was in the 1640s in East Anglia after the chaos of the Civil War, when the infamous Mathew Hopkins found great profit in hunting witches. Many – most – of the accused were poor women who were old, infirm, without influence or friends. Each town paid a fee to Mathew Hopkins for finding a witch. More witches, more money.

The son of a Puritan vicar, Mathew Hopkins called himself the Witchfinder General. It is estimated that he accused more than 250 people, mostly women, of whom 100 were executed. The first trial was at Manningtree, Essex, in 1645. At Chelmsford, nineteen of the women he had accused were hanged in a single day. He was paid £23 for his efforts. Between 1645 and 1647, trials were held at Stowmarket, King's Lynn, Ipswich, Aldeburgh, Yarmouth and at Bury St Edmunds, where sixty-eight died. Both Aldeburgh and Ipswich decided to raise local taxes in order to pay for the service of hunting witches; Aldeburgh paid £6 and Stowmarket the considerable sum of £23. 'Proof' of guilt for witchcraft was found in various ways: a weighing chair, ducking in a pond or river, or being forced to walk all night. Finding certain marks on the body might also prove their guilt.

Jane Wenham, Witch of Walkern

Tried as a witch in 1712,[7] the trial of Jane Wenham (c. 1642–1730) was a sensation followed as far away as London, where pamphlets were printed about the Witch of Walkern. A small Hertfordshire village, Walkern was Jane's home. She was a poor, old widow who took in washing to earn money. As Norah Lofts points out in *Domestic Life in* England,[8] an old woman living alone who quarrelled with her neighbours was vulnerable to being accused of anything from putting a curse on their cows or their spinning wheel to causing deaths in their household. Everywhere, witchcraft is usually a 'woman's crime'. In Hertfordshire, between 1573 to 1621, twelve men were accused among some fifty cases of witchcraft.[9]

Jane Wenham's trial, held at the Hertford Assizes, included the accusation that she had been seen flying by night. The judge, Sir John Powell, did offer up the fact that there was no law against this, but he could not alter the jury's verdict. This would have meant death, but Sir John managed to obtain a royal pardon from Queen Anne. Though she was spared in the end, Jane Wenham was one of the last witches in England condemned to death.

Jane could not return to Walkern and the neighbours who had accused her, so local landowners kindly offered protection and a place to live. When Jane died in 1730, she received a Christian burial at St Mary's Church near Hertford. To be buried in consecrated ground was an important symbol for her, as it meant she was not a witch in the eyes of the Church but a true Christian.

Jealousy would sometimes create an accusation such as that levelled at Jane Wenham. Such is the case for Barbara Gilmour (d. 1732), who returned to Scotland having lived in Ireland for a time. She married a farmer, John Dunlop, and brought with her a splendid new recipe for cheese (known as Dunlop cheese) which became popular. Indeed, it was so tasty that her neighbours accused her of witchcraft, though she was found innocent. These days, Dunlop cheese – with a delightful nutty taste – is still made in Ayrshire, where Barbara first made it.

Elizabeth Peacock: A Witch and Her Will

A few decades before Barbara Dunlop and Jane Wenham, Elizabeth Peacock (d. 1675) and others were accused of witchcraft in Malmesbury, Wiltshire. The charges included the 'killing and murdring [sic] of Margery Neale by witchcraft', and being in league with the Devil.

Elizabeth had already been accused in 1670, when the Webb family claimed their son Thomas was bewitched by her, but she was found innocent on that occasion. Two years later, in 1672, Thomas again was ill and this time he named the people harming him. Elizabeth Peacock was accused together with her sister Judith Witchell and Anne Tilling, who immediately confessed. Tilling named nine other women and two men. Perhaps she hoped that if more people were arrested she might be pardoned. Instead, three local magistrates were summoned to the town. Sir James Long, a fourth magistrate, arrived later and was immediately sceptical about Anne's 'confession' as well as Thomas's claim he could 'see' the women in his room. Sir James recommended caution; sending so many to the Salisbury Assizes on flimsy evidence would make a laughing stock of Malmesbury in the rest of the county. We know such details because Sir James wrote a pamphlet on the subject in 1686, during a national debate about the reality of witchcraft.

Caution did prevail, and so fewer women were sent to trial: Elizabeth Peacock, said to be the leader, along with Anne Tilling, Elizabeth Mills and her sister Judith Witchell. Only two, Judith Witchell and Anne Tilling, were found guilty of injuring Thomas Webb by witchcraft. They were hanged at Salisbury.

Research by historian Tony McAleavy[10] has uncovered new documents, including Elizabeth Peacock's will. He believes that because Elizabeth Mills and Elizabeth Peacock refused to confess they could not be found guilty. But what happened to them after the trial? It might not have suited those who sent them off to be tried, but the two women simply returned home to Malmesbury and continued their lives as normal.

Elizabeth Peacock died in 1675, and in her will asked to be buried in Malmesbury Abbey. As in the case of Jane Wenham, this is a most illuminating request; the abbey grounds were consecrated, proving she was no witch but a true Christian. Elizabeth's will declares her hope that her soul will be saved through the passion of Jesus Christ, claiming her right 'to be buried in a decent manner' as a Christian. Her sister Mary Browne received her cottage (worth £4 10s) and her clothes, valued at 10 shillings. Her goods overall were valued at £5 10s, and from this the funeral costs and debts were to be paid. An 'old fflock [sic] bed with bedstead, bolster and appurtenances' was given to William Witchell, presumably a relative of the Judith Witchell hanged as a witch.

Modern Witchcraft

Do we still believe in black magic and witchcraft? Some of us keep lucky items and superstitions have not disappeared. Just think of walking under ladders and Friday the 13th, both still considered to be unlucky. Even people who are otherwise perfectly rational avoid travelling or attending meetings on that inauspicious date. In Boscastle, Cornwall, you can visit a Museum of Witchcraft and Magic with thousands of books and more than 3,000 objects. Among them is a weighing chair, used in earlier centuries to see if a woman was guilty of being a witch.

Thomas Waters, in his book *Cursed Britain*, claims that these early beliefs and black magic have not disappeared. Recent events also remind us of the surviving belief in such things, especially in other parts of the world. An example was the torture and terrible murder of eight-year-old Victoria Climbié in 2000. Victoria was born in the Ivory Coast and lived in London with her great-aunt, who at her trial claimed her niece was possessed by the Devil. Belief in witchcraft still survives in the Ivory Coast, where, as in Nigeria and Angola, children are sometimes punished for supposed witchcraft.

If those prosecuted and found guilty of witchraft could not make a binding will, why include them in this book at all? Their 'bequest' to history is of course as innocent victims of patriarchal societies, but while the executions were appalling, there are several surprising facts that in some ways contradict the accepted view. Firstly, in the UK an accused witch was not automatically doomed: the conviction rate was about 50 per cent. Secondly, most were accused not by men, but women. Thirdly, accusations do not seem to be a way of suppressing secret female knowledge of medicine, aimed at midwives, wisewomen or 'cunning' women. Such women were accused, but they do not predominate. Accusations were a way for neighbours to explain everyday misfortunes. Accusations were, as bizarre and terrible as it may seem, 'normal'.

4

THE EXTREME DANGER OF DYING IN CHILDBIRTH

> Thinking myself to be with child in lawful marriage...
> The will of Mary I, March 1558

The housewife in earlier times had many domestic chores to fulfil in addition to looking after her family and any young children. The dairy, the brewhouse and the baking, the laundry, a kitchen garden and preserves were all part of domestic life.[1] If she was sufficiently rich, then there were servants and nurses to look after the children, such as a wet nurse to breastfeed the new baby in place of the mother. The tradition of a wet nurse is found in Saxon times and existed much earlier, in ancient Egypt. In Greek mythology, Odysseus was said to have had a wet nurse.

Without modern medical knowledge, each and every pregnancy might prove lethal. Large families were not unusual. Elizabeth I's cousin Catherine Carey, Lady Knollys, had sixteen children: eight sons and eight daughters. Susannah Wesley (b. 1669), mother of the founding Methodists John and Charles Wesley, had eighteen or possibly nineteen children. Even by seventeenth-century standards this was a large brood. Queen Anne had eighteen pregnancies but only one living child, who died at the age of eleven.

Every pregnant woman in earlier centuries knew that the risk of death was very great. All families would have known the grief and sorrow for a mother, daughter, sister, sister-in-law, friend, neighbour or aunt who had died in childbirth. Sometimes the baby survived, but just as often the death of the mother meant the death of the baby as well. Many church monuments can be found dedicated to mothers who died in childbirth, among them one at York Minster for Jane Hodson (d. 1636), who died at the age of thirty-eight. The monument says she was the mother of twenty-four children.

Even when a child survived, the rates of infant mortality were high. Indeed, they hardly changed from medieval through to Victorian and Edwardian times. Evidence from London, for example, reveals that nearly half the burials during the 1730s were those of children under the age of five.[1] Earlier, during the Restoration years of the 1660s, half of all deaths in London were those of children younger than ten.[1]

Superstitions for a Safe Birth

During medieval times, women might use a saint's girdle during childbirth in the hopes of ensuring an easy delivery as well as a safe outcome for both mother and the baby. Westminster Abbey owned one girdle attributed to the Virgin Mary, but during the Reformation almost all were destroyed as superstitious trappings of the old Catholic faith. We might suspect that many families continued to use their own, however, and who can blame them for attaching importance to such safeguards? The Wellcome Collection in London has one rare girdle made in the late 1400s from a religious parchment.[2] Amulets of eaglestones and toadstones were also thought to make childbirth easier during the medieval era.

The danger of death in childbirth only significantly altered after the 1860s, when superstition and old wives' tales were slowly replaced by improved medical knowledge and understanding of the critical importance of hygiene. Antiseptics were developed around this time, and the rudimentary anaesthetic chloroform was invented too. When Queen Victoria used it during the birth of her eighth child, Leopold, in 1853, she described the pain relief as 'delightful beyond measure'. Some doctors opposed the newfangled idea of chloroform for ordinary births, believing that women should suffer pain in childbirth as nature had intended. However, most of Victoria's loyal subjects preferred to follow her example if they could.

In 1871, Florence Nightingale was one of the first to analyse the data and review the number of deaths at lying-in (maternity) wards and hospitals. Finding that the mortality rate was higher there than among mothers giving birth at home, she concluded that regardless of how basic the home might be, women were safer giving birth there.

The Cholmondeley Ladies

A Tudor painting from the early 1600s depicting two new mothers is known as *The Cholmondeley Ladies*. These women, who are sisters, sit stiffly upright in bed, fully dressed in their finest clothes. The painter was clearly keen on precision; fine details are included on their necklaces, which are almost identical, not to mention their heavily starched high double ruffs, the embroidery of their dresses and the tiny bows on their sleeves. No wonder they appear uncomfortable in such elaborate, expensive clothes.

The Cholmondeley Ladies is one of the most popular paintings in the Tate Gallery, and it is easy to see why. The sisters are so realistic that they seem as if they might get up and walk towards the viewer at any moment. They stare straight out with a rather mysterious, sphinx-like expression. Each cradles a newborn babe, wrapped in swaddling and ornate, bright red christening robes. The crimson robes provide a vivid splash of colour against the silver sheen and expensive blackwork embroidery of the women's dresses, the pattern of which matches that of the swaddling robes. Dating from around 1604, the painting was for many years in Vale Royal House, Cheshire, the Cholmondeley family home. The legend in gold on the painting tells us their story:

The Extreme Danger of Dying in Childbirth

Two Ladies of the Cholmondeley Family,
Who were born the same day, Married the same day,
And brought to Bed [childbirth] the same day.

The painting celebrates the birth of a son and heir for both sisters. Lettice, Lady Grosvenor (d. 1612) and Mary, Lady Calveley (d. 1616) were the daughters of Sir Hugh Cholmondeley and Lady Mary.[2] Lettice's son Richard was born in 1604 and would inherit Eaton Hall, the large country estate where the Grosvenor family remains resident today. Lettice married into a local gentry family, although most of the advantage then was for the bridegroom, as the Cholmondeley family ranked second in the county. The Grosvenors were lower down the social order, ranking fourteenth. Later generations did prosper, however, becoming dukes of Westminster.

Pregnancy Portraits – Revealed and Concealed

The photo of a nude, heavily pregnant Demi Moore on the front cover of the magazine *Vogue* in 1991 was profoundly shocking to many. Her hands preserved her modesty, but the profile view emphasised her large stomach. However, it often surprises people to discover that the idea of 'pregnant and proud' was not new and had in fact been pioneered many centuries earlier.

Early 'pregnancy portraits' from the sixteenth and seventeenth centuries show mothers deliberately posed to reveal their pregnancy bump, but keeping all their clothes on as would have been expected at the time.[2] Such paintings capture the pride of the family and the intense focus of the expectation on a woman to be fertile and produce the all-important son and heir. Among the famous examples are Lady Mildred Burghley (1563, attributed to Hans Eworth); Lady Catherine Knollys (1562); Barbara, Countess of Leicester (1596); Lady Anne Pope (also 1596); and Lady Alice Caesar (1597). The 1611 portrait of Lady Maria Thynne by Daniel Mytens is another, produced a year after Marcus Gheeraerts' painting of a pregnant Lady Mary

Neville. Later, in the 1620s, Marcus Gheeraerts painted *Portrait of a Woman in Red*. The sitter was Lady Anne Fanshawe, and it is a sad and sombre painting as Anne died from that pregnancy, aged twenty-one. The child, who was her first, survived and was named Anne in honour of her mother. There also are some van Dyck pregnancy portraits from 1636, including one for Queen Henrietta Maria. The painters were the most important artists of their day.

However, by the Victorian era fashions had changed and pregnancy itself is hidden behind other phrases: 'in the family way', 'increasing', or 'in an interesting condition'. A concealed pregnancy can be seen in Joshua Reynolds' portrait of Theresa Parker (1775), in which a cloak hides her baby bump. Tragically, she died giving birth.

Concealment of pregnancy continued through to the twentieth century when modest maternity dresses were preferred. Attitudes did change, and by 1974 a statue of a nude pregnant woman was placed outside University Hospital, North Tees. But the matron of the maternity ward was shocked, petitioning against the statue as 'inappropriate'. Many agreed with her, so it was returned to sculptor Eddie Hawking. He had modelled it on his wife Audrey, and fortunately kept the sculpture as some decades later, in 2021, it was reinstated outside the building, no longer considered inappropriate or outrageous.

Men risked their lives going to war, but women also risked theirs with each and every pregnancy. In the Tudor age a first marriage might last only for around five years, though it was death rather than divorce which decided this as so many young women died in childbirth.[3] If there was a new baby every twelve or eighteen months, this cycle of almost continual pregnancy must have been both physically and mentally exhausting. Nafis Sadik, who did so much to help poor women in rural Pakistan during the 1950s, found that constant childbirth made the women 'so anaemic, so ill'.[3] The situation would have been the same in Britain in earlier centuries.

Four of Jane Austen's sisters-in-law died in childbirth, so it is hardly surprising she held a rather bleak view of a woman's destiny. Writing about her niece Anna Lefroy, who eventually had seven children, Jane said, 'Poor Animal, she will be worn out before she is thirty – I am very sorry for her.'

I Am Likely to Die

Across the centuries, many expectant mothers wrote wills. In fifteenth-century Renaissance Florence, for instance, it is thought most pregnant women made one.[4] In 1312, Queen Isabella received her husband's permission to make a will, though the document itself was lost; she survived, and the boy who would become Edward III was born. Sarah, 1st Duchess of Marlborough, had similar concerns in 1690 when she wrote a will just before her second son was born. One Victorian example came in 1892, when Vita Sackville-West's mother, Victoria, felt that same bleak expectation of death. Neither the will nor the farewell letter she wrote for her husband were necessary, however, as both mother and daughter happily survived.

Mary, Queen of Scots and her Pregnancy Will

Cousins Mary Stuart, Queen of Scotland and Mary Tudor, Queen of England made pregnancy wills. The latter was expecting a child in March 1558, her first pregnancy at the advanced age of thirty-eight, although it did not come to pass. Her cousin Mary, Queen of Scots was herself pregnant in 1566, also with a first child, but was in her twenties at the time.[5] Both mother and child survived, though shortly afterwards she was forced to abdicate in favour of the boy who became James VI of Scotland and I of England.

Many bequests in the pregnancy will of Mary, Queen of Scots concern her jewellery. Some belonged to the Scottish Crown while other items were her own, from France when she was married to the Dauphin. Her uncle did suggest when she left France that it would be safer if the jewels stayed there, but her reply was that if it was safe for her to go then it was safe for her jewels. Hers was a magnificent collection, with diamonds, rubies, emeralds, exceptional black pearls and garnets. The inventory still exists in the National Records of Scotland, containing notes in the will against different items, showing who was to receive what. Some of the jewels had belonged to her mother, Mary of Guise.

The queen bequeathed her wedding ring to her husband, Lord Darnley, whose murder the following year would contribute to her downfall and abdication. Various other jewels were destined for her mother's Guise family in France, and for her ladies-in-waiting and friends. Her Latin and Greek books, intended for St Andrews University, never did arrive.

In the desperate power struggle after the birth of James, Mary's half-brother became Regent of Scotland and confiscated Mary's jewels, giving some to his wife. Others were secretly sold in order to bolster Scottish finances. Elizabeth I bought a handsome, most expensive, black pearl necklace and she wears it in the famous 'Ermine Portrait' of 1585 by Nicholas Hilliard. In Mary's pregnancy will, the pearls were to be divided between the Crown of Scotland and her mother's family.

Mary fled to England in 1568, only to be imprisoned for nineteen years before being executed in 1587. Buried first in Peterborough Cathedral, her grave was then moved to Westminster Abbey on the orders of James when he became King of England.

The English queen Mary Tudor's will[5] and pregnancy tell a different story. Instead of the son and Catholic heir so desperately wanted, hers was instead a phantom, false pregnancy which modern medicine regards as a symptom of ovarian cancer, from which she is believed to have died soon after. The birth of a son and heir was of such national importance that the queen's pregnancy had been proclaimed in Parliament, and then at St Paul's Cathedral, with bells rung at what turned out to be the false announcement of a son.

The Extreme Danger of Dying in Childbirth

The will begins:

> Thinking myself to be with child in lawful marriage between my said dearly beloved husband and Lord ... forseeing the great danger which by Godd's ordynance remaine to all whomen in ther travel of children, have thought good ... to declare my last will and testament ...

The nursery was prepared, servants and a wet nurse readied, while the queen retired with her ladies to a lying-in chamber at Hampton Court Palace. After a long wait it became clear to everyone, including the queen, who perhaps believed the longest, that there would be no son and heir.

Queen Mary's will was written in March 1555. She died three years later, in November 1558, aged forty-two. One request was that her mother's tomb be moved from Peterborough to Westminster Abbey to be near to her. It never did happen, and Catherine of Aragon still rests at Peterborough Cathedral. Queen Mary left £500 to each of the Catholic religious houses which had been re-established at Syon and Sheen. Gifts were also left to the poor, as well as legacies for her servants. Of the two executors named, her husband, King Philip of Spain, was not in England at the time while her faithful servant Cardinal Pole, who was to receive £1,000 for his troubles, died the same day as the queen.

The Duke and his Duchess ... and her Lover's Child

In 1791, Georgiana, Duchess of Devonshire wrote a will in the certainty that she would die in childbirth. For centuries, the will lay forgotten in the family archives at Chatsworth. It was only discovered in the twenty-first century when Amanda Foreman came across it while combing the archives in the process of writing Georgiana's biography.

Georgiana already had a young family, but the baby[6] that was due just weeks after she wrote her will was the result of a love affair with a young, promising politician named Charles Grey (later Prime Minister the Earl Grey). In order to avoid scandal, she planned to lie low with her sister Harriet until after the baby was born. However, upon discovering what had happened William, Duke of Devonshire came to Bath to confront his wife, who was by now six months pregnant. There were unpleasant scenes when the duke shouted and Georgiana cried.

The duke offered a choice: her lover or her children. The latter choice meant going abroad to have the baby and returning without the child. The former meant divorce and never again seeing her young children. This was a cruel ultimatum, and hypocritical as well considering the duke's affair with Georgiana's closest friend Lady Bess Foster. But law, as well as every social convention, was firmly on the husband's side. He had all the rights while a wife had none.[7]

What a wretched business. Such a tragedy for Georgiana, who did go away to the Continent, travelling with her sister, her brother-in-law and her mother. Ironically, Bess also joined them. As the birth of the baby drew near, the duchess became convinced she would die. Along with a will, she wrote farewell letters to her children – the blessing in the letter to her son she wrote with her own blood. In the will, Georgiana left 'as a remembrance' to her husband a green antique ring which Bess had given to her.[7]

Georgiana did not die in childbirth. The will was eventually lost, forgotten among the family papers at Chatsworth. The baby, named Eliza Courtney, was sent to Charles Grey's parents. As she grew up, her father was presented to her as her older brother – a pretence families often used to hide such shameful secrets.

Georgiana could meet her daughter when the Greys came to London, but she could only write letters to her as if she were an aunt or godmother. In the meantime, the duchess was one of the most popular women in the country. Expensive addictions to gambling and laudanum went side by side with society life as she continued her close friendship with Bess. Their children were brought up together in London and at Chatsworth House in

Derbyshire. A strange ménage à trois continued for over twenty years, with two illegitimate children between the duke and Bess. It was an 'open' secret in polite society, as a few years before the duchess's affair Betsy Sheridan had written to her sister Alicia of the rumour that Bess and the Duke were romantically involved.[7] Georgiana's mother, Lady Spencer, would never stay at Chatsworth when Bess was there.

When Georgiana died in 1806 of a liver abscess at the age of forty-eight, her letters and private papers were left to Bess, who was also executrix of the will. Some papers were then destroyed or damaged, with pages taken out or paragraphs inked over. She probably removed anything which made her look bad or scheming. Three years later, she married the duke – a triumph which, while not unexpected, was much resented by Georgiana's children. The marriage was brief, as the duke died before their second wedding anniversary. He was buried in the Cavendish family vault at Derby Cathedral alongside Georgiana. A decade later, when Bess died in Rome, her body was brought back to the family vault. So, in death as it was in life, the duke and his two duchesses are together.

Only after the duchess died did Eliza learn the truth; she later named her own daughter Georgiana in memory of the mother she never knew.

Christening Gowns and Family Heirlooms

White christening gowns often became family heirlooms, passed down through generations. An example can be found in the British royal family. A dress made in 1841 for Victoria, first child of Prince Albert and Queen Victoria, is still in use today. A modern copy has also been made, and reputedly dipped in tea to mimic the shade of the original lace. Similarly, two late nineteenth-century gowns were given to Buckland Abbey in Devon by one Mrs Soper of Tavistock because there was no new generation to receive them.

It wasn't always a gown. In Tudor wills we sometimes find a christening sheet rather than a gown, as in 1521 when Johan Morcott, a widow in Bedfordshire, left two sheets to her daughter Agnes.[8] Christening sheets were also popular bequests much earlier in medieval London,[9] and presumably elsewhere.

To Die in Childbirth

The risk of death in childbirth was always high in previous centuries. These days the birthing room is a much safer place but there are still certain mysteries which need resolving. For all our medical knowledge, for example, we do not fully understand why a quarter of million pregnancies each year end in miscarriage, equal to around one in five pregnancies. A few mothers who died (or nearly died) in childbirth throughout history are shown below.

1134 Empress Maud (d. 1167), daughter of Henry I, nearly died giving birth to a second son Geoffrey and so made a will.

1316 Marjorie Bruce died at the age of nineteen. Her son survived and became Robert II of Scotland. Marjorie's mother Isabella of Mar died at a similar age when giving birth to her.

1503 Elizabeth of York, wife of Henry VII, died aged thirty-seven after the birth of her seventh child, a daughter named Katherine who lived only a few days.

1537 Jane Seymour, third wife of Henry VIII, died aged twenty-eight after the birth of her first child, the future Edward VI.

1548 Katherine Parr, the sixth wife (and widow) of Henry VIII, died aged thirty-six, a few days after the birth of her first child, Mary. After Henry's death she had married Sir Thomas Seymour for love. Her will reads, 'I, Katherine Parr, etc., lying on my deathbed, sick of body but of good mind and perfect memory and

The Extreme Danger of Dying in Childbirth

discretion, being persuaded and perceiving the extremity of death to approach me, give all to my married spouse and husband, wishing them to be a thousand times more in value than they are or [have] been.'[10]

1605 The saddest memorial brass in Wormington church, Gloucestershire, has a portrait of Anne Savage. She died in childbirth aged twenty-five and the brass shows her lying in bed while her tiny baby, which did not survive either, is wrapped in swaddling clothes beside her.

1775 Theresa Parker, Lady Boringdon *née* Robinson, art patron and designer, aged thirty-one, died after the birth of a second child, a daughter named after her. She oversaw the interior design and golden age of Saltram House in Devon.

1797 Mary Wollstonecraft, author of *A Vindication of the Rights of Woman*, died aged thirty-eight after the birth of her daughter, future author Mary Shelley.

1855 Charlotte Brontë was thirty-eight and died during her first pregnancy. The child also died. Modern medical experts now generally agree that the cause of death was severe morning sickness, *hyperemesis gravidarum*. She wrote her will on 17 February and died on 31 March.

1924 Andolyn Lewis died giving birth to a daughter who was named after her. In the Welsh tradition, baby Andolyn – later Lady Marjorie Clark – was christened over the coffin of her dead mother.

1927 Edith Jenkins *née* Thomas, mother of actor Richard Burton, died aged forty-four after her thirteenth child, Graham, was born.

The Original Princess Diana

In 1817, Princess Charlotte died aged twenty-one after a nightmare labour of fifty hours. Heir to George IV, her death was a national tragedy akin to the death of Princess Diana in modern times. Charlotte was immensely popular, the darling of the nation and the hope for something better after her father's dissolute life.

The tragedy of a young princess dying was made all the more dreadful by the death of her baby son. When Diana died in 1997, cathedrals such as Winchester opened books of remembrance and it was particularly touching to see mothers and daughters going together to sign such books across the country.

Princess Charlotte was much younger in 1817, but there was a similar outpouring of shock and grief. The royal family at court went into mourning, and so did many others. The nation seemed to close down. Shops in many towns hung black drapes of mourning, and London shops and the law courts closed entirely for two weeks. Some blamed the death of the princess on Dr Richard Croft, who had attended the birth; a few months later he committed suicide after attending another difficult delivery.

5

FEWER WILLS AND FAR LESS TO LEAVE

'To daughter Elizabeth Hellier her best petticoat, her best gown, best smock and best woollen smock, her 2 best cross kerchiefs, best apron, best hat and 2 best partlets [a collar or ruff].'

Elizabeth Bantonn, widow,
11 June 1599, proved 29 October[1]

'To wife of John Hopttan, cutler, of St Peter's Parish, her grogrem gown, her best red petticoat, best kerchief...'

Elizabeth Waker, widow,
26 April 1597[1]

Fewer Wills

While it is true that in earlier times both men and women mention clothes as bequests, it is more common among women's wills. Sometimes we find precise details about what is to be given, as in the extracts above by Elizabeth Waker and Elizabeth Bantonn. A daughter may be singled out, or a godchild, granddaughter or niece; sometimes there is a wide network of female relatives and friends.

Confusingly, we find mention of 'the worst petticoat' or gown in wills, which may seem strange, but still these were likely to be valued by someone not as wealthy as the deceased. Aprons, hats, smocks, and kirtles are all mentioned as well as coats, head napkins (scarfs), and safeguards worn over skirts when horse-riding or travelling.

In wills from seventeenth-century Suffolk,[2] clothes mentioned include the best waistcoat, best ruff or neckerchief, a cloth gown, red petticoat, best stammel stuff petticoat (a worsted cloth that was often red), a best hat, serge kirtle, an old ruff, azure cloth petticoat, best gown and two best petticoats, gown, best cloak, best hat lined with velvet, green petticoat, taffety (thin silk) aprons, a green say (serge) apron, a linsey wolsey (coarse inferior cloth combining linen and wool) apron, watchet (light blue) petticoat, two worst petticoats and two worst waistcoats, and best apron, a pair of gloves, crimson stuff (worsted) petticoat, petticoat of shag bayes (mixed cloth with velvety nap on one side), four coifs (close-fitting caps covering the top, sides and back of the head), a gold coif, best holland (fine linen from Holland) apron, a new russet petticoat and an old petticoat.

Some of these would have been everyday clothes, but a silk apron was kept for Sunday or belonged to someone wealthy.

'My Red Petticoat'

In 1624, Abrie Boteman, a spinster from Badingham, left bequests to her cousins. Aunt Packerall was to receive the biggest kettle and all her woollen clothes.[2] As in this case, we sometimes learn about the variety of materials used – wool was for everyone, but linen, silk, damask and velvet were not. Red petticoats were popular in the Tudor era as the colour was considered to bring health to those wearing it. But of course red is also striking, and must have created a brilliant splash of colour among all the drab colours prevailing in those times. A crimson satin petticoat mentioned among the clothes of Queen Mary I would have been of the very best quality.

A few generations later, in 1635, a butcher's widow in London left 'to my Cosen Mary Brockett ... my best scarlett Petticoate or the value thereof in money'. She is Catherine Yarwood, the mother of John Harvard, who died the year before her son emigrated to America and founded the famous college that bears his name.

Clothes given to the Church or religious foundations were always acceptable as luxury materials could be reworked into altarpieces or vestments. Dame Jane Neville in 1470 gave blue velvet gowns to her local church in Warwick to be made into vestments for the priests.[3]

Blanche Parry (d. 1590), Elizabeth I's favourite lady-in-waiting, gave a most expensive skirt of Italian silk and cloth of silver as an altar cloth. Originally the skirt had belonged to the queen, and the embroidery on it is both fantastical and delightful, studded with butterflies, frogs, flowers – even a bear and a sea monster above an empty boat!

One wonders what the parishioners made of this strange artwork at Bacton church in Wales. The same place of worship boasts a monument to Blanche Parry, though her actual grave is in Westminster, London.[3]

Most wills belong to widows or single women, as married women by law could not make a will without their husband's permission for centuries. In one survey of over 2,000 wills from Lincoln, Bath and Wells between 1327 and the early 1500s, it was found that roughly 90 per cent of the wills were for men.[4] Later in Tudor times, in Shakespeare's hometown of Stratford-upon-Avon the situation is almost identical: only 9 per cent of wills belong to women.[5] In Uffculme in Devon, in a period spanning the sixteenth and eighteenth centuries, only seven of more than 250 inventories (lists of belongings left by the deceased) belong to wives.[5]

In larger towns such as Colchester there were some signs of progress over the years, with the amount of wills representing men down to 81 per cent later on in the period.[6] This trend can be seen to continue in Hertford between 1660 and 1725, when 20 per cent of the wills belonged to women, mostly widows and spinsters.[7] In the small Fenland town of Ramsey, the earliest wills are exclusively by men; in all its history up to 1600, there were fifteen wills made by women; all were widows.[8]

The larger number of women's wills in Colchester and Hertford perhaps reflects a greater freedom enjoyed by the fairer sex in larger towns. With constant trade and busy markets to London and the Continent, together with the constant churn of migrants moving through, women might have had greater opportunities for financial betterment. If they were more likely to prosper, they were more likely to have belongings or property to leave after they died.

The number of women testators in Tudor Bristol is also relatively high at 24 per cent. As a bustling and wealthy port, the same rule as applies for Colchester and Hertford may well be in evidence here.[1]

A Widow's Inheritance

Widows often found their inheritance controlled by the terms of their husband's will. In 1471, John Fellowe, a barber from St Albans, left a tenement to his wife Joan – but only for her lifetime. After her death it was to be sold and the funds were to be used to employ a priest who would pray for his soul, as well as those of his parents and his former wives.[9]

Sometimes a widow would lose her inheritance if she remarried. In 1604, for instance, John Pasco of Trewey forbade his wife Jowana to marry again.[10] This looks like a form of coercive control from beyond the grave. One justifying motive might be a concern that a second husband and additional children resulting from the new marriage might take some, or indeed all, of his children's inheritance. However, if the widow is clearly given a chamber, livestock and harvest from the land (that her son must provide), then her rights are clear until such time as she might remarry. Similar provisos occur in medieval times as well as much later into the nineteenth century, as shown by Harriet Barker's study of wills from Liverpool and Manchester.[11]

Despite these considerations, there were no children to worry about in the case of Anne Lister, who in 1840 left a life interest in Shibden Hall to her lover Ann Walker. If Ann Walker should ever (legally) marry, the bequest would cease and cousins would instead receive the estate 'as if the said Ann Walker should have then departed this life'. Anne Lister had no intention of letting Ms Walker marry a man and forget her, perhaps because this did happen earlier with another woman she had loved.

Known locally in Halifax as 'Gentleman Jack', Anne Lister dressed like a man and seemed to have lesbian affairs. She certainly visited the Ladies of Llangollen, a famous upper-class Irish couple, during the summer of 1822 with her aunt, though she puzzled over whether theirs was a platonic or a lesbian friendship. She envied the idyllic way of life led by Eleanor Butler and Sarah Ponsonby, who lived together in their own house.

Anne Lister's journals were considered so shocking and sexually explicit when first deciphered that the owner of Shibden Hall was advised to burn them. Instead, he hid them carefully so somebody else might discover them in a more tolerant future. This indeed happened, and Helena Whitbread's book became the basis of the 2019 BBC series *Gentleman Jack*.

The Squire's Wife

A widow was often appointed to administer her husband's will, as in the wills at King's Langley, Hertfordshire dating from 1498 to 1659.[11] One study of probate records from the late sixteenth through to the middle of the eighteenth century found that most married men appointed their wife as executrix.[11] J. T. Cliffe's survey of country society during the 1600s similarly recognised women's central role in family affairs. Most squires – important landowners in their local area – named their wife executrix.[11] The same is true in earlier Tudor wills in Colchester studied by Laquita Higgs,[6] even among a lower Yeoman social class than the landed gentry.

Studies of wills from seventeenth-century Sudbury, Suffolk, show that women were named as sole executrix (rather than appointed jointly with a male executor) in 55 per cent of wills. The same can be found when examining the wills of actors in the early London theatre between 1558 and 1642. In 1618, Richard Burbage, one of the most famous actors of the time, appointed 'his wellbeloued wife Winifride Burbadge [sic]'.[12]

'Quishons and Bedde Stockes'

Modest bequests by poorer women are always present in local collections of wills, as attested in Bedfordshire, Bristol, Northampton, Devon and Suffolk. In a seventeenth-century survey of wills from St Helens, Lancashire,[12] only a few women could leave the relatively large sum of £5 or £6 for a funeral. Most wills contain items connected to daily life, work and toil, and are focussed on smaller household items:

> Blanketes, curteynes, sheetes, fryinge pann, corne unthreshen, bees, one syde saddle [a side saddle], and nine pair of bedde stockes [bed socks].

Such strange spellings, which are typical of a time when there were hardly any formal rules for grammar or spelling, can be found in wills throughout the history of English. Indeed, in examining texts for this book we observe whimsical spellings like bedstid (bedstead) and quishon (cushion). Pettycoat is fairly straightforward, as is 'my white rugge'. Another is 'the great brase poot and a spinning while' left by Ellin Downall of Sutton to her son Roger. Ellin's inventory of goods also mentions 'cheares' and 'stooles'. From bees to bedsteads, almost all the items in the wills from St Helens have value, either practical, financial or possibly sentimental, as in the three examples below:

> ... and the Cradle, I do give and appoynte them to my son Thomas, as heirelooms formerly given to him by his Grandfather.
> Margarett Winstanley, Billinge, 1633

Item I doe give to alise [Alice] the wif of Roger barton my best hatt and asmock [a smock].

Elline Ashurst, Billinge, 1638

I give Mary Roughley senior the red petticoat.

Elizabeth Baines, Sutton, 1684[12]

My Dear Grandchild

Jane Davies, a widow from Waen Isa in Wales, made a will at the end of the eighteenth century. It was kept by the family and it featured on the *Antiques Roadshow* during a visit to Mold in Flintshire. A rare Georgian document, and rather fragile, it was written on 13 November 1793. Jane Davies did not sign the will but instead 'made her mark', as it was known, with a cross. This often happened for wills, leases, legal documents or marriage certificates as many people were unable to read or write. The will included a special bequest to her granddaughter: 'the best feather bed … and bedstead to my dear Grandchild Elizabeth Price as a token of my regard'.

'My Best Beaver Hatt'

In a Hertfordshire will written in the seventeenth century, Elizabeth Joyce gave a 'damaske petticoat of sea-green colour' together with 'my best beaver hatt' to her sister-in-law.[13] Was the hat fashionable, sentimentally treasured or simply valuable? Perhaps it was a combination of all three. Beaver fur was certainly expensive, so even an old hat would have value, and Elizabeth had been precise in specifying her 'best' one. To give an idea of the value, Samuel Pepys once paid 45 shillings for a beaver hat. It was a most respectable item.[13]

Wills from St Albans mention many small items. For a goddaughter named Agnes there is 'a good sheet', while in another will a goddaughter receives 'my third best gown'.[9] In the Bedfordshire wills another Agnes, a granddaughter, receives a sheet while Alice Johnson, who died in 1521, left sixpence to every novice nun at nearby Chicksands Priory.[14]

A Woman's Will

Two pence for the mother church was a frequent bequest in Bedfordshire wills of the early sixteenth century, and although no one knew it at the time, this generation was to be among the last to be Catholic. Just a few years later, Henry VIII, for reasons of succession and financial acquisition as opposed to religious fervour, declared that England was now a Protestant nation. The Crown confiscated the monasteries and convents, taking the land and everything they owned. The king replaced the pope as head of the Church of England – as every monarch has been since. Thereafter, the Catholic bequests for Masses and prayers 'to save my soul' abruptly cease as the faith was forbidden. Anyone brave enough to disagree was guilty of treason.

> To the cathedral church of Lincoln 2 pence, to the high altar 12 pence.
>
> Johan [Joan] Wynne, Steventon, 1522

> To the lady abbess of Elnestow [Elstow Abbey] and the convent 10 shillings to be equally divided between them.
>
> Elizabeth Munke, Elstow, 1523

> To the friars of Bedford for a trental [thirty] of masses for the souls of the testator [Johan] and her husband Thomas Butler 10 shillings.
>
> Johan [Joan] Butler, Temmysford [Tempsford] 1525

> To bells 8 pence.
>
> Margaret Coore, Potten, 1527[14]

In an earlier Cornish will, the godchildren and servants are remembered as well as the local church:

> Two pence to each of my godchildren; two pence to each manservant or woman servant of my son John; to Holy Trinity

Church, two pence; to the fabric of the church of Maramchurch [a few miles from Bude] one cow.

Joan Pomeroy, 1435[15]

My Loyal Servants

Queen Catherine of Aragon died in early January 1536, aged fifty. Her marriage with Henry VIII had finally been annulled in 1533, though she never would accept their divorce. Instead, she was exiled from court after nearly thirty years as queen, having even been appointed queen regent when Henry was away in France. Only a daughter had survived; other children were stillborn, and the all-important son and heir lived for just two months.

Catherine of Aragon had relatively little to leave at the time of her death, but her will carefully sets out numerous small bequests to those who served in her household, even remembering the woman who did the laundry:

> Item, I ordain that my launderer be paid of that is due unto her, and besides that of her wages for the year coming.[16]

Queen Catherine asked that a pilgrimage be made on her behalf to Walsingham, the Norfolk shrine she and the king had visited decades before in the hopes that it would help in their quest to have a male heir. No pilgrimage was made. Nor was she buried at the Observant Friars in Greenwich as she had asked. Instead, the funeral was held at faraway Peterborough, and not in the name of Queen Catherine; the king insisted her title must be Catherine, Dowager Princess of Wales as this was her title before they married.

Her last letter to Henry was signed 'Katherine the Queen' with the words, 'Mine eyes desire you above all things.'

All the Katherines of England

Queen Catherine's grave was damaged during the Civil War, and to add insult to injury the local bishop took its black marble stone for his summerhouse in the eighteenth century. Only in 1895 was a new stone installed after a national campaign. This was organised by Katherine Clayton, wife of one of the Cathedral canons (later bishop) at Peterborough, who asked all the 'Katherines of England' to each donate a penny towards the new stone.

Henry VIII's fourth wife, Anne of Cleves, also gave money to her servants in her will. She further asked princesses Mary and Elizabeth, her stepdaughters, to take some of the servants into their households.[17]

A wealthy woman often left sufficient money for the household to continue for some months after her death, sometimes even as long as a year, providing them with sufficient time to find employment elsewhere and rewarding their loyal service. When Lady Margaret Beaufort died in 1509, the household servants were paid for another six months. For three of those months the household was continued, supplied with food and so on, as if she was still there. In 1578 her great-granddaughter Margaret, Countess of Lennox left a year's wages to all her servants, while in 1612 Jane Dormer, Duchess of Feria similarly asked that her household remain together for two months after her death.

Philippa Russell, Medieval Brewer and Singlewoman

Philippa Russell followed her parents into the brewing trade. Her mother Alice and father John had been members of the Guild of Brewers, this being one of the few trades in which women could be involved in the medieval era.

In 1458, Philippa Russell (sometimes Russel) made her will.[18] She had never married and was somewhere between thirty and forty years old when she died. Hers is one of only fifteen wills by single women in the City of London dating between 1450 and 1500, and it intrigued historians a good deal when it was first discovered. The fact that Philippa describes herself in the will as a 'singlewoman' was unexpected, as it had previously been assumed that this term described prostitutes. Clearly not, as Philippa was a most respectable single woman with a successful business.

Mostly written in Latin, the will is a long and detailed document with a codicil added a few months later. The four executors named included an alderman and a wax chandler who had probably known Philippa's family for many years. Many of her bequests concern church and charitable donations, with £5 for the marriage portions (or dowries) for ten poor girls in the Walbrook ward where Philippa lived. The girls were to be of 'good repute and honest behaviour', a clause often found in other wills to ensure those who received such charity were worthy, honest and virtuous.

Philippa also left bequests of money to repair roads and bridges. This was then considered part of a citizen's duty, as seen in a later Bedfordshire will when Elizabeth Aulaby (d. 1537) left 13s 4d for Puggihill (Puddlehill) – the name conjures up a muddy image of just how bad this road might be in a dreary winter or a wet springtime.[18]

Philippa Russell's estate was worth slightly more than £220, which was a considerable sum for those times. She also gave money to various London prisons including the Fleet, Marshalsea, Ludgate, Newgate, the King's Bench and the Abbot of Westminster's Bench. Her will included the conventional requests for prayers, 300 masses, gifts to the Church and to the poor to help save her soul. Prayers were also requested for the souls of her mother and her stepfathers.

Philippa wished to be buried beside her mother at St Mary Borthwick and gave generously to four other London churches with family links, as at St Swithin's where her father and one of her stepfathers were buried. Churches in Middlesex and Kent also received bequests and their parishioners were asked to pray for her soul; these also perhaps had family connections.

One curiosity is that Philippa left a loan chest and a sum of money to her own parish to be used over the next forty years to help needy parishioners, who could pledge silver or other goods against a loan. Usually, loans involved high interest rates so this practical bequest to the parish offered financial help without any interest payable.

Margaret Warde, one of Philippa's servants, received £10 and half of her household goods as well as twelve silver spoons. To a former apprentice of her stepfather, Philippa left 26s 8d. A large debt of £120 is mentioned in the will, which insists that the tailor John Spencer be sued in law 'as swiftly as they [the executors] can'.

Neither a Borrower nor a Lender Be

Having examined Philippa Russell's will we did not find evidence of loans made in a similar fashion in London, though there is plenty of evidence for this practice elsewhere. In Bristol and Southampton, York and Oxford, there are sufficient examples to show that loans were an accepted part of everyday life. In Tudor and Stuart wills[19] from St Helens in Lancashire[11] and Hertford,[7] loans also seem to have supplied a valuable income stream for women.

Always, though, there must have been a worry about whether the loan would be repaid. In 1666 in the inventory of the possessions (and estate) of Mary Stephens the final item includes the words 'in debt hopeful, £50', followed by the much bleaker phrase 'in desperate debt, £20'.[20] Whether the money was recovered or not is unknown, but £70 was a considerable amount to risk and it was left to Mary's son William as executor to recover the debts if he could.

Other wills belonging to women from Bristol also mention debts, both large and small, but one who apparently was not so entangled is the innkeeper Elinor Biggs. This may at first seem rather surprising, because she kept The Lamb Inn on Wine Street in the heart of Bristol, exactly the sort of occupation where she could be expected to deal with customers asking to put orders on a tab. Perhaps the reason she did not do this was because there would probably, almost certainly, have been too many requests once she set a precedent. And it is easy to imagine the disappointment if a customer was then refused a loan knowing that their neighbour, or another customer, had been given credit.

Angry words might occur, souring the all-important atmosphere or, even worse, causing a melodramatic and noisy exit.

Memento Mori

Many bequests are keepsakes or *memento mori*, by which to remember the deceased. The phrase is from the Latin 'remember you must die'. Bridget Mathew from Earls Colne, Essex, who died in 1671, left to 'my loving friends' George Cressener and his wife Mary three old 20-shilling pieces of gold[21] with which to buy rings.

Mourning jewellery was worn by men and women. Sometimes it was inscribed, set with a lock of hair from the deceased. When Jane Austen died, her sister Cassandra took some locks of hair to set into jewellery. There is a bracelet made with the hair of the aforementioned Princess Charlotte and set with a miniature painting of her eye. If this seems macabre to our modern tastes, there is a fairly recent idea in jewellery to include the cremated ashes of the deceased. The current Duchess of Northumberland has decided her ashes will be put into hourglass egg-timers, one for each child so that they will remember her every breakfast time! This is unusual but undeniably practical, as with another duchess, who commissioned her coffin in her lifetime. Queen Elizabeth II (and Prince Philip) had similarly pre-ordered their coffins – lead-lined and made of English oak, which is now so rare as to be prohibitively expensive.

Early wills from Tudor and Stuart times reveal another, rather more cheerful tradition to end this chapter – one associated with brides.

Alice Crawley of Stopsley and her Bride Cart

Local historian James Dyer, in writing about wills from Stopsley in Bedfordshire,[22] has connected us to the world of Alice Crawley, a favourite daughter. She is left an honest 'brydcart', or bride cart, in 1551 by her father Richard. This was used to carry the bride's dowry and her wedding presents from her father's house to her new home. We can imagine Alice travelling down the small lanes with the bride cart, from the farmhouse 'Plenties', Lane Farm in Putteridge Road, to her new house nearby. Putteridge Road is still there, and Lane Farm existed into the 1930s. (Later generations of the Crawleys became wealthier; by the 1740s it was one of the leading families in Luton.)

Some forty years later we find a bridewain (or cart) mentioned in two Yorkshire wills from Giggleswick, in each case left by a father for his unmarried daughters.[22] The cart doubtless held various pieces of household furniture as well as pewter plates, linen and bedding, some bought for the wedding and others given as gifts for the bride and groom. The local tradition in Giggleswick was for the cart to be drawn not by horses but oxen, with their horns decorated with ribbons – an intriguing touch as we still decorate wedding cars with pretty ribbons. These gifts were made by prosperous men, yeoman farmers who could afford to send their daughters off in some style with a good dowry of household goods to set them up in their new house.

In Warwickshire a bride cart is mentioned not in a will but in a marriage agreement which is now held in the County Record Office. Dated 20 May 1687, it concerns one John Spyer the younger and Sarah Hitch, 'spinster'. Sarah is to have a marriage portion of £65 – quite a large amount of money – plus a 'bride cart to the value of £15 (at least)' according to the contract signed by her brother Bartholomew. The bride and groom lived in neighbouring villages only 10 miles apart, and one can imagine the jolly procession as the loaded cart and happy bride trundled through the lanes from Dunton Bassett in Leicestershire, crossing over the country boundary into Warwickshire, towards her new home at Burton Hastings. It seems likely that then, just as now, neighbours and friends would turn out to see the bride passing, the inhabitants of both villages joining the celebrations while the local children skipped along behind the cart – rag, tag and bobtail.

Sarah Starr of New England and her Wedding

These wedding traditions existed in Bedfordshire, Yorkshire, Durham, Leicestershire, Warwickshire, and Kent, so it seems reasonable to assume that bride carts were widely popular. The tradition was even exported to the United States, as a bride's cart is mentioned in the early 1800s in a history of the Starr family who had emigrated to Boston, New England, as early as 1635. They hailed from Ashford in Kent, and it is the new bride Sarah Starr who is described as travelling on an ox cart with her furniture after the wedding feast on the way to her new house. Neighbours and friends came from their houses, bringing their glasses to be filled with the wine left from the feast. They toasted the couple, wishing them health and prosperity for a happy marriage.[22]

6

A GREEN PARROT, TWO GRANDSONS AND SUTTON HOO

> I give you my son John ... to kepe hem as hys owne chylde
>
> Joan Harve, Bedford, 1529

It is the year 1529 – we even know that it is 26 October – when a widow named Joan Harve made her will. She lived and died in Bedford, and in this sad will she gave her son, John, to the town's bailiff, William Thomas:

> He [Thomas] to kepe hem as hys owne chylde [child] and so to fynde hem mette and drenke and clothyng as he kepe on of hys owe childerne ... and to this end she bequeaths him all the goods that she has in this world.[1]

Whether John lived and prospered in the bailiff's family we do not know, but it was likely the only option for his mother. Without relatives or friends to help, this was the best place to leave him. Hoping that he would have a good life, Joan gave to the bailiff all the goods that she had.

The future for Joan's older son, Richard, was also uncertain though his mother could have no idea of what troubles lay ahead for him. Richard was a friar probably at the Franciscan Greyfriars in Bedford, and his mother left him a pair of sheets, a mattress, a blanket, a bolster, two platters, two candlesticks, a coverlet and a chafing dish (used to keep food warm). But within ten years all the monasteries were dissolved by Henry VIII and Richard lost this safe home for his old age. The religious properties were surrendered to the king's commissioners, who came to inspect, value and sell everything. All the gold and silver treasures, together with the saintly relics, were either confiscated or destroyed.

Beaulieu Abbey, founded in 1204, was dissolved (to become home to the Montagu family) and Woburn Abbey, now owned by the dukes of Bedford, was the site of a trial concerning Abbot Robert Hobbes and two of his monks in June 1538. Found guilty of treason for refusing to acknowledge Henry VIII as Supreme Head of the Church of England, they were hanged from an oak tree near the front of the Cistercian Abbey. The site is still marked on modern Ordinance Survey maps as 'Abbot's Oak'.

At Tewkesbury, the Benedictine abbey was sold to the town for £453 – the price of the lead on the roof and the metal in the abbey bells. It became the parish church. The bells at Furness Abbey, meanwhile, were sold to the men of Kendal for the bargain price of £80. At St Albans, forty monks were expelled and the abbey sold to the town for £400. A slimmed-down version of the abbey became the parish church. The lady chapel for the next 300 years was the town's grammar school. In London, land owned by Westminster Abbey was taken by Henry VIII to become his personal hunting ground; we know it today as Hyde Park.

Just a few years later, we find another mother trying to win friends and influence people through her will in order to ensure the safety of her sons after she has died.

'My Green Parrot ... I Have Nothing Worthy Else for Her'

Jane Dudley (*née* Guildford), Duchess of Northumberland (d. 1555) made her will shortly after her husband was executed for treason. Her life had truly been turned upside down; just a short while before, they had been one of the most important families in the realm. The duke had been Lord Protector, guardian and virtual regent for the young Edward VI, but now they were disgraced, traitors to the Crown and the new queen, Mary Tudor. The duke's bold plot to seize the throne had failed, and now ruin beckoned for his family. Their sons were imprisoned in the Tower of London, and though the duchess was released the queen refused to grant her an audience.

The Duke of Northumberland had attempted to change the succession by declaring his daughter-in-law Jane Grey as queen after the death of Edward VI. Secret plans made during the last few weeks of Edward's life created a charade that he was merely ill rather than dying. In the meantime, the Tower of London was fortified and the aldermen of London persuaded to support the new regime as the City's backing was vital if the coup was to succeed.

Letters were sent to Mary and her younger sister Elizabeth as if from Edward, asking them to visit him in London. Princess Mary had already left her house at Hunsdon before receiving a warning of the trap and instead turned east towards friendly Norfolk, specifically Kenninghall. Northumberland's soldiers followed close behind and burnt Sawston Hall, arriving just after she left. Elizabeth also stayed away from London, and supporters slowly but surely rallied around Mary.

Even those who previously supported the duke began to waver, with some of his closest allies changing their allegiance. Such moments in history are fraught with danger, a murderous game of musical chairs: end up on the wrong side and you're a traitor. The punishment could be hanging, drawing and quartering, while the family lands would be forfeit to the Crown.

Soon it was clear that Mary had the most support. The duke was never popular, and regardless of her Catholic faith Mary was Henry VIII's eldest child. Many people therefore considered she should inherit the throne despite her pious beliefs; most also knew that she was next to succeed as set out in Henry VIII's will. The duke's plot might well have succeeded if Elizabeth and

Mary had been tricked and taken prisoner. Instead, the duke was the one captured and later executed. A few months later, his son Guildford and daughter-in-law Lady Jane Grey were both executed.

To Protect My Sons

Duchess Jane could not change the fate of her husband, nor her eldest son, but Queen Mary did show some leniency towards the younger sons. The manor house at Chelsea was also returned to the duchess, though much else – her belongings and family property – was confiscated.

One son who had been held in the Tower of London was released in October 1554, though he died shortly afterwards. Three others were released a few months later, in January 1555, though they were not pardoned. The fact that they were Protestants in what now was a fervently Catholic nation only worsened their vulnerability.

Jane Dudley wrote her will that same month, making a final attempt to influence the Spaniards, who were close to Queen Mary. Her green parrot was bequeathed to the Duchess of Alba, the most important of the Spanish women at court, asking her 'to be a good Lady to all her children [Jane's children] as she has begun'. The Spaniards were part of the inner circle at court as they had accompanied Philip of Spain when he arrived to marry Queen Mary. The gift must have been quite delightful, as parrots were very rare. 'I have nothing worthy for her else,' she wrote.[2]

Another of the Spanish courtiers, Don Diego de Mendoza, also received a valuable bequest: the contents of an entire room, together with a golden book clock. Again, the Duchess of Northumberland requested his continuing friendship to help her children.

Don Diego de Acevedo, a favourite of the new king, Philip, received a bed of green velvet along with a plea that he continue to be a father and brother 'to my sons ... now their mother is gone'. Centuries later, these remain powerful words. Other gifts in the will were diplomatically left to Queen Mary and King Philip. The king had also been asked to be godfather to Jane's grandson Philip Sidney. The will also has a most unusual request that reflects perhaps what many other women of those times might fear most about death:

> In no wise to let me be opened after I am ded; I have not loved to be very bold before women, moche [much] more I wold [would] be loth [loath] to com into thands [to come into the hands] of any lyving man, be he phisicion or surgeon.

Was She Murdered?

The duchess could not know that, after all this misery and suffering for the family, there would be some good fortune ahead for her children. A week after she died, her sons were pardoned. The Dudleys managed to survive the next few troubled years of Mary's reign, when Protestants were persecuted. Many were martyred, burnt at the stake for refusing to become Catholics.

The next queen, Elizabeth, had been a friend of the Dudleys from earlier years when her own life was in danger. Jane's sons Ambrose and Robert were fortunate to receive some of the new queen's earliest court appointments, while her daughter Mary Sidney became a lady-in-waiting. This was a most sought-after role as these women were so close to Elizabeth in all of her public and private life.

Robert Dudley, handsome and debonair, seemed particularly blessed. Indeed, his star rose so high as favourite of Elizabeth that for many years it was expected that they would marry. Theirs could not be a happily-ever-after ending, however, not least because Lord Robert was already married. His wife, Amy, died in suspicious circumstances: she was found with a broken neck at the bottom of a staircase, having died when the servants were conveniently absent from the house. A formal inquest was ordered, and cleared his name, but even that could not stop the chattering voices, which effectively ended any chance of a royal marriage.

Let us now consider grandmothers and grandsons of the Churchill family. The first is relatively modern, taking us back to just after the First World War.

Two Grandsons: Winston Churchill and Chartwell

Winston Churchill received a bequest from his father Randolph, who himself was the grandson originally mentioned in a family will written in 1865, a decade before Winston was born at Blenheim Palace. Though he never knew his great-grandmother, the inheritance that was passed to Winston provided one of the most important gifts for any ambitious politician: financial stability.

Frances Anne Vane-Tempest (1800–1865) was a leading light of fashionable society in London as well as in Vienna, where her husband was ambassador to Austria. To her four grandsons, including Randolph, she gave the estate of Ireland's Garron Tower in County Antrim, to be held in trust[3] with a careful plan for the order of succession.

The inheritance provided a significant income of between £4,000 and £5,000, sufficient for Winston to go house-hunting. In Kent he found Chartwell House, which was offered at the knockdown price of £5,000 rather than the original asking price of £6,500. Still, cautious folk might have argued Chartwell was far too big – true. And far too expensive to run – true again. But Winston's grandparents lived in Blenheim Palace, compared to which lovely Chartwell must have seemed modest. There was also the major problem of dry rot. However, Winston took care to mention the dry rot when offering his lower bid for Chartwell. It would become his beloved family home for nearly forty years. Now owned by the National Trust, Chartwell remains a memorial to a great Prime Minister who led the country to victory in the Second World War.

For the second inheritance from a grandmother of the Churchill family, we must skip back a number of generations to the eighteenth century and the first Duchess of Marlborough.

Two Grandsons: Althorp and John Spencer

Sarah Churchill, 1st Duchess of Marlborough (1660–1744), could be a faithful friend, a loyal wife and a loving mother and grandmother. To this she added less appealing qualities. She was quarrelsome, opinionated and difficult, some might say cantankerous. There were frequent quarrels with her daughters, and the eldest, Henrietta, went so far as to stipulate in her own will that she was not to be buried at Blenheim Palace alongside her mother.[45]

John Spencer was the grandson who eventually received most of Duchess Sarah's large fortune. Family tradition says that John's good luck was a result of avoiding argument or disagreement with his grandmother. When the duchess told him it was time to marry and sent him a list of potential brides, John Spencer obligingly proposed to the lady named at the top of the list.

John Spencer did not, however, have long to enjoy this wealth as he died of alcoholism just two years later. Instead, it was his son, also John, who inherited the Althorp estates with an immense income of nearly £30,000 a year. The younger John Spencer could afford diamond-studded shoe buckles and built one of the grandest London townhouses. Spencer House, just off Pall Mall, is one of the last London palaces still standing, and although it is no longer used as the family's townhouse it remains in their hands. At Althorp House there is a room commemorating the duchess and the inheritance she gave.

Sarah's will decreed that her grandson John should not hold political office – other than the rangership of Windsor Park, an appointment the duchess once held. The catalyst for this unusual stipulation was her final quarrel with Queen Anne. Once she had been the queen's beloved friend and favourite as Keeper of the Privy Purse, of such importance (and perhaps demeanour) that some disparagingly called her 'Queen Sarah'. But Sarah was dismissed, something she viewed as a betrayal after such a long friendship with Anne. This was all the more bitter because Abigail Masham, who took her place as favourite,[5] was Sarah's cousin, a poor relative she had introduced at court as a favour. This had all happened long ago, in 1711, but thirty years later it remained fresh for Sarah. In the event that her grandson John did take office, he was to be cut from her will.

The duchess changed her will on many occasions. All in all, the will was rewritten twenty-six times.[6] This may sound like chronic indecision, but in her defence there were many family disputes in this time and Sarah was extraordinarily rich. In every age before and since, wealthy grandmothers have enjoyed dangling a sizeable inheritance over the younger generations. Manipulating family members by dropping hints about her will created confusion. Everyone is kept on their best behaviour, paying close attention to all of the old lady's whims and wishes. Only when the will is read does everyone finally know who is to receive what.

The South Sea Bubble

Regardless of her argumentative ways, Duchess Sarah was blessed with an excellent business brain and occasionally lent money to the Bank of England. One of her most profitable investments was in the South Sea Bubble.* She timed her intervention to perfection, taking out her money shortly before the bubble burst in 1720. Earlier, she had lent to those desperate to invest in the marvellous scheme before it all went wrong.

---

* The South Sea Company created a national frenzy of investors desperate to put money into the scheme. Many risked everything they had or even borrowed money – as the expected high returns were so tempting. A good deal of smoke and mirrors deceived even the cleverest; the great mathematician Isaac Newton is thought to have lost £20,000. When the bubble burst in 1720, there were daily suicides in London by those who had lost everything.

Having persuaded her husband to cash in his money at the same time, Sarah enjoyed immense financial gain. At a time when thousands were ruined, John and Sarah Churchill tripled their investment. When he died in 1722, the duke was worth around £1 million (not counting Blenheim Palace). Sarah had £750,000[5] with over twenty landed estates. The duchess was so rich and famous that her will was published as a pamphlet by M. Cooper of London and printed in *The London Magazine*.

Sarah Churchill was one of the few women of her age with sufficient income to build on a grand scale. Blenheim Palace, Wimbledon Park and Marlborough House owe much to her taste and her love of grand construction projects. She was fearsome, with a reputation as someone who kept a sharp eye – many said miserly – on all the costs. Her tiered garden at Chilworth Manor in Surrey, purchased in 1725, is another delight. A new 'Marlborough' wing was added to Chilworth, and was inherited by John Spencer. The garden can still be seen today.

Despite her reputation for penny pinching, Sarah gave generous bequests to her loyal servants and in particular to her maid Mrs Grace Ridley, who had been with her for many years. Grace received the generous sum of £16,000, equivalent to around £1.9 million today. There was also a bequest for the marriage of Grace's daughter plus half of Duchess Sarah's clothes. The other half of her clothes were to be shared by Sarah's other two maids.

The next part of this chapter takes us back many centuries to a Saxon king and his treasure-laden ship burial.

Britain's Own Valley of the Kings

It is 1,300 years ago. A group of hand-picked warriors moor a boat on the River Deben near Woodbridge in Suffolk, a short distance from the palace of King Raedwald. The ship takes on its precious cargo: the body of the fallen king. He is carried on his final voyage. Perhaps also on board or in other smaller boats would have been women from the royal family, to help in the ceremony and to weep and grieve for their king. There would have been a feast, and many practical items would have to be brought to the burial site.

There was much work to be done. Not only did they have to make the grave and build a wood-lined burial chamber, but the grave had to be big enough to contain the boat itself. Once a trench was prepared, the vessel was then manoeuvred into place. With ropes pulled by skilled teams of strong men and horses, the boat was taken 600 yards up the steep slope from the river onto the hill above. The ship itself was immense, some 90 feet long, and was to be used upright to create a magnificent grave.[7] Just imagine the engineering and effort involved in all of this.[8]

Once the ship was in the trench, a wooden burial chamber was prepared. Though no trace of the body was later found, the king was laid in the chamber and ceremonially surrounded by many of his possessions. Most important were the items of war: a wooden shield, a sword, a collection of spears and his favourite helmet. There was a variety of other household items, including luxury imported pieces like silver bowls. When all was finished it looked like a chamber in the palace, with everything carefully displayed in the best way. The boat was then buried under a huge mound of soil.

These ship burials were a Viking tradition reserved for great warriors. Only three have so far been discovered in England, all in East Anglia.

King Raedwald ruled East Anglia, and dating of the items in the tomb align closely with his death in AD 624. His palace at nearby Rendlesham, excavated in 2016, revealed a vast site with a large Anglo-Saxon hall some 75 feet by 30 feet. This is almost identical to the size of a royal hall at Lyminge in Kent, which was another wealthy Anglo-Saxon kingdom. Excavations of the Great Hall at Ad Gefrin in Saxon Northumbria reveal a similarly large building capable of accommodating around 230 people.

The Rendlesham Palace finds revealed evidence of international trading links and wealth, even a few gold and garnet beads among some 4,000 items including weights and coins. The royal site is immense, covering some 120 acres.

A Magnificent Gift to the Nation

Fast-forward into the early twentieth century and the ship burial is rediscovered. Colonel Frank Pretty and his wife Edith had bought Sutton Hoo house near Woodbridge in East Anglia. There were mounds close to the house, but it was only after the colonel's death that Mrs Pretty decided to find someone who could excavate them. She hired Basil Brown, a well-known amateur archaeologist who was about to discover the find of a lifetime.

By one of those delightful twists of fate it was a keen amateur who quickly recognised what was being revealed by the traces left in the soil – the stains of the ship's timbers and some rusty iron rivets or nails.

In the beginning, in 1938, with help from the gardener and a gamekeeper, the search must have seemed hopeless. The first mound had been robbed in the seventeenth century, but fortunately Mrs Pretty decided to continue the following year in May. This time, at her suggestion, they put a trench through the largest mound and quickly struck gold – loose ship nails or rivets, actually – but there was also real gold in among the grave goods.

Before it was turned into a mausoleum, the ship had probably sailed on the sea with twenty, possibly up to forty rowers. The actual evidence of the wooden ship in the soil was scarce but sufficient to reveal the details of how it was built and its massive size. The body in the burial chamber was also missing, the bones having disappeared due to the acidity of the soil. Nothing like it had been found before in England, nor has it since.

The grave goods placed with the king reveal luxury imports from the Continent. His was a sophisticated life, with a lyre wrapped in a beaver-skin bag, as well as superbly crafted weapons and jewels. There are exquisite gold shoulder clasps for a cloak, set with millefiori glass and garnets from faraway Sri Lanka, a favourite stone in Saxon jewellery as the dull purple and deep red colours shimmer and enhance the strong colour of solid gold. (A 2022 excavation at Harpole, Northampton uncovered a rare bed burial of a woman from Saxon times, an early Christian. The body was gone but a dazzling gold thirty-piece necklace of semi-precious stones remained, set with Roman gold coins and garnets. It is the richest Saxon necklace found to date.)

The Sutton Hoo helmet is terrifying and ferocious. Only six Saxon helmets have been found, and this iron example has empty eyes. Such details were only discovered after some 500 fragments were pieced back together. A 'face' with large eyebrows and a moustache contrive to make the man extremely lifelike. Helmet decorations include warriors and dragons while the eyebrow section is inlaid with red garnets upon foil to intensify the colour. Only recently was it discovered that the left eyebrow is dull and empty, copying the mythology of Odin, Norse god of war and wisdom, who sacrificed his left eye for knowledge.

Originally the king's body had been laid in a large coffin and covered with a yellow cloak. Close by were his sword and helmet, a long knife or seax, a purse with gold coins and a solid gold belt buckle with ornate decoration.[7] An enormous wooden shield hung on the wall at the head end of the burial meant the king had everything necessary for the afterlife. The gold coins were French[8] and dated to between AD 610 and 635.

The importance of Sutton Hoo was at once recognised, as in one newspaper headline: 'Britain's own Valley of the Kings'. Until its discovery, many historians believed Anglo-Saxons lived simple lives with crude weapons in what was termed the Dark Ages. The gold and glory of Sutton Hoo completely dispelled this myth.[8]

A modern, full-size replica of the Sutton Hoo ship, crafted with traditional Saxon tools and construction methods, will be launched by the Sutton Hoo Ship's Company in spring 2024. Built within a short distance of the original Sutton Hoo burial, it will set sail on that same river, the Deben.

Treasure Hidden under the Bed of Edith Pretty

On the first night of the discovery at Sutton Hoo, some items had to be stored for safety inside the house under Mrs Pretty's bed. The local police were asked to provide a guard, keeping watch together with the butler. The amazing news was sent to the British Museum, and one story from those first few days of discovery tells of an expert who came by train to see some of the grave goods. At the meeting, held in the waiting room of the small local station, he was so amazed that he nearly fainted at the sight of the glories revealed.

As the film *The Dig* (2020) revealed, there was then a disgraceful battle wherein the snobbish professional archaeologists tried to oust the self-taught Basil Brown from his own excavation rather than appreciating his expert skills in recognising the importance of what was uncovered. Only after Mrs Pretty's insistence did he remain at the excavation.

A treasure trove inquest of fourteen jurors decided in August 1939 that the finds rightfully belonged to Edith Pretty as landowner; otherwise they would have gone to the Crown. But within a few days Mrs Pretty decided to donate Sutton Hoo to the nation, gifting it through the British Museum.

Born into a rich family, Edith Dempster had been the second daughter and enjoyed all the social advantages that came along with a good income. Both girls were brought up with a keen sense of duty, and Edith was one of the first women magistrates. Together with her sister she served with the Red Cross in France during the First World War. Edith and Frank Pretty had known one another for many years before their marriage; the wedding was after her father's death, and they soon moved to East Anglia.

Edith unfortunately would never see the Sutton Hoo helmet restored, nor any of the other treasures, as she died of a stroke in 1942 aged fifty-nine. She had suffered ill health for many years since catching typhus during her pregnancy. Her estate was valued for probate at £398,976 1s 0d. It was put into a trust for her only child, Robert Dempster Pretty. Her will also gave Robert the right to excavate in the future and to keep any finds. Robert, who was only twelve when his mother died, went to live with his aunt Elizabeth and her family. However, portraits of what was once a happy family remain at Sutton Hoo House. Painted by Cor Visser, Colonel Frank is shown on horseback; Edith's portrait is more formal, with her seated inside the house. Young Robert most appropriately carries a toy wherry boat, modelled after the local vessels still used in Suffolk at the time.

What Happened to the Saxon Ship Nails?

On the last day of the Sutton Hoo dig in August 1939, Miss Mercie Lack was given the ship nails excavated from the site. It seems strange to us now that the archaeologists regarded these rivets as something to be given away, but so it appears they were.

Mercie Lack and her friend Barbara Wagstaff were teachers enjoying a summer holiday near Sutton Hoo when they first heard about the excavation. Curious to know more, they visited the site and asked if they could return each day to take photos as they were keen amateur photographers with high-quality Leica cameras. Even better, they had just bought two rolls of the latest colour Agfa slides, only recently available in England.[9]

During daily visits to the dig, Barbara and Mercie faithfully captured the painstaking excavation work, taking over 400 photographs plus precious colour slides. Their photos became more important later on as all the excavation field notes were lost during the war. Even the photographer sent by the Science Museum with a large-format plate camera only took twenty-five photos.[10]

And the ship nails or rivets? Well, when Mercie Lack died in 1985 she bequeathed the rivets to the British Museum along with the Sutton Hoo photos (and most importantly the copyright). After the war, Barbara and Mercie had sent their photos to the Royal Photographic Society and been awarded associate status. This was a great achievement for both women, who were in the right place at the right time with the right skills to help record this important moment in British archaeology.

7

A CASTLE IN NORFOLK AND FEATHER BEDS

> Item I bequeath to Joan Dyve, my natural [illegitimate] daughter ...
> one feather [bed]...
> Ricardina Mose, wife of Robert Mose, 1473[1]

Isabella, Rebel Queen

Isabella of France (1295–1358), Queen of England, led an extraordinary life and took equally extraordinary actions in her reign, changing the course of British history. Her dynastic marriage to Edward II, King of England in 1308 was conventional enough in the beginning. It was relatively happy for many years, producing four children including the all-important son and heir. By the 1320s, however, much had changed. The marriage was troubled. Even so, in 1325 Isabella was sent to negotiate a peace treaty on behalf of England with the French, led by her brother, Charles IV.

After the treaty was signed, Isabella failed to return home. Staying in Paris, she wrote home with excuses and later with demands for Edward to banish Hugh Despenser, his favourite, who effectively ruled the country. Through Despenser's influence, Isabella's lands had been confiscated, her French servants dismissed, and worst of all her younger children had been taken away from her. She was bitterly humiliated. As her influence over the king waned, so the Despenser family became increasingly important.

Isabella's absence during 1325 caused international ructions. Even the Pope intervened, advising the French king that as a dutiful wife his sister should return to England. Her own view of the situation was the reverse:

> ... someone has come between my husband and myself, trying to break this bond [of marriage] ...

The queen put aside fashionable clothes, adopting instead the sombre black colours of a mourning widow. This was a masterstroke, painting her as the injured wife in the dispute. Perhaps by then she had already made the decision not to meekly return to England.

A Knight in Shining Armour?

In the meantime, Isabella took a lover, the exiled Roger Mortimer, who was already King Edward's enemy. With the king unwilling to compromise, all might have ended with a separation; but Isabella's determination was fixed. She raised money from her dower lands in France and, in a stroke of brilliance, negotiated an alliance with the Count of Hainault.

To seal this agreement, a marriage was arranged between Isabella's son Edward, heir to the English throne, and Philippa, the Count's young daughter. The marriage contract, signed on 27 August 1326, stipulated that if the marriage did not take place within two years, Edward would be fined £10,000[2], which was a vast amount of money. (Some decades later, in 1395, a castle in Northumbria cost far less to build. In fact, Embleton Tower cost a mere £40.) The marriage contract is an exceptionally rare surviving document from the fourteenth century, and in 2019 it was auctioned for £150,062 – rather more than that proposed fine![3]

Philippa's dowry was paid in advance and so could be used to hire mercenaries to invade England. The count's military support included eight war ships, as now there was a possibility his daughter might become Queen of England. A month after the marriage contract was signed, Isabella and Roger Mortimer landed on the east coast of England with a modest army of only 700 soldiers. The troops provided by the Count of Hainault were matched by similar numbers from other English exiles, but by any estimate it was a tiny army.

The rebels nonetheless had certain advantages. The first, and possibly the best, was surprise. While a French invasion was expected, it was predicted to come from the south rather than the east coast. The king was also now deeply unpopular, while the Despensers were reviled. As a result, the rebels met with little resistance save for a short siege at Bristol. The rebel army moved across the country, passing through Dunstable and towards Oxford and the West Country, while the capital quickly declared for Isabella. Parliament would also help, convincing the king to abdicate in favour of his young son.[4]

This meant the kingdom had to formally withdraw its allegiance to the monarch. The principle of swearing allegiance still applies today; Queen Elizabeth II and Charles III both swore a coronation oath to the kingdom on the Bible, while a newly elected prime minister (as with Boris Johnson in December 2019 and Rishi Sunak in 2022) swore an oath in Parliament declaring allegiance to the monarch.

The Despensers were captured and executed. The king was imprisoned, but soon died in mysterious circumstances. For the next four years, Isabella was regent for her son, ruling with Roger Mortimer. Frustrated at being side-lined by his mother and her lover, young Edward III waited until he was old enough before staging his own rebellion, a swift coup d'état which ended with Mortimer's execution and his mother's imprisonment.

All Is Forgiven

Initially placed under house arrest at Berkhamsted Castle, Isabella was soon allowed to join her son and Queen Philippa at Windsor

Castle, though she was still under house arrest and her lands and income were forfeit to the Crown. But in truth her troubles did not last long. Rebellion, regicide, adultery – all were forgiven. Isabella was once more queen dowager, with a large allowance and her own household.

By the end of 1331, her lands were restored to her. In the following year, Edward and Philippa named their daughter in her honour. Edward began his war against France in 1328, which would become acknowledged as the beginning of the Hundred Years War, claiming his right to rule France through his mother Isabella, which he declared made him the closest male relative to the last French king. For the final part of her life – which would last thirty years – Isabella regularly visited court, though never with the same degree of influence and power as when she had been regent.

In 1336, Isabella set up a chantry at Eltham Palace for her husband's soul, a place where they had often stayed in their early married life. Her main residence was Castle Rising in Norfolk. It is a ruin these days, but it was a most splendid, fortified castle. In her will the castle was left to her favourite grandson, Edward the Black Prince, along with all her estates, including Leeds Castle and Hertford Castle.

Her library was divided between her son Edward III and her daughter Joan, Queen of Scotland, including a psalter, a Bible and an Apocalypse (an illuminated manuscript) written in French in 1313, which survived and now is in the Bibliothèque Nationale de France.

Isabella wished to be buried in her wedding mantle or cloak, perhaps recalling those happier years as a young bride. Or was this an expression of regret for her treachery to her husband? She also wished for a silver casket holding the heart of her husband to be buried with her in 1358 at Greyfriars in London. Heart burials were well known in medieval times, with a separate grave site reserved for them.

Christina, Peasant and Brewer

Christina Cok, a peasant, was born sometime around the year 1285 in the village of Codicote in Hertfordshire. Details about Christina were only rediscovered during the filming of a BBC programme by Michael Wood in 2008 using records which survived in the local archives. Perhaps most surprising of all is the fact that Christina left a will. Though in most respects her life was as far removed as possible from that of Queen Isabella, it was a better existence than might be expected. We rarely think of peasants owning land, but she did; even more than that, it was a family inheritance that ran for three generations.

Christina inherited property from her father, Hugh, and in turn was able to pass it to her daughter. Theirs was a feudal world with a good deal of hardship and danger, not least considering the presence of the Black Death and the Great Famine (from 1315 to 1322), which killed perhaps as many as 20 per cent of the population. Peasants like Christina's father Hugh held land (small strips usually) from the Lord of the Manor, which for Codicote was the local abbey at St Albans. Hugh and his wife Agnes also brewed ale, as Christina did in her turn, which would provide a good, steady income. In medieval times people drank weak beer instead of water, which was unsafe to drink.

Gradually Hugh managed to purchase small pieces of land, a house and a market plot in Codicote from which he sold fish. The Church at this time decreed three meat-free days each week, so a fishmonger could make a good living. During his lifetime, Hugh decided to give Christina his house and the market plot when she was in her late 20s. By 1319 we know she had two children – Alice and John – and her husband William had died around this time. We also know of a dispute, heard at the local court, when Christina had to prove that she and her husband had jointly owned a property.

Christina Cok died in 1348 when the Black Death came to Codicote. Her children survived the plague years. Alice was by now married (or widowed), as in Christina's will she has another surname. There was a death duty of 4 shillings to pay (an amount equal to approximately two weeks' wages for a labourer). The will deals with what was most important – her hope for her soul to be saved by God and a wish to be buried in the local churchyard. There was a gift to the local church, and only one item of clothing is mentioned, which Alice is to receive.

> In the name of God, Amen I mak myn wylle in this wyse. First I comytte my sawle [commit my soul] to God and me body to be beryed in the chirchyerde of Seynte Giles. And I beqwethe unto the lyghtes of the chirche fower busshellis of barley [four bushels of barley]. And I beqwethe unto Alyce Whyte, my coate.

St Giles Church in Codicote still stands today.

And So to Bed ...

... and in particular to the popularity of featherbeds in earlier centuries. Peasants like Christina Cok might only have had a straw mattress to lay upon the floor, possibly not even that, but in other wealthy wills we find four-poster feather beds draped with hangings or curtains to keep out the cold, plus quilts or coverlets and bed linen. Often made from velvet, damask and silk, these were prized bequests. Tapestries were similarly important, high-status objects among the elite. In the inventory of the palaces of Henry VIII, some 2,000 are recorded.

Beds, embroidered hangings, tapestries, quilts and curtains were also mentioned in Anglo-Saxon wills, a tradition which continues right through to the eighteenth century. When in 1771 the Austen family moved the short distance to Steventon rectory, just a mile or so from nearby Deane, we have the delightful image of Mrs Cassandra Austen, Jane's invalid mother, making the journey on a feather bed atop a cart full of household items.

The 1427 will of Cecily Harom, from Scarborough in Yorkshire, mentions bed hangings embroidered with the arms of the Earl of Northumberland to emphasise and boast of her family connection with the aristocracy.[5] Beds were valuable bequests abroad, too, as in 1390 a woman left the English hospice in Rome (founded for English pilgrims) her three best beds with the best pillows, sheets and coverlets.[6] One Scottish example illustrates just how many might be needed for a draughty castle. In 1545, Urquhart Castle was raided by the dreaded MacDonald clan, who plundered twelve featherbeds and bolsters, blankets and sheets. It was an excellent haul considering that they also took the castle gates and 2,000 cattle!

Founding Fathers... and Founding Mothers

One of America's Founding Mothers, Elizabeth Howland (née Tilley, 1607–1687) was born in Henlow, Bedfordshire. Her family were among the first settlers, seeking religious freedom and sailing to New England on the overcrowded *Mayflower*. That first winter was so harsh that Elizabeth's parents, aunt and uncle died. Indeed, fewer than half of the settlers survived until the first Thanksgiving. Another family took in Elizabeth, and their servant John Howland would inherit part of their property. Elizabeth was first his ward and later his wife, though she might have been neither if John had not been rescued from the waves on the voyage when he fell overboard.

Elizabeth Howland's will is highly important as one of the first made in New England. By 1687, she had been widowed for some fifteen years. She wrote her will the year before she died at her daughter Lydia's home. It was Lydia (written as 'Lidia' in the will) who received the best feather bed, while Lydia's husband was given the 'great Bible'. Another feather bed and bolster went to her son Jabez, while her 'wearing clothes linnen and Woollen' went 'unto my three Daughters ... to be equally Devided amongst them ...'

Elizabeth and John Howland had a large family of ten children, who all continued in the same vein. In the next generation there were eighty-eight grandchildren, and they have millions of living descendants today.

William and Anne Shakespeare's Second-best Bed

William Shakespeare's bequest in 1616 was 'unto my wife my second best bed with the furniture'. Otherwise, there is no mention of Anne (*née* Hathaway) in the will. Shakespeare certainly loved his children, but did he really love his wife? The meaning of this bequest has been much debated by experts and academics such as Katherine Duncan-Jones. According to some, this reveals how little he cared for his wife. So often is this myth repeated that there is a danger of it being accepted as fact.[7]

However, Michael Wood points out in his work *In Search of Shakespeare* that by custom a widow inherited a third of her husband's estate, so this did not need to be included in the document. Far more likely is that the second-best bed was a special, sentimental bequest. The year before her marriage, Anne received a bed in her father's will; in all likelihood this was William and Anne's bed. Later, when a new bed was bought, it became the 'second-best' bed but stayed as an important part of their memories. Thanks to recent discoveries by the National Archives and the British Library, we also know that this bequest, along with other remembrances for friends, were added to the will the month before Shakespeare died. The will was first drafted in winter 1616 by his friend and lawyer Francis Collins, who returned to Stratford on 25 March to make these final changes.

A Pair of Hempen Sheets

An earlier will from King's Lynn, made in 1341 by a wealthy merchant's widow named Joan de Thornhegge, concerns bedding. Her two daughters, and their daughters, received in equal shares the contents of Joan's bedroom including blankets, pillows, bed, linen and quilt.[8] Tudor wills from Bedfordshire have similar bequests of bedding and beds to daughters or a granddaughter, as shown below, although sometimes to a son:

To daughter Elysabeth ... the best featherbed with the appurtenances [furnishings such as covers, hangings and curtains].
Margaret Coore of Potten, widow, 1527

... 2 pair of flaxen sheets; a pair of hempen [hemp] sheets; 2 pillows ... [to my granddaughter Alys]
Agnes Butt of Elnestow [Elstow], 1524

To son Reynold ... the hangings of her bed, the best coverlet ... and a pair of sheets; to Walter Pickok a blanket and a pair of sheets ...
Johan Picok of Kyshoo [Keysoe], 1523[9]

A Spangled Bed, a Quilt and a Rabbit

State beds can still be found in some grand houses, such as Holkham Hall in Norfolk, and they often became family heirlooms. Queen Caroline's six-mattress bed, made in 1715, is still at Hampton Court. It sounds most uncomfortable, but presumably the opposite must have been true. Sometimes a marriage bed arrived along with a new bride, furnished with expensive silk, velvet or damask curtains, embroidered hangings, coverlets and quilts.

One special bedspread at Holkham Hall, though much repaired, dates from the early 1700s. When examined by experts from the Victoria and Albert Museum in the 1980s, it was concluded that the bedspread was produced professionally rather than made at home. The design combined traditional styles with the latest fascination for sparkle and spangle. The central embroidery is dull green today, but originally it would have shimmered and glittered as it contained gilded silver thread. In candlelight it would sparkle gloriously, offering diffuse and subtle shades of silver.

The quilt's embroidered picture shows a rockery, some of which is padded to accentuate and show off shells, feathers and a small rabbit, who also appears on one of three matching cushions. The Holkham archives mention a quilt bought in 1719 for the considerable sum of £101 1s. This was purchased a year after the wedding of twenty-one-year-old Thomas Coke and the eighteen-year-old Lady Margaret Tufton, just when a couple might wish to buy such an expensive quilt. Some fifty years later, in 1765, it is again mentioned in an inventory of Lady Leicester's belongings as an embroidered quilt kept in a chest.[10] All household linen and blankets in a grand house would be kept either in a linen store or in blanket boxes under lock and key.

A quilt was also a treasured possession in Jane Austen's family, as described in the next chapter.

8

JANE AUSTEN AND THE REGENCY ERA

> I appoint my said dear Sister the Executrix of this my last Will & Testament...
>
> Jane Austen's will, April 1817

Jane Austen's pretty turquoise ring was passed down between the women of the Austen family until 2012. One of only three pieces of jewellery owned by Jane, it was nearly lost to the nation when American singer Kelly Clarkson bought it at auction, paying five times the reserve price. Justifiably, this news caused an outcry and the government agreed to an export ban (with a tight deadline) to see if sufficient money could be raised to stop the ring leaving England. The amount required, £152,450, was quickly mustered, including an anonymous donation of £100,000.

The ring is now in Chawton Museum. It might be said to have gone back to where it belongs, as this was Jane's home for the last eight years of her life and where she did much of her writing.

The Genius of Jane Austen

Jane never did see her actual name on her published books – they were not published in her name until after she had died. *Gentlemen's Quarterly* duly noted her death in 1817, and the titles of her four novels, and although it was some 200 years late *The Times* did graciously publish an obituary in 2017, the bicentenary of her death, acknowledging that this accolade was somewhat late.

There was a general prejudice against women writers at the time. Having sent some early poems to the Poet Laureate Robert Southey in the 1830s, Charlotte Brontë received the reply, 'Literature cannot be the business of a woman's life, and it ought not to be.' Charlotte fortunately ignored this advice, although she did publish *Jane Eyre* under a male *nom de plume*.

Jane Austen's first book, *Sense and Sensibility*, was published anonymously in 1811 and the author was identified only as 'a Lady'. Two years later, the three-volume *Pride and Prejudice* was 'by the author of *Sense and Sensibility*'. One of our greatest novelists, Austen has an amazing ability to put across in just a few words the greed, hypocrisy and selfishness of some of her characters, as well as the love and sacrifices others make.

Even in the early years, Jane Austen had admirers. The Prince Regent bought a copy of *Sense and Sensibility* before it was advertised in the newspapers and owned two copies of *Pride and Prejudice*. She was invited to dedicate *Emma* to him, though we know from her letters that she hated his cruel treatment of his wife and cousin, Caroline of Brunswick. Many of his more respectable subjects felt the same. Indeed, it was hard to find much to admire in the Prince Regent's dissolute life. A reckless *bon vivant* obsessed with fine clothes and gambling, he was the perfect target for cartoonists such as James Gillray, whose satirical prints were often displayed in London shop windows so that the public might ridicule him.

Jane's will was written at the end of April 1817, just a few months before she died on 18 July. The year had begun well, with time spent on a new manuscript. In January, Jane wrote to her friend Alethea Bigg asking for her receipt (recipe) for orange wine from Seville oranges. Then, just a month before making her will, Jane stopped writing for good. The manuscript, which eventually became *Sanditon*, was kept by the family and only published after the First World War, in 1925.

Written in Jane's elegant handwriting, the will is short and businesslike, fitting on a single sheet. It was not witnessed; perhaps that seemed too final. Instead, family friends later had to swear that it was written in Jane's handwriting.

Jane Austen's will read as follows:

I, Jane Austen of the Parish of Chawton do by this my last Will & Testament give and bequeath to my dearest Sister Cassandra Elizth every thing of which I may die possessed, or which may be hereafter due to me, subject to the payment of my Funeral Expences, & to a Legacy of £50. to my Brother Henry, & £50 to Mme de Bigeon – which I request may be paid as soon as convenient. And I appoint my said dear sister the executrix of this my last Will & Testament.

Jane Austen, 27 April 1817 (TNA, PROB 1/78)

Her brother Henry had been in dire financial straits. His bank, Austen, Maunde and Tilson, had failed a year earlier. Madame Francoise Bigeon was Henry's housekeeper and had lost her savings when the bank collapsed. This no doubt is why the money was 'to be paid as soon as convenient'. Everything else went to Cassandra, with no mention of her turquoise ring or the manuscripts of her novels; indeed, it is only from such manuscripts that we have discovered an alternative earlier ending to *Persuasion*.

Cassandra organised her sister's mourning jewellery with great care, as described by Margaret Wilson in her book *Almost Another Sister*.[4] There were gold chains for Louisa Knight, Jane's goddaughter, while another niece was asked if a lock of hair was to be set as a ring or a brooch.

Two almost identical necklaces – chains with a topaz cross – belonged to Jane and Cassandra, having been presents from their youngest brother Charles. As a lieutenant in the Royal Navy in 1801, he had helped capture a French ship and spent some of his £40 prize money on these elegant trinkets. Jane called them spoils of war when writing to Cassandra, saying that though Charles would be thanked he would also be 'well scolded' for extravagance. Later, their names lived on in Charles's family as his daughters were christened Cassandra and Jane. The necklaces were passed through his family.

An elegant patchwork quilt made by Jane, Cassandra and their mother also belongs to Chawton Museum, home of her famous ring. The fine needlework of the diamond-shaped quilt is expertly done; the Austen ladies were typical in taking pride in such sewing and embroidery skills. A handmade stitched shirt or an embroidered purse was quite an acceptable present. While not as valuable as the Holkham quilt mentioned earlier, this quilt was kept and treasured by the Austen family.

We also know what they liked to cook, as a recipe book was kept by Martha Lloyd, a friend who shared Chawton with Mrs Austen, Cassandra and Jane. Every self-respecting housewife kept such a book, exchanging and comparing recipes between friends and relations exactly as people do today. Much later, when Martha was in her early sixties, she actually became an Austen as she married Francis, Jane's brother. Martha Austen kept the recipe book, including the aforementioned recipe for orange wine and another for a trifle topped with sherry syllabub. Safely preserved by later generations, it has been published by Maggie Black and Deirdre Le Faye; another by Julienne Gehrer uses the original manuscript.

Letters Kept and Letters Destroyed

The recipes, the turquoise ring, the diamond quilt – the provenance for each is quite precise. The ring was first Cassandra's, then given to Eleanor Jackson on her engagement to their brother Henry. Eleanor died in 1863 and bequeathed the ring to Caroline, Jane's niece, and so it was passed on through the women of the family. Few people outside of the family knew it existed until the auction in 2012.

Jane's possessions, her writings, a few revisions of her books, a brown silk pelisse and a portable writing desk were all safely guarded by Cassandra, who lived until 1843. The manuscripts and papers, small keepsakes, and treasures with detailed instructions are mentioned in Cassandra's will. Anna Austen Lefroy, her niece, received the unfinished manuscript with eleven chapters of *Sanditon* together with some handwritten chapters of *Persuasion*. The *Sanditon* manuscript was eventually given to King's College, Cambridge by Mary Isabella Lefroy, Jane's great-great-niece. The writing desk, a present to Jane from her father, descended through James Austen's family until in 1999 Joan Austen-Leigh, a great-great-great-niece, gave the desk and three pairs of spectacles to the British Library.

Fanny Knight, a niece, received some of Jane's letters, leaving them in turn to her son Lord Brabourne, who edited them. They reveal Jane to be as witty as in the novels, as we see from a letter in 1796:

> What dreadful hot weather we have! It keeps one in a continual state of inelegance.

Cassandra destroyed many letters. Fewer than 200 survive, although it is estimated there might have been as many as 3,000. Were they too ordinary and dull, saucy or downright acerbic? As Jane became more famous, parts of letters were cut out and given away or sold, but still this hardly accounts for so many lost letters. If only somewhere there might be a cache of letters neatly tied with a ribbon just waiting to be discovered in an attic somewhere. It could still happen.

A Royal Feud

Jane's estate was worth a little less than £800, a most respectable sum for those times, and not accounting for the sales of *Northanger Abbey* and *Persuasion*, published at the end of 1817. But this is as nothing compared to the wealth of Queen Charlotte, who died the following year. Wills were regularly published in newspapers in this period, and *The Times* declared her estate to be worth around £140,000. Frogmore House in Windsor was given to Augusta, her eldest unmarried daughter. The splendid Arcot diamonds from India were to be divided equally among her four youngest unmarried daughters:

> I give and bequeath the jewels received from the Nawab of Arcot to my remaining daughters, or to the survivors or survivor in case they or any of them should die before me, and I direct that these jewels should be sold and that the produce ... shall be divided among them, my said remaining daughters or their survivors, share and share alike.

This temptation was too great for her son the Prince Regent, who decided to keep the Arcot diamonds for himself and had them set into his new coronation crown.

There was also a most unfortunate family dispute over other jewels mentioned in Queen Charlotte's will. Her own wedding jewels were bequeathed to her family in Hannover, Germany, rather than to her English family. As often happens, this brought out the worst on both sides. The ensuing legal tussle lasted some twenty years and was only resolved in 1857 when a court decided in favour of Hannover. Queen Victoria had always hoped to win the dispute, and it was with reluctance that she handed over her grandmother's jewels.

Two other Regency characters concern us next: a horse thief and a soldier's wife.

To Follow the Drum

At the age of thirty, Catherine Exley (*née* Whitaker, 1779–1857) left England to follow her husband, Joshua, a soldier in the Duke of Wellington's army. Known as 'Following the Drum', this was a tough and uncertain life. The women experienced all sorts of dangers during the Peninsular War campaign, from food shortages, indifferent housing, vermin and lice to bandits and every type of extreme weather.

Joshua was not an officer but a lowly infantry soldier in the 34th Regiment of Foot. He served in and survived the toughest campaigns in Portugal and Spain. Three of Catherine and Joshua's babies died during this time. Her travels with him lasted for ten years, and the journey she took with their children is both fascinating and more dreadful than many of us can imagine. One of the most awful things must have been the search over a battlefield to see if her husband's body was there – a thousand years before, Saxon women had undertaken the same gory task.

Catherine's mother was a Quaker, and she herself was a Methodist, and so it was perhaps her strong religious belief that enabled her to survive all the hardships. Even in the most difficult situations she felt certain God would protect her.

Records of life for ordinary foot soldiers in this period are rare, let alone accounts of women following them. There is only Catherine's diary. It was written when she was back home in Yorkshire but then lost to the family. Miraculously, it was published in 1923 in a local paper, *The Dewsbury Reporter*, in which form it was rediscovered by a descendant. Nearly 100 years after that, the diary of Catherine Exley's remarkable life was finally published in full. These recollections were her legacy to her family and to all who would like to know what life was like for the women who went to war.

Exile as Punishment
The Regency is known for both elegant, fashionable high society and desperate poverty. By 1775 some towns already had a workhouse for the poor; one in Luton, Bedfordshire held eighty inmates, and the Endell Street workhouse in Covent Garden was so vast that it was transformed in the First World War into a hospital with 573 beds. One at Berkhamsted survived until the 1930s.

This also was the age of cheap gin, 'a penny a quart', which was twice as strong as it is today. It was known as Mother's Ruin, which indeed it was – the heroin of its day, but on a far larger scale. Slums and the accompanying prostitution were found almost everywhere in London, which boasted thousands of gin sellers. There were countless brothels or bawdy houses, and it is estimated that around one in five Georgian Londoners were treated for syphilis by their mid-30s.[1] Child prostitution was commonplace in the capital and elsewhere right through to Victorian times when the age of consent was thirteen. It was only only raised to sixteen in 1885 after public campaigning.

Punishment was harsh even for minor crimes. Stealing goods worth more than 40 shillings might mean a death sentence. In Halifax, on market day, a guillotine was used for such executions as a grisly warning to others. Fraud was a hanging offence, as was stealing a loaf of bread, while Elizabeth Johnson of York was hanged in 1800 for using a forged £1 note. The idea was that a draconian system would deter crime. Perhaps it did for some, but in extreme poverty theft could be the only way to stay alive. Stealing ribbons, umbrellas, clothes, shoes or handkerchiefs could get you transported to Australia or sentenced to hard labour, as could trespassing, night poaching or breaking into a house. It is unimaginable now that stealing seven ducks (in 1835) or, in another case, ten rabbits (in 1850) would be punished with seven years' transportation, but it was.

Britain exported its criminals to far-flung colonies. Until 1793, criminals were sent to America, often becoming slave labour for the cotton plantations. After the battles of Preston (1715) and Culloden (1746), the defeated Jacobite prisoners were also sent to the Caribbean and Carolina in America. After American independence, British convict ships sailed in the opposite direction to Australia, another British colony. The First Fleet in 1788 gives you some idea of the scale of the operation, as eleven ships arrived in Sydney Cove with 751 convicts, among them men, women and children.

Transportation would continue until 1868, by which time thousands of prisoners (among them 25,000 women) had reached Australia. Deborah Oxley's detailed study *Convict Maids* challenges the view that these women were hardened criminals. She found that many were transported for minor thefts or even first offences, as in the case of young Mary Haydock from Bury in Lancashire.

The Horse Thief

Mary (Molly) Haydock (1777–1855) was a servant before she made the terrible mistake of running away from her employers in 1791. After successfully hiding disguised as a boy for five months, she was caught and tried for the theft of a horse. Although she was only fourteen, the court sentenced her to transportation.

Forty-nine women were aboard the ship taking Mary to Australia, along with 300 men, on a long and dangerous journey that lasted more than 100 days. When the ship arrived at Botany Bay, as she waited to go ashore, Mary Haydock wrote a letter home to her aunt Penelope. You might think she would be frantic, if not suicidal. Instead, commenting on how pleasant the bay looked, Mary writes with amazing youthful optimism and *joie de vivre*. She has now been told the sentence is for life rather than seven years, but she will try to escape after two or three years and 'will make myself as happy as I can'.[2]

Mary worked as a maid and aged seventeen she married Tom Reibey, a sailor who had received land to settle in Australia. The young couple began farming and then trading goods by boat, a business which did exceptionally well. Tom died in 1811, leaving the business to Mary, now in her thirties and with seven children. She decided to continue with the trading business.

In those early colonial years, men and women often quickly remarried, but Mary did not. Before long she had a warehouse and a hotel in Sydney, and within a few years two ships were taking goods over to Tasmania. Eventually the family could afford to buy 2,000 acres on Tasmania, an astonishing achievement and testimony to how well the business prospered.

By the 1820s, Mary could afford to return to Britain. She visited Lancashire and her hometown of Bury with her daughters Celia and Eliza before embarking on a grand tour of London, Liverpool, Manchester, Glasgow and Edinburgh.[2] Mary was well off by now, and had become respectable. Keen to disown her convict past, from the first census of 1828 she claimed to have arrived 'Free' just a few years before, just as many other ex-convicts did. Such deceit was by no means unusual.

Mary lived a long life, dying in 1855 at the age of seventy-eight, and was buried in Sydney alongside her husband and their eldest daughter, Celia. Mary left bequests for her three surviving daughters, stipulating that their gifts be free from the control of their husbands, who otherwise could claim them.

Mary's estate was sold after her death, and within a few generations some of the money made its way back to England. No doubt she would be amazed to know that her money was used in the 1930s to buy a fine Tudor manor house in Devon. Lottie William-Powlett and her husband were then renting Cadhay Manor, where they found the Powlett family coat of arms (the three swords of the Paulets or Powletts) carved in stone above the fireplace. Lottie considered this was fate and so decided to use her family inheritance to buy the manor. Lottie was born a Reibey and brought up by her grandfather James, who was Mary's grandson. Nowadays, Lottie's great-grandson Rupert Thistlethwayte owns Cadhay.[3]

A Convict in the Family

For many years Mary's convict story was the kind of family secret that few families wished to discuss even as late as the 1990s. Fortunately, we are these days more enlightened and such taboos have largely disappeared. As a pioneer founder of Sydney and a successful businesswoman, Mary became famous. Her grandson Thomas did particularly well, becoming Prime Minister of Tasmania in 1876. Mary's fame was such that her portrait was put on the $20 dollar bill. Instead of what some might imagine a convict to look like, there is instead a portrait of a sweet old lady who is wearing glasses with a shawl around her shoulders. She is the perfect picture of respectability.

Australia provided many convicts with opportunities for upward social mobility that would have been unavailable to them back home in the United Kingdom. A few generations after Mary Hadock in the 1830s, Caroline Gadbury was transported for stealing in London. These days her great-great-grandson is a supreme court judge in New South Wales, most definitely on the right rather than the wrong side of the law.[2]

For My Dear Friend Lucy

One of the more unusual gifts between friends just after the Regency is a delightful painting that depicts guardsmen riding past Buckingham House, which a few years later was renamed Buckingham Palace after improvements commissioned by the Prince Regent. A label on the back of the painting tells its story: 'For my dear friend Lucy, Mrs Holbeche, June 1826.' A small oil painting measuring roughly 9 inches by 12 inches, it was sold by the Holbeche family in 2018. The artist was named as Mrs Phipps, but little was known about her. However, Huon Mallalieu proposes that most likely she is Maria *née* Thellusson (1771–1834), wife of the Honourable Augustus Phipps.[5]

Another dear friend some fifty years earlier in 1774 is mentioned by Sarah Deschamps of London. A widow, one of the French Huguenot refugees who were granted refuge in Protestant England, she left the 'remainder [of her estate] to my worthy and most esteemed friend and executrix Mrs Mary Bonouvrier'.[5]

The Prince Regent's Secret Wife

In every age, pearls and diamonds were mentioned as bequests. Some Regency diamonds were given by the Prince Regent to his secret morganatic wife, Mrs Maria Anne Fitzherbert (*née* Smythe, 1756–1837). His infatuation came at a high price; by one estimate, he spent £54,000 buying her jewels.[6] However, in order for a marriage to be legal every royal marriage needed the king's consent – impossible when Maria was a Catholic and twice widowed. Instead, the couple married secretly in 1784 and lived for some years in great style and in separate establishments at Brighton, where the Prince Regent amused himself with a lavish renovation of a villa near the seafront, Brighton Pavilion.

The jewels were passed down through the female line of Minnie Dawson-Damer, who was adopted by Mrs Fitzherbert, and were included in a major exhibition called 'The Four Georges' held in 1931.[6] Among other items was a locket given by the Prince Regent, known as the Maria Fitzherbert jewel. It bears his miniature portrait painted on ivory, surrounded with eighteen diamonds and covered with a portrait diamond. The family only auctioned off this glorious jewel in 2017, for the seemingly rather modest sum of £341,000.[6] Two matching lockets were made for the lovers; the one made for the Prince Regent contained Maria's portrait and was buried with him at the end of his life according to his wishes.[7]

The Prince Regent eventually left Mrs Fitzherbert to make a diplomatic marriage with his cousin Caroline of Brunswick, spurred on by the prospect that his mountain of debts would be settled. It was a disastrous marriage, and the couple quickly separated. They had one child, Charlotte Augusta, born early in 1796. On the night she was born, the Prince Regent wrote his will, leaving all his property to

> my Maria ... the wife of my heart and soul. Although by the laws of this Country she could not avail herself publicly of that name, still such she is in the eyes of Heaven, was, is, and ever will be such in mine.[6]

To his wife Caroline, he left one shilling[8] – the traditional gift in a will to ensure that the person in question does not receive a penny more. Mrs Fitzherbert kept the will, along with their marriage certificate.

9

ACTORS AND MISS BURDETT-COUTTS, THE WEALTHIEST WOMAN IN ENGLAND

> For a poor man at the play house 6 pence; Toys for her sons ... several nightgowns, dresses, and a pinke & white Lutestring Coate – 12 shillings ...
>
> Nell Gwyn's household accounts

Nell Gwyn (1650–1687), one of the first female actors of the Restoration, is best known to us these days as the mistress of Charles II. Born into poverty, Nell was only thirteen when she and her sister began selling oranges to theatre audiences. Within a few years she was on the stage and, helped by her pretty face and neat figure, she soon became a popular comedy actor. She could not read, so instead learnt her lines by heart.

The idea of women acting had always been controversial, but in the earlier Puritan regime Oliver Cromwell had gone further and closed all theatres for being frivolous and immoral. He also banned Christmas and music in church services. Before this, public theatre and extravagant court masques had been popular since the reign of Henry VIII. They were the delight of Queen Anne, wife of James I; she even directed some of them herself, usually staged to accompany a marriage or an important celebration. When their daughter, Princess Elizabeth, married in

1613 there were two months of lavish celebrations with four masques on the wedding day, including one by George Chapman.

The staging of Ben Jonson's *Masque of Queens* in 1609 with set designs by Inigo Jones cost the immense sum of £3,000. Jonson wrote fourteen masques, and these paid so well that for ten years he did not write any plays. This quite magical form of entertainment involved elaborate scenery, special effects, lavish costumes and the best music. The queen and her ladies took part in the acting and dancing, a tradition happily continued by Henrietta Maria, French wife of the next king, Charles I.

These were examples of the highest form of theatre, and it was acceptable for women to act in them as they were private events held at court. Some people thought it immodest, to be sure, and in public theatres only men and boys could act. Indeed, at Elizabethan theatres like the Globe Theatre, all of Shakespeare's female characters – from lovestruck Juliet to murderous Lady Macbeth and both of the Merry Wives of Windsor – were played by teenage boys. These young lads were called upon to act as young maids, great queens like Cleopatra and wits like Beatrice in *Much Ado about Nothing*. Of course, if they did a bad job of it then at least in the comedies this simply added to the entertainment. (Mark Rylance's production of an all-male *Twelfth Night* in 2002 revealed another level to the comedy to those of us fortunate enough to be in the audience.)

With the Restoration of the Monarchy in 1660, women were allowed to act – something witnessed in Italy and France by the young Charles II during his exile on the continent. The London theatres reopened, and in December 1660, at Lincoln's Inn, the first Shakespearean actress appeared in *Othello* as Desdemona. Nobody took the trouble to record her name, but the general belief is that it was Anne Marshall.

Soon, female actors were all the rage. Moll Davies, Peg Hughes and Nell Gwyn[1] attracted the young men from court, who came to admire and ogle. If willing to pay the large sum of 4 shillings, the men were allowed backstage to watch the actresses dressing – no doubt more enticing to some than the play itself.

Nell Gwyn inspired at least thirty portraits. One risqué pose as Cupid shows her armed with a bow and arrow but rather lacking in clothes. It was so admired by Samuel Pepys that he kept a copy above his desk at the Admiralty. Another portrait appeared in 2012 and was sold by Nell's descendants in the same year as the National Portrait Gallery's exhibition about the first actresses.[2]

Pepys was smitten when he saw Nell Gwyn's earliest plays, calling her 'pretty, witty Nell'. One of the most famous stories of her sharp wit involves her carriage being mobbed by a crowd of Londoners who thought she was the king's deeply unpopular mistress the Duchess of Portsmouth, a foreigner and a Catholic. From the carriage, Nell called out to the crowd, 'Pray good people be silent, I am the Protestant whore.'

A Silver Bed for the King's Mistress

A few items from Nell's household accounts and papers, auctioned by Sotheby's in 2008, give us an idea of what a comfortable life she led. The accounts and all the receipts survived as the items, including an amazing silver bed, were to be paid for out of the king's coffers. There was a delightful town house at 78 Pall Mall, the most fashionable London address. Charles gave it to her in 1671, making it one of the few houses on the south side of Pall Mall that did not belong to the Crown. It would be her home until her death in 1687.

Nell's supper parties were famous. Whenever the king attended, his favourite meal of pigeon pie would be served. Her accounts for 1675 include:

For orinages [sic] & lemons – 2 shillings 6 pence
    Considerable quantities of meat and fish including up to three barrels of oysters a week at 3 shillings a barrel)
    Tarts and cheesecakes & drink

Carriage, mostly by sedan chair: For a Chaire carring my lo: from the dutches of Portsmou[th] – 1 shilling; for Careing [carrying] you to Mrs Knights and to Maddam younges and to madamms Churchfillds [Arabella Churchill] and wating fowre oures [four hours] – 5 shillings

For a poor man at the play house [theatre] 6 pence

Toys for her sons: 2 Colering broshes [colouring brushes]

Milliners [hat makers] for the purchase of several coifs and coronets

Glove-makers for 12 pare of Childrns gloves colerd and witt [12 pair of children's gloves coloured and white] – 12 shillings

Dressmakers for several nightgowns, dresses, and a pinke & white Lutestring [textured silk] Coate – 12 shillings

Silversmith John Cooques: two receipts acknowledging total payment of £500.

The last entry above concerns the aforementioned silver bed. Silver furniture was not only expensive but the latest, most extravagant French fashion. Some pieces survive at Knole House and in the Royal Collection, such as a mirror rediscovered at Windsor Castle in 1902 after languishing in a store room for centuries. Nell's bed included a headboard decorated with a relief of Charles II's head together with cupids, an acrobat dancing on a rope, crowns and eagles.

In all likelihood the silver bed was the most expensive item of furniture in the house. It would have been special even in any of the king's palaces. According to Nell's biographer Derek Parker,[1] the bill for the ornaments to the silver bed alone came to a total of £1,135 3s 1d. For context, the typical wages for a maidservant were less than £10 a year.

Beyond acts of sexual passion, Nell later said that the king would tell her 'who was my friend and who was not', which perhaps explains how she managed to survive the constant intrigues and jealousies at court. With Charles having so many mistresses, it must have resembled a harem at times. The king had fourteen illegitimate children, and not a single legitimate child to inherit his throne.

Nell's son by the king, also named Charles, was sent to France when he was young. Later, as a soldier, he deserted the army of the Catholic James II, who had succeeded to the throne, supporting instead the Protestant William of Orange. This was a wise choice, as William swept to power with James's daughter Mary in what is known as the Glorious Revolution.

Nell only survived Charles II by two years, dying aged thirty-seven from an apoplexy (or stroke) in November 1687. She was buried according to her wishes in St Martin-in-the-Fields, London, in her mother's plot. Her will, dated July 1687, calls her 'Ellen Gwynne spinster'. The main heir was Charles, 'my said dear son', described in the will as a 'natural' or illegitimate son. By now he was Duke of St Albans. There was £200 for her sister, Rose, and there were gifts for her servants. To the poor of her parish she gave £100 with an added £20 so that her son would release debtors from prison each Christmas Day. Another legacy was £50 to poor Catholics, intended 'for showing my charity to those who differ from me in Religeon'.

Nell also had debts. Some jewels were sold,[34] including a magnificent pearl necklace which had once belonged to Elizabeth, Queen of Bohemia. It had cost £4,250,[5] making it even more expensive than the silver bed!

Nell never did learn to write, signing her will with the initials E. G. for Eleanor Gwyn; the same letters were engraved upon her silver dinner service.

Being a mistress had given Nell the good life, and it lasted beyond her lifetime. Her descendants, the Beauclerks, continue down to the current 13th Duke of St Albans, the title and surname given to her son.

Since the Restoration actresses have continued to play an important role in our popular culture. Many, almost all, of the fifty-three portraits in the National Portrait Gallery's 2011 exhibition 'The First Actresses' were painted by the leading artists of the day, demonstrating how an early celebrity culture flourished almost as soon as women first stepped onto the stage. Both Joshua Reynolds and Thomas Gainsborough painted actresses, including the famous Mary Robinson (d. 1800), an early love of the Prince Regent.[1] Elizabeth Farren (d. 1829) was also popular, known for some twenty years as the Queen of the Theatre Royal in Drury Lane. She was mistress and then wife of the Earl of Derby and is depicted in a fashionable portrait by Thomas Lawrence in 1790, a few years before her marriage.[2]

The Incomparable Mrs Siddons

Sarah Siddons (*née* Kemble, 1755–1831) was born in Brecon, Wales. Her parents ran a company of strolling players but still opposed the idea of her acting, so her first job was as a lady's maid and then as a companion. Only after she married at the age of eighteen did she act. Her first roles on the London stage were unremarkable, and she moved out to the provincial theatres for a few years. During this time she changed her approach considerably. She began listening to the entire play to find what we now call the 'psychological depth' and emotions of a Shakespearian character such as Lady Macbeth. The dramatic intensity borne of this new approach gave her the marvellous stage presence which made her name. Her own favourite role was as Queen Catherine in Shakespeare's *Henry VIII*, a play rarely performed these days.

With the success of Sarah Siddons, actresses in particular and acting more generally became far more respectable in the eyes of the public. Returning to London, she was the star of Drury Lane and then of Covent Garden. By the mid-1780s Sarah was part of London's high society, accepted and admired by fashionable people. Nearly 400 portraits of Mrs Siddons were painted, including some by Reynolds and Gainsborough, the foremost artists of their day.

Believing herself to be destined for more than just acting, Sarah later turned to sculpture. Her diary, letters and memoirs were willed to the Scottish poet Thomas Campbell, who published her biography in 1834. Her funeral took place in 1831 at St Mary's

Church, Paddington, and attracted a crowd of more than 5,000 mourners.

Sarah's will bears a codicil adding two important theatre gifts to her children. Her youngest daughter, Cecilia, who was unmarried, was to have all the money that might be in the house or in the bank at the time of Sarah's death; her son George, meanwhile, was given an inkstand made from the mulberry tree planted by 'the immortal Shakespear – and also the Gloves which were worn by him'.

Celebrity

Victorian and Edwardian actresses were among the first celebrities, their fame fuelled not just by paintings but by new inventions such as cigarette cards, *cartes de visites* (calling cards) and postcards in the second half of the nineteenth century. Actors male and female, as well as music hall artists and singers, often featured in their own postcard collections. Gertie Millar can be found on countless colour postcards, both hand-tinted and plain. Miss Hilda Hanbury (grandmother of the actor Edward Fox), Isabel Jay, Edna May, Marie Studholme, Margaret Scudamore (grandmother of the actress Vanessa Redgrave), and sisters Zena and Phyllis Dare regularly published new postcards. It was all the rage to collect such postcards, especially among the dedicated admirers of prominent artistic figures.

Celebrity culture was soon booming. When the American actress Mary Pickford and her husband Douglas Fairbanks came to London in the summer of 1920, they stayed at the Ritz Hotel. The day after the couple were mobbed by fans, a large crowd consisting mostly of women waited to see Mary leave the hotel. Breaking through the police cordon, some fans desperately clung to her bonnet or the steps of her car as it drove away. *The Times* reported, 'They have caused probably the biggest stir in London since the first Zeppelin was brought down several years ago.'

Queen of the Poor

Harriot Mellon (1777–1837) was another actress who moved up the social scale with the help of a good marriage. In fact, she made two good marriages; the second made her a duchess. However, first she was the mistress and then the wife of the wealthy banker Thomas Coutts, founder of Coutts Bank. Coutts' daughters were firmly opposed to the marriage, perhaps having correctly guessed what would happen later as he left all his money to Harriot.

When Harriot herself died, she left the money in her will to her favourite step-grandchild, Angela Burdett (1814–1906), who was the youngest of six children. Not only was it a surprise inheritance, but it represented incredible wealth: a 50 per cent share in Coutts Bank and a sum of £1.8 million. These days it would be worth somewhere in the region of £160 million. The capital could not be touched, but the annual income of £50,000 was still enormous, being rather more than the £30,000 spent on building Euston Station, which opened the following year.

Harriot's will required Angela to add Coutts to her surname.[6] Furthermore, if she married a foreign national then the inheritance would be forfeit.[7] This may seem a rather strange condition, but at that this point in the nineteenth century there was strong anti-French sentiment. It was unthinkable that a British bank might be owned by a Frenchman.

Shortly after news of the will reached the public, Miss Burdett-Coutts received countless offers of marriage. Some men called at the house to propose, while others sent formal letters. A great hoarder, Angela kept all such letters, so we even know what they said. Instead of marriage, however, Angela began what was to be a lifetime of remarkable philanthropy.[8]

Cheek by Jowl, Wealth and Destitution

There was such desperate poverty everywhere, from towns like Carlisle down to Hitchin, where the slums close to St Mary's Church were only cleared in the 1920s. London was filled with endless poverty in its teeming narrow streets, courtyards and alleys with families crammed into tiny rooms. Open sewers were common, as were the resulting outbreaks of deadly cholera and typhoid.

When Charles Booth set out to colour code and map the streets of London by different incomes and social classes, the results were unsurprising. The maps revealed the huge gulf between the elite, whom he called the 'upper wealthy', and those he termed 'very poor'. Around 35 per cent of Londoners lived in abject poverty, their children often afflicted with rickets or scurvy. It was not only the capital that suffered so; there were similar numbers in distant York, for instance. Britain's population by 1901 was 41 million, representing an immense growth from a mere 9 million in 1801, and with this came countless social evils such as overcrowding, poor housing and disease.

Landowners had to pay poor rates to those living on their estates, but as agriculture became more mechanised this became an increasing financial burden. At Petworth in Sussex during the 1830s the Earl of Egremont, with other local landowners, offered his tenants free travel to Canada, though of course this was a single rather than a return ticket. This was evidently not an altruistic offering, but the fact that nearly 2,000 men, women and children from the Petworth estates and surrounds chose to accept gives some idea of the poverty that was rife.

Until 1834, every parish was required by law to keep a workhouse. Occasionally conditions were decent but mostly they were not, as the main idea was to discourage what was perceived as idleness. Families were separated as men were split from women and children. Old folk dreaded the workhouse, fearing that once in they would never leave. In some, unmarried mothers wore a uniform to distinguish them and highlight their disgrace, their supposed sin.

Entering the workhouse with its bleak conditions was a last resort. Once there, if starvation and cold did not kill the poor then one of the many epidemics of typhoid or cholera might do.[9] Life expectancy was low, with half the population born in 1880 predicted to die by the age of sixty.[9] By 1909, when the government first introduced a general pension – 5 shillings a week – life expectancy had hardly changed. This is important because to claim a pension you had to be at least seventy years old!

Blessed Are the Philanthropists

One project in Shepherd's Bush, London, supported by Miss Burdett-Coutts was controversial for helping homeless women and prostitutes, then considered to be sinful and wicked. Her decision to support this charity was a bold one, and many criticised her. She also gave generously to the Church, supporting volunteer nurses who went to the African campaign (the Boer War) in the 1890s. She had previously helped fund Florence Nightingale's nursing efforts during the Crimean War.

Columbia Market in London's East End, begun in 1840, marked the transformation of one of the poorest parts of London into an area with decent social housing plus a food market of 400 stalls. It was philanthropy on a most practical level to improve the lives of those who lived there.

In a slum area of Westminster, land was bought for a new church, a vicarage and three schools – one for girls, one for boys and one for infants. This was a crucial investment as there was no state education at this time. In 1851, Baroness Burdett-Coutts was one of the first supporters of the Royal Marsden Hospital, providing an interest-free loan for the building and an annual subscription thereafter. This was the first hospital dedicated to cancer research, offering free treatment. The National Health Service would not arrive until much later – introduced by a Labour Government in 1948.

Marriage, Tiaras and Some Rare Books

Angela Burdett-Coutts loved jewels, cherishing a famous collection including a tiara once owned by Marie Antoinette. She later began purchasing other expensive objects, including early English portraits, fine china and rare books such as two First Folios of Shakespeare's Complete Works. (Both now belong to the Folger Library in America.)

Queen Victoria was among Miss Burdett-Coutts' many admirers, and Charles Dickens spent many years as a friend and advisor on matters of philanthropy, dedicating *Martin Chuzzlewit* to her. In 1871 the queen made her a baroness in her own right, and in the following year the City of London took the royal hint and gave her the Freedom of the City; she was the first woman given this honour. (Florence Nightingale was the second.)

However, in 1881 the baroness decided to marry. This was most controversial. Firstly, there was the considerable age difference between the couple: William Lehman Ashmead-Bartlett was in his twenties while his bride was in her sixties. Making matters even worse, William was her secretary rather than a gentleman, which perhaps shocked people more than the age gap in the rigid class hierarchy of those times. Queen Victoria went so far as to write to a mutual friend advising against this mad marriage.

An Expensive Marriage

Some called her 'Baroness Chequebook' because she could buy a husband. This was hardly a fairy tale beginning for the couple, but according to her biographer Edna Healey it was mostly a happy marriage, lasting over twenty-five years. However, under the terms of Harriot Coutts' will there was a price to pay. William had been born in America, making him precisely the foreign national forbidden by the will. Her sister Clara duly challenged the will.

An agreement was only grudgingly agreed between the sisters, narrowly avoiding what would have been a lengthy and most expensive lawsuit. Angela was to have two-fifths of her original income while Clara received the remainder, totalling £30,000 per annum. Clara had married the Reverend James Money, making her the appropriately named Mrs Money-Coutts.

Angela Burdett-Coutts died of acute bronchitis in December 1906. Around 30,000 people came to pay their respects before her casket at her house in Stratton Street. Her estate was worth £79,482 15s 4d, and she left it to her husband, who continued with her many philanthropic projects. She always preferred giving money to causes where it would make a difference rather than patronising merely the accepted, fashionable charities of those times. It is estimated that she gave away somewhere between £3 million and £4 million during her lifetime, which today represents a sum in the region of £350 million. Little wonder that to Londoners she was Queen of the Poor, a title thoroughly deserved. *The Times* also thought so highly of her that they published an exceptionally long and reverential obituary notice a few days after her death.[10]

Westminster Abbey Is Deceived

The baroness was to be buried at Westminster Abbey in a state funeral. This was a great honour, but the dean insisted on cremation rather than burial, which was then a controversial new idea to create more burial space, and all was agreed with William. Then, the day before the funeral, the dean discovered there had been no cremation – nor would there be!

A year earlier, the great actor Sir Henry Irving had been buried at the abbey. His close friends had made the arrangements, among them Angela and her husband. Irving was cremated as required by the abbey, and his ashes duly placed in a narrow coffin below Shakespeare's statue. This knowledge was now used by William, who instructed the funeral directors to make a new, much smaller coffin that would fit into such a narrow space. The men worked through the night in order to get a new coffin ready – but it was for a burial, not a cremation.

State funerals are major events, and once the dean understood that Angela was not going to be cremated it was too late to cancel the event, not least because all the great and good would be there to pay their respects, including Edward VII and Queen Alexandra. Finding himself tricked, the dean made his disapproval known by staying away, leaving his deputy to take the service.[10]

Only one other burial has since been allowed at Westminster Abbey, for the grave of the Unknown Warrior after the First World War.

Miniature of St Aethelthryth, Queen of Northumbria and founder of Ely Abbey in the seventh century. Her land at Ely was a marriage gift in 652 from her first husband, Tondbert. (British Library, fol. 90v, illustration from *The Benedictional of St. Aethelwold*, late tenth century, owned by the Bishop of Winchester, with permission from the British Library)

The gold gospel book commissioned by Countess Judith of Northumbria (see chapter 1) sometime before 1066. Bound in gold and studded with gems, the illuminated book was probably made in Canterbury. Later Judith married the Duke of Bavaria and at her death bequeathed this and other gospel books to Weingarden Abbey, Bavaria. It is an exceptionally pious gift and would have been highly valued. It is a little smaller than an A4 piece of paper and so could easily be carried by a wealthy lady. (© The Morgan Library & Museum with permission. MS M.709. Purchased by J.P. Morgan in 1926)

The Great Gate of Christ's College, Cambridge, which was re-founded in the early 1500s by Lady Margaret Beaufort, mother of Henry VII. Priests at the college were to say prayers in perpetuity for their founder, her ancestors and descendants who today include Charles III. The heraldic crest above the Great Gate includes the mythical yales of the Beaufort family, beautiful beasts which are part goat and part antelope, also used in the royal crest of Henry VII. (Author's collection)

Known as the Cholmondeley Ladies, two sisters sit upright in bed, fully dressed, wearing their best clothes and holding their babies in swaddling clothes (see chapter 4). In wealthy and royal families the most important thing was the birth of a son and heir to continue the family line. Henry VIII divorced his first wife, Catherine of Aragon, for not producing a male heir to the Tudor dynasty. (© The Tate Gallery with permission)

Mary Share and Share alike. And I do hereby ...
nominate constitute and appoint my Daughter Jane
Price sole Executrix of this my last Will & hereby revok
all former Wills by me at any Time heretofore made
In Witness whereof I have hereunto set my
Hand and Seal the thirteenth Day of September
one thousand seven hundred and ninety three.

Signed sealed published and
declared by the Testatrix Jane Davies
as and for her last Will and Testament
in the Presence of us, and in her presence
have subscribed our Names as Witnesses

The Mark of
+
Jane Davies

An extract of the handwritten will of Jane Davis of Flint, Wales, 1723, who left a featherbed to her granddaughter. (Flint Archives, Wales with permission)

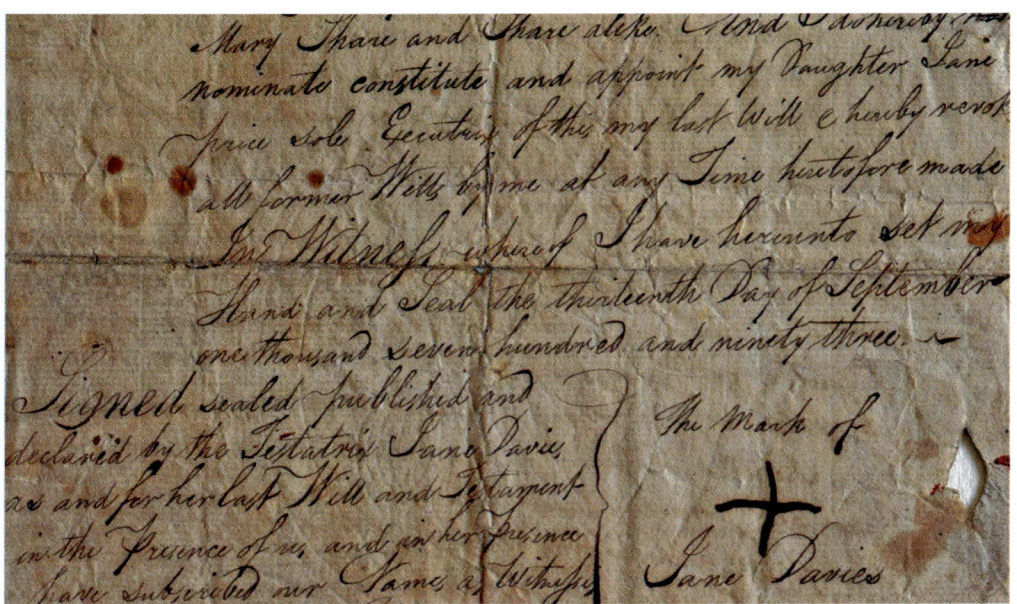

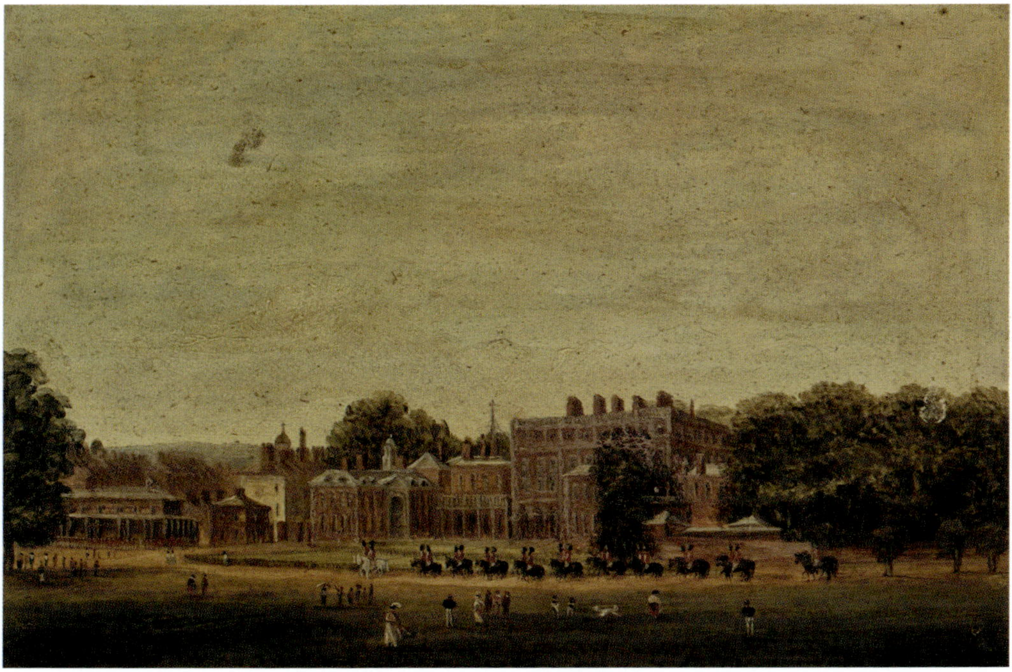

An early painting of Buckingham Palace when it was merely Buckingham House (it only became a palace after building work commissioned by the Prince Regent). This was painted by Mrs Phipps as a bequest to her dear friend Lucy Holbech and remained in the family until auctioned by Sotheby's in 2019. A label on the reverse of the painting declares, 'Gifted to Mrs Lucy Holbech, Farnborough Hall, Warwickshire, in June 1826.' (© Sotheby's 2018 with permission)

Above: The Swan at Swinbrook. Deborah, Duchess of Devonshire was one of the six famous Mitford sisters and grew up in Swinbrook. On her later visits to the village near Oxford the duchess became friends with Miss Bunce, who decided that as she had no close relatives the Swan pub and Mill Cottage were to be offered at a low price to the duchess. The bequest recognised their friendship as well as the love they shared for Swinbrook and the local area. (Author's collection)

Left: Two topaz crosses owned by Jane Austen and her sister Cassandra. (© Jane Austen's House Museum with permission)

Below left: Coverlet or quilt made by Jane, Cassandra and their mother. (© Jane Austen's House Museum with permission)

Right: Jane Austen's portrait by her sister Cassandra. (© Jane Austen's House Museum with permission)

Below: Chawton House is now a museum for Jane Austen. It was her home, where she lived with her sister and mother for the last eight years of her life. (Author's collection)

Left: Miss Marianne North at her painting easel (chapter 12). (Courtesy of Kew Gardens © with permission)

Below: The interior of Kew Gallery, designed by Marianne North to hold many of her paintings. (Courtesy of Kew Gardens © with permission)

Bottom: Mount Fujiyama, painted by Marianne North. (Courtesy of Kew Gardens © with permission)

Above: One of the first colleges for women, Girton had a fierce principle of making its students independent and set up its own fire brigade. The first chief fire officer of the London Metropolitan Fire Brigade, Captain Sir Eyre Massey Shaw, helped teach female students how to use firefighting equipment. Girton retained its own women's fire brigade from 1878 to 1932. (© Archive reference: GCPH 10/2/3 taken by RH Lord. With permission of The Mistress and Fellows, Girton College, Cambridge)

Above right: The Hendon Sunningdale Ladies Tennis Club, *c.* 1890. (© The Francis Frith Collection, with permission)

Below right: Lady cyclists of Barnstaple, 1906. Photograph taken in Boutport Street. (© The Francis Frith Collection, with permission)

Postcards of some celebrity actresses and those famous from opera and the Edwardian music halls. Left to right, from top to bottom, are Zena and Phyllis Dare, Gertie Miller, Isabel Jay, Doris Stocker, Dame Ellen Terry, Maude Dainton, Grace Arundale, and Barbara Deane. Isabel Jay was so popular that over 400 different postcards featuring her were published. (Author's collection)

A postcard from the early 1900s on the Mer de Glace, Chamonix, France, shows a group out on the mountains. Regardless of their long heavy skirts the ladies manage the difficulty of alpine weather and mountaineering. (Author's collection)

Above left: A woman tennis player at the turn of the twentieth century. (Author's collection)

Above middle: Cambridge postcard, posted in 1903, of a women's rowing team. (Author's collection)

Above right: A Davidson postcard entitled 'The Belle of the Ball' celebrating a lady golfer. (Author's collection)

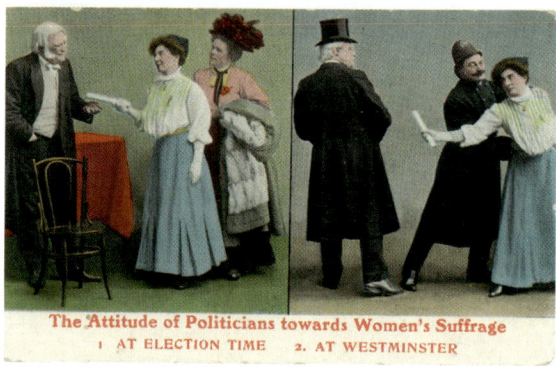

Above left: A witty Suffragette poster dating from before the First World War, c. 1912: 'What a Woman May Be, and Yet not Have the Vote. What a Man may Have Been, and Yet not Lose the Vote.' It was not until 1918 that some women were given the vote, and not until 1928 that all women were given it. (© Museum of London with permission)

Above right: Defaced Edward VII penny, 1906, stamped with 'Votes for Women'. (Author's collection)

Left: Two panels on a postcard from the early 1900s. The left-hand side shows the politician as a great friend to women (at election time), but the right indicates that once elected he is uninterested and the lady is hustled away by a policeman. (Author's collection)

Below left: 'Why Should I Want a Husband?' A satirical cartoon postcard by Donald McGill from the early 1900s where a single lady outlines a few reasons why she does not need a husband.

A photograph of a nurse from the First World War. The encouraging words 'Thumbs up!!!' are handwritten on the margin. (Author's collection)

Cheshire munitions workers on a postcard from Northwich dating from the First World War or possibly a few years earlier. On the back of the postcard is written, 'On the right is Miss Mary Hitchen of 132 Delamere Street, Winsford.' Theirs was extremely dangerous work involving large amounts of explosives. (© Courtesy of Cheshire Archives & Local Studies c11232 with permission)

Black Cat cigarette cards featuring women in war work, with illustrations on one side and descriptions on the other. (Author's collection)

WOMEN ON WAR WORK

No. 3. POSTWOMAN.

IN country districts even before the war there were women employed for delivering letters. Now nearly all this work even in the big towns is being done very capably by women.

Issued by
CARRERAS LIMITED
ESTAB. 1788
LONDON & MONTREAL
ENG.   QUE.

WOMEN ON WAR WORK

No. 25. GARDENING.

ALTHOUGH there were not many women gardeners before the war, this is work which is very suitable for women. A great many estates now employ only women gardeners, and even after the war there is no doubt that this will be one of the careers many women will adopt.

Issued by
CARRERAS LIMITED
ESTAB. 1788
LONDON & MONTREAL
ENG.   QUE.

WOMEN ON WAR WORK

No. 7. DRIVING GOODS DELIVERY VAN.

SINCE War started, the able-bodied young men who used to drive delivery waggons have been called up and their places have been taken by women. They make just as good and careful drivers as the men, and it is quite a common sight to see women driving the Royal Mail Vans, as well as delivery vans for private firms.

Issued by
CARRERAS LIMITED
ESTAB. 1788
LONDON & MONTREAL
ENG.   QUE.

WOMEN ON WAR WORK

No. 41. BUS CONDUCTOR.

VERY smart and workmanlike are these girls, and on the whole they are very good-natured in spite of all the difficulties and trials such work brings. Their work is fatiguing, their hours are long, but they are "doing their bit" in this very useful way.

Issued by
CARRERAS LIMITED
ESTAB. 1788
LONDON & MONTREAL
ENG.   QUE.

WOMEN ON WAR WORK

No. 16. PREPARATION OF SOLDIERS' DINNERS.

IN order to release for active service a large number of men who were employed as army cooks, the Military Authorities have enlisted women for this work. The experiment has proved a huge success.

Issued by
CARRERAS LIMITED
ESTAB. 1788
LONDON & MONTREAL
ENG.   QUE.

WOMEN ON WAR WORK

No. 5. FLOUR MILL.

SOME of the work in a flour mill requires a good deal of muscular strength, and in peace days such work was considered unsuitable for women. However, when the need came the women proved themselves quite equal to the strenuous tasks required of them.

Issued by
CARRERAS LIMITED
ESTAB. 1788
LONDON & MONTREAL
ENG.   QUE.

WOMEN ON WAR WORK

No. 38. WOMAN WAGON WASHER.

WOMEN are employed in livery stables, garages, and on railways, as wagon washers. It is not too easy, and in peace times is not regarded as "women's work" at all, but while the war lasts the gentler sex are ready to do all they can to keep things going.

Issued by
CARRERAS LIMITED
ESTAB. 1788
LONDON & MONTREAL
ENG.   QUE.

WOMEN ON WAR WORK

No. 19. MECHANICS.
Electrical Engineering.

SINCE so many men have been called up, while at the same time a tremendous amount of extra work has been thrown on the engineering trades, it has been found that women make very satisfactory substitutes, particularly where a light and delicate touch is required for precision work.

Issued by
CARRERAS LIMITED
ESTAB. 1788
LONDON & MONTREAL
ENG.   QUE.

WOMEN ON WAR WORK

No. 47. BREWERY WORKER.

THIS is work which requires a good deal of muscular strength, consequently only really strong women are able to do it. Still, there are plenty of fine, strong, able women who are willing to turn their hands to this, as to many other equally strenuous tasks.

Issued by
CARRERAS LIMITED
ESTAB. 1788
LONDON & MONTREAL
ENG.   QUE.

WOMEN ON WAR WORK

No. 13. AMBULANCE SERVICE.

THE Red Cross Service has been very glad to avail itself of the services of capable women drivers, in conveying the wounded to hospital.

Issued by
CARRERAS LIMITED
ESTAB. 1788
LONDON & MONTREAL
ENG.   QUE.

Above: The Portpatrick lifeboat *John Buchanan Barr*, funded from a bequest of £2.6 million from Katherine Barr in memory of her husband Dr John Barr, a Glasgow doctor and GP. The boat was launched in 2011. (© Courtesy of the Royal National Lifeboat Institute/ Nicholas Leach)

Left: Studio photograph of Emily Green with her grandson Michael, *c.* 1940s (Author's collection)

A brooch from the collection of Anne Hull Grundy, given to the Higgins Museum in Bedford in the 1970s. Dating from around 1850, its empty acorn signifies loss and is an example of Victorian mourning jewellery. (© The Trustees of the Cecil Higgins Art Gallery (The Higgins Bedford) with permission)

Elton House is now a handsome and imposing Georgian townhouse in the centre of Bath given to the Landmark Trust by Miss Philippa Savery. In the early 1980s she was searching for a shop where she could sell antiques and found Elton House. No longer the grand family home it once was, it had been divided into various properties and rented out. It took years before she could empty the house of tenants and renovate back to its former glory. (© Landmark Trust with permission)

Left: Mrs Helena Cooper gave the Landmark Trust Obriss Farm, which her father worked before the days of modern intensive farming; it was a farm since Tudor times. (© Landmark Trust with permission)

Below: The Castle of Mey looking out towards the Orkney Islands. (Author's collection)

10

THE TALE OF PETER RABBIT AND THE NATIONAL TRUST; VOTES FOR WOMEN

> 'All my books to the people of Zimbabwe.'
> Doris Lessing's will, 2013

Are modern women's wills so very different to those made by their grandmothers and earlier ancestors? In the inclusions and omissions, in what is left and to whom, each will tells a story of secrets and kindnesses, great loves and expectations disappointed. There are some positive differences today, not least the fact that far more women now control their own financial destiny. One of the wealthiest, Dorothy Rothschild (d. 1998), made history in that her will dealt with the largest sum of any will in English history, some £96 million. It is not surprising that it belongs to a Rothschild – after all, theirs is a very wealthy banking family – but it is significant to find it is a woman's rather than man's will.

One constant across the ages is women's love and appreciation for education, books and learning. From those first illuminated manuscripts in Saxon times through to present-day bequests this is clear. There are countless bequests for schools and universities in the twentieth century, and so much generosity is evident, as with the novelist Doris Lessing, who died in 2013 in her nineties. Her first novel was set in Rhodesia (now Zimbabwe), where she grew up and lived for over twenty years. She bequeathed her entire book collection, some 3,000, to Harare City Library. The terror and chaos prevailing in the country meant that most public libraries had few books, and sending the books was her way to help the people of that nation.

Another thread from ancient times through to the modern age is philanthropy. Miss Georgina Cotton-Browne (d. 1944), who owned Walkern Hall, was long remembered in the Hertfordshire village of Walkern for her many kindnesses and care for the local people. She always gave most generously, not least in providing Christmas parties, and in her will she left £1 to every child in the village.

Vera Lynn (d. 2021), famous during the Second World War as the Forces Sweetheart, is another example. Almost a quarter of her £1.1 million estate was willed to the charitable trust she and her husband established in 1989. Her daughter, the main beneficiary, received more than 600 paintings from her mother, whose artistic talents were known to few outside of the family.

A third constant is the support network between women and their female friends and relatives. In 2013, one woman in Birmingham selected small items of jewellery for her husband to give to her closest friends after the funeral. Each received a bracelet, ring, necklace or brooch as a particular remembrance. In earlier centuries remembrance rings were given by those who could afford them, enamelled black on the outside if a woman was married or white if she was not, with the name of the deceased and their date of death inscribed inside. Often a skull or some other reminder of death was part of the ring's design.

The close bond between some grandmothers and their grandchildren has likewise remained; no doubt it will continue for every future generation, whether in modest or expensive bequests, such as the two grandmothers in chapter 6. For a granddaughter (or great-granddaughter) it might be a pearl necklace. This was a popular choice in aristocratic and well-off families in a time when pearls were even more valuable than diamonds. Since Victorian times, trust funds have prospered – money invested to later pay for a good education or simply to provide financial security.

Women in the Twentieth Century: Revolution Not Evolution

The huge social upheaval from two world wars, along with women's own ambitions for independence, created an era of great opportunity for women. They could finally attend university, and after a long, bitter campaign they had won the right to vote. In 1918, only a limited number of women were eligible and they had to be thirty or older; only in 1928 would all women be given the vote. And if this seems late, then consider that women were not allowed to vote until 2015 in Saudi Arabia.

The early years of the twentieth century were marked by major changes for women in politics and elsewhere. In 1919, the Sex Disqualification (Removal) Act 1919 meant women could officially become magistrates and join professions such as law; women had practised as solicitors during the First World War. Just before Christmas, the first seven women magistrates were appointed: Lady Londonderry, Lady Crewe, Mary Augusta Ward, Beatrice Webb, Gertrude Tuckwell, Elizabeth Haldane and the Prime Minister's wife, Margaret Lloyd George. Selected from different political parties and areas of Britain, they were followed the next year by a longer list of 172 women. Ten years later, there were 1,775 women magistrates. Today women make up 56 per cent of the magistracy.

Also in 1919, the Metropolitan Police recruited twenty-five female officers as a one-year experiment. They could not make arrests and were paid less than the men. Sophia Stanley, the first Superintendent of Women Police, designed their uniform, which was manufactured by Harrods. In 2019, Westminster Abbey held a service of thanksgiving marking 100 years of women in the Metropolitan Police.

The next year, in 1920, six women were appointed for the first time as jurors at Bristol Quarter Sessions. This major event was covered with a photo of the women in the *Bath Chronicle and Weekly Gazette*. The pioneers were Agnes James, Florence Pope, Harriett Parker Wake, Virginia Dadge, Ellen Elizabeth Hudd and Florence Cox.* Lincoln, Nottingham and Leicester also had similarly mixed juries for the first time in this year. We take such equalities for granted now, but in the early 1900s a woman could not be a jury member, a solicitor, a barrister or a judge.

In 1921, Marie Stopes opened the first birth control clinic in London amid considerable public opposition, including from church leaders. Many people thought that offering advice would increase promiscuity. Free advice was available – but only for married women at first. Much later, after the contraceptive pill was introduced in the early 1960s, it was similarly available only to married women (until 1967).

The year 1922 saw the first female barrister, Miss Ivy Williams. According to *The Manchester Guardian*, Miss Williams said it had been her dream and that of her father, an Oxford solicitor. In the same year, Carrie Morrison became the first female solicitor. Early in 1923, Maud Crofts, Mary Pickup and Mary Sykes followed. Lord Halsbury, Lord Chancellor at that time, had been among those who objected to women being admitted. In Scotland the breakthrough was slightly earlier, with Madge Anderson qualifying in 1920.

Nancy Astor, the First Woman MP

Most importantly, in 1918 women could stand for election to Parliament. Lady Nancy Astor's victory in a by-election at Portsmouth Sutton made her the first woman to sit as an MP in the House of Commons. Before this, women's continuing political interest across the centuries was as political hostesses, mistresses of politicians or the wives of Prime Ministers. Certainly, they might be influential and important, especially the political hostesses, but it was always the men who had held the formal appointments.

---

* With thanks to Anne Buchanan, Bath Record Office, for discovering the names from the Quarter Session records.

The Tale of Peter Rabbit *and the National Trust*

Nancy Astor's husband had held the seat before, so this was an ideal opportunity to win a safe seat, though evidently she suffered endless indecision about whether or not to stand. Fortunately, on balance, she decided it was worthwhile. However, it would be another sixty years before a woman was Prime Minister, when Margaret Thatcher won the general election of 1979.

The Times covered Lady Astor's arrival with the headline 'Ladies Day in the Commons', describing the event as 'the capitulation of a fortress which had been exclusively masculine for over 600 years'.

Lady Astor's supporters included many female friends, who watched the scene from the Strangers' Gallery. Her fellow MPs were less welcoming, jeering her entrance and crowding around so that she had to push through the mêlée in order to gain her seat.

On the same day, almost unnoticed, there was another and rather unexpected breakthrough:

> … two women journalists, greatly daring, sought and secured admission to the Press Gallery for the first time in its history.

Lady Astor, who died in 1964, was always stylish. In Parliament she dressed simply, in a dark jacket and skirt with a white blouse that blended perfectly with the men's dark suits. She wanted to set an example to other women who followed her into Parliament, and who might only have the MP's salary of £400 a year, rather than the Astor family wealth.

For their part, many male MPs resented Lady Astor and began their own war by not speaking to her. Such bad behaviour only made her more determined to stay, though in an interview years later Nancy Astor said it was a great day when a second woman MP joined.

A Brilliant Partnership

The second woman MP, who won the election in the constituency of Louth in 1921, was Margaret Wintringham. A headmistress first, she was married to the incumbent MP for Louth when he died in office. After she decided to stand in his place, it was not considered proper for her to canvas for votes as she was a widow in mourning. Fortunately, women from Girton and Newnham Colleges turned out to help with the campaigning and Margaret was duly elected.

With a shared bullish intelligence, Margaret and Nancy made a brilliant partnership, an alliance which led to close friendship. When news of Margaret's election was announced, Lady Astor sent a telegram of congratulations, saying to reporters,

> I rejoice to welcome another woman to the House of Commons. Although differing in politics, I feel that at this time when women are so needed to put forward the women's and children's point of view, and to press for improved legislation on their behalf, the claims of party need be no barrier to co-operation.

Nancy Astor was a champion of women's issues, successfully campaigning to lower the female voting age from thirty to twenty-one in 1928. She received many letters from women asking for help and regarded this as an important part of her parliamentary duty. Her salary matched the men's. If only such a rule had been applied thereafter in every sector! Pay inequality would not then have been such a vexed issue for every following generation of working women – as it still is. In 1921, *The Times*, when announcing the admission of women into the Civil Service, said that the pay would not be equal 'for the simple reason that the cost would be too great'.

Outside of her political career, Lady Astor was extremely wealthy. She had a smart London townhouse and also Cliveden, one of the nation's foremost stately homes, set high above the River Thames. Another unusual friendship developed between Lady Astor and Rose (Rosina) Harrison, who came into her employment as lady's maid in 1929. Lady Astor's reputation for being difficult was such that the other servants were certain Rose would not stay long. Instead, they developed a lifelong friendship lasting over thirty years. Sometimes voices were raised between the two women, and Lord Astor, listening in from the next room, tried to hear what it was all about. More often, though, he heard laughter as her ladyship entertained Rose with the day's events. Lady Astor was a strong-minded, wealthy American socialite used to getting her own way, but Rose could be equally fierce, proud to be a plainspoken Yorkshire lass. As she grew older, Lady Astor increasingly relied on Rose, making her promise to stay with her until she died.

Rose later became a minor celebrity, publishing *My Life in Service to Lady Astor*, and was invited to take part in Radio 4's *Desert Island Discs*. When Lady Astor died in 1964, Rose received £1,000 in her will plus an annuity of £500.

Save Our Heritage!

The money that charities receive as legacies are critical for their survival. In 2021/22, for example, £63.6 million was left to the National Trust in wills. Women played a key role in the early days of the National Trust, as we have seen. Their generosity gave the National Trust grand country houses and mansions, art collections and estates, establishing it as a custodian of our national heritage.

In 1908, in the year of her mother's death, Rosalie Chichester handed part of Arlington Court to the National Trust. The remainder went to them as a bequest at her death aged eighty-four in 1949. The Chichester family, one of the most important families in the county, had lived at Arlington Court in Devon for eleven generations. Miss Chichester lived there nearly ninety years, unmarried and with no children to inherit. The last of the Chichester family, she was cremated according to her wishes, with her ashes buried by the lake at Arlington Court.

The Tale of Peter Rabbit *and the National Trust*

One of the most important patrons of the National Trust was a writer by the name of Mrs Heelis, far better known as Beatrix

Potter (1866–1943). She bought a large amount of farmland in the Lake District, bequeathing it to her husband and after his death, to the National Trust. As with Fanny Talbot, who gave the first piece of land to the National Trust, there was a close friendship between the Potter family and Canon Hardwicke Rawnsley, one of the founders of the trust.

Beatrix Potter's first purchase of an old farm at Hill Top was made possible by a small legacy from her aunt and early royalties from her books, among them *The Tale of Peter Rabbit*. Published in 1902, the book has never been out of print. Her watercolour pictures, which illustrate more than twenty books, are entrancing, as are the stories of Mrs Tiggywinkle, Ginger and Pickles, Squirrel Nutkin and of course Jemima Puddle-Duck.

Beatrix Potter eventually moved to the Lake District, where the family had spent many holidays.[1] And when she did marry later in life, at the age of forty-seven, it was to William Heelis, a local solicitor who had helped her find and buy other farms and land. Her parents opposed this match as much as they had disliked her first engagement so many years before. William Heelis was only a mere country solicitor, and socially inferior to the Potter family. But they did marry.

In 1930, Beatrix Potter made one of her largest purchases: the Monk Conniston estate, which developers had wanted for commercial forestry. In the end, she owned more than 4,000 acres; when this was transferred to the National Trust in 1943, it became one of the largest bequests they had ever received. She had been concerned about the threat of development, as big a danger then in the Lake District as it is now everywhere across the land. Hill Top Farm was to be kept exactly as it had been when she first lived there, and not let to tenants. Having written many of her books there, she considered it a very special place. On the fell farms, Beatrix stipulated that the sheep must be pure Herdwicks (still a rare breed). She was particularly proud to be President of the Herdwick Sheep Breeds Association. Also, hunting was banned:

The Tale of Peter Rabbit *and the National Trust*

I declare that hunting by otter hounds and harriers shall be forbidden and prohibited over the whole of my Troutbeck property.

Beatrix Potter was always concerned about preserving the Lake District, leading a campaign to ban the noisy trials of seaplanes before the First World War. Winston Churchill, as First Lord of the Admiralty, disagreed. He asserted that the trials were critical to develop a modern air force.

In her will, Potter insisted that the National Trust keep farm rents at modest levels. In later life, long after the instant fame of *The Tale of Peter Rabbit* in 1902, she much preferred country life rather than any success or celebrity. Nor was she as fond of children as might be imagined of someone who wrote such magical stories for them. In fact, she could be quite brutal. In the 1920s, a six-year-old Roald Dahl turned up at Hill Top, telling Beatrix that that he'd come to meet her. She replied, 'Well, you've seen her now – buzz off.'

Concerns to preserve our national heritage can be found in every county and in so many towns, as in East Grinstead, Sussex. Sackville House, close by the church, is a rare survival of an early Tudor house with an original long, narrow garden plot and was given to the Landmark Trust in 1995 by Ursula Webb. Polesden Lacey, a fine country house in Surrey, along with an art collection was left to the National Trust by Dame Margaret Greville (1863–1942).

Mrs Greville, a Tin Box and Some Diamonds

Few women would keep expensive jewels in an old tin box, but Mrs Greville did for a very good purpose: disguise. Her home address was painted on the side in the unlikely case it should be lost or forgotten, so you might imagine it held boots and shoes rather than some exceedingly valuable diamonds. A clever ruse to fool any diamond thief.

Margaret Greville's father founded McEwan's Brewery in Scotland, which made him exceedingly rich. His only child, she would inherit all. Her marriage to Captain Ronnie Greville, a close friend of Edward VII, was perfect; with her wealth and his social connections, Margaret could become an important society hostess. It truly was the good life – the very best, in fact, with top chefs and the finest wines. They travelled in style, staying at the smartest hotels.

Mrs Ronnie, as she became known, enjoyed 'collecting' royal visitors to her weekend parties at Polesden Lacey. The Duke of York and his wife, later George VI and Queen Elizabeth, spent part of their honeymoon at Polesden Lacey and Mrs Ronnie was so proud of this close connection that a photograph of them taken on the garden terrace was always kept on display.

The Grevilles took trips to South America (for five months) and to Japan, as well as making a constant round of visits to well-connected friends, in addition to the society events each season. After the captain's death, she decided to keep their house in Mayfair, London; it was ideal for the London season.

A Friday-to-Monday stay at Polesden Lacey was a much sought-after invitation. It boasted vintage champagne and a French chef – essential assets for any aspiring hostess in Edwardian times. Polesden Lacey was left to the National Trust by Mrs Greville in memory of her father, together with 1,000 acres of land. Her original intention had been to leave it to the Duke of York and his wife, but his brother Edward's abdication in the 1930s meant that he was king rather than a younger son without a country house. She also left money for the upkeep of the house, which was crucial as maintaining grand country houses can be ruinously expensive.

The queen (later known as the Elizabeth the Queen Mother) had to pretend she knew nothing about her dazzling inheritance, even when Mrs Greville's solicitor came to visit her with the details of the will and those fabulous jewels. The gossips must have been buzzing with the secret news! The estate was worth more than £64 million in today's terms; back then the precise sum for probate was £1,623,191 17s. Death duties alone came to

£830,120 which was rather more than the sums left in many wills at that time and now.

Inside the tin box were outstanding jewels including Marie Antoinette's necklace, a Cartier diamond necklace of five strands, and large pear-drop diamond earrings designed by Cartier in 1938. The Greville diamond honeycomb tiara was refashioned in the 1920s by Boucheron, one of the leading French jewellers. Even tiaras go in and out of fashion, and it was one of the most important pieces in the Greville collection.[2]

Maggie Greville had no children and chose to give her magnificent jewels with 'loving thoughts' to the queen. In 2002, they were inherited by her daughter Queen Elizabeth II. Occasionally, the Greville jewels come out for special occasions, as in 2019 when Camilla (then Duchess of Cornwall) wore the honeycomb tiara for a state banquet at Windsor Castle in honour of US President Donald Trump. Princess Eugenie wore another of the Greville tiaras, set with emeralds, for her wedding in 2021.

Amusingly Unkind?

Not everyone liked Maggie Greville. Cecil Beaton, for one, called her a snobbish old toad. Exceptionally kind to some, she nonetheless had a sharp tongue, often making fun of people. Even her closest friends were not safe. Henry 'Chips' Channon confided in his diary, 'No one on earth was so skilfully malicious as old Maggie.'

Yet her kindness and wit were appreciated as well. 'I shall miss her very much indeed ... so shrewd, so kind, so amusingly unkind, so sharp, such fun, so naughty,' wrote the queen in a letter shortly after Mrs Greville's death. Having declared, 'Everybody else leaves their money to the poor – I am going to leave it to the rich,' Maggie Greville spent her final days in the Dorchester Hotel. To the last, she loved wearing her many sparkling diamond rings.

Polesden Lacey and her London house were filled to overflowing. It took James Lee-Milne weeks to complete the cataloguing of her valuable paintings, silver and furniture. In the meantime, his acquaintances hoped they could look through the London house for a memento or that an earlier present to Mrs Greville might be returned to them. Queen Mary even went as far as to hint she would like to look round Polesden Lacey. A dedicated collector of objects d'art, she was well known for her acquisitiveness; a host or his lady might feel compelled to offer a piece which had caught her interest. In some households, ornaments would be tidied away before their royal guest arrived.

My Servants, My Friends

For all her snobbery, Miss Ronnie was egalitarian when it came to her servants. Many had been with her for years, such as Adeline Liron, first her lady's maid and then her companion. Mrs Greville left 'to my valued friend Marie Adeline Liron' the care of her pet dogs and a large legacy, items of jewellery as well as the right to stay on at Polesden Lacey, which she did until her death in 1959.

There was such a huge gulf then between servants and their employers, but Margaret Greville's own background makes it easy to understand why she ignored this. Her mother had been housekeeper to Mr McEwan when Margaret was born, and only later did they marry. The chauffeur Sidney Smith received 'all my motor cars with accessories and the garage furniture at 11 Hays Mews' (the London townhouse). Francis Bole, the steward and butler, had worked for Mrs Greville for over forty years. He was both a friend and someone she trusted completely. Even his drunkenness rarely got him into any serious trouble. Entrusted to destroy her private papers and letters after her death, he received her valuable collection of modern silver plus £1,000 and an annuity of £500.

11

EMILY TINNE'S WARDROBE AND EMILY GREEN, A SERVANT

'I will haunt the British Museum'

Emily Tinne and Emily Green were children in late Victorian times. They lived through two world wars, the introduction of the motor car, telephones and planes as well as dramatic social changes for women. Not least of these was the right to vote on equal terms with men.

Emily Tinne Goes Shopping

From 1910 to 1940, Emily Tinne (*née* McCulloch, 1886–1966) regularly went shopping in Liverpool. Bold Street, known as the 'Bond Street of the North', boasted shops on a par with those lining the more famous London thoroughfare. For women who could afford to do so, shopping here would have been the favoured pastime. They could see the latest fashions, meet friends for tea and then head back to a house with servants where dinner was prepared and all the chores taken care of.

An illustration of just how much shopping went on at this time can be seen in details from 1937, when the department store D. H. Evans, on Oxford Street in London, opened a restaurant on its fifth floor; it could serve 1,000 people at any time. Most customers were women.[1]

Emily Tinne trained as a teacher in domestic science. She moved to Liverpool and in 1910 married a doctor and gave up her job.

This was normal if there was sufficient income to do so, and there certainly was as her husband inherited a large sum of money in the mid-1920s, £161,830 to be precise. They lived in a large house and owned an expensive, exclusive Daimler, which was the first car in Liverpool. The family could afford servants as well as an excellent education for the children. The sons went to Eton while the girls attended local schools.

Emily was born in India but her missionary parents sent her back to England to attend boarding school. Until she married, Emily owned few clothes; her wardrobe had a few simple, practical outfits for everyday wear. It must have been an austere life, and many years later her daughter suggested it was probably this background that lay behind Emily's desire to follow the latest fashions.

Only when Mrs Tinne died did the family discover the full extent of her shopping habit. Squirrelled away in various places around the house, even in outbuildings and the cellar, was a vast collection of clothes. In later years, expensive new items were carefully packed into tea chests. There were hats, underwear, and shoes (relatively few), coats and cocktail dresses, everyday dresses and suits, fur coats and evening gowns, plus some children's clothes and servants' uniforms.

One of Emily's favourite milliners was Madame Val Smith, who had a smart shop in the centre of Liverpool. No doubt 'Madame' added that indefinable glamour to reassure customers that all the fashions came direct from Paris. Emily's daughters remember how when they were young their mother would go shopping most afternoons, and that some of the fur coats were bought so that a female shop assistant might earn commission on the sale.

Some clothes were never worn, packed away in pristine condition in the original boxes with the written bill inside just as they had been delivered. Other items were reduced or discounted items, which is rather puzzling. Did Emily perhaps set herself an allowance every month, and so reduced items meant she could buy more? Maybe, like many of us today, she simply could not resist a bargain. She does sound like a 'shopaholic', although that word was yet to be invented. This was an obsession rather than a passing interest.

A Museum Collection

Emily's sizeable collection was offered to the Walker Gallery in Liverpool, and for months Emily's daughter would leave two tea chests of clothing outside the house to be collected each week. Gradually the curators sifted through the offerings, finding sufficient examples to create an exhibition in 2020 of seventy outfits – 'An English Lady's Wardrobe'.[2] It is a time capsule of fashion between the wars. Few other such collections exist, though Brighton Museum has the Messel family collection. Some 500 items showcase fashion trends from 1879 through to 2005, representing six generations of stylish women. Put together with exquisite taste, a veritable passion for fashion and the necessary bank balance to buy expensive and couture items, it provides us with a valuable snapshot of what the female *bon ton* wore.

Another Emily, who was much less wealthy, makes an appearance later in this chapter. First, though, let us talk about Mrs Hull Grundy.

Anne Hull Grundy's Jewellery

Another unique collection – this time of jewellery – was put together over a period of many years. Mrs Anne Hull Grundy (*née* Ullmann, 1926–1984), though born in the mid-1920s, had that Victorian love of jewellery. She could afford to indulge her passion for buying jewels from the eighteenth and nineteenth centuries with a collectors' eye, and she was shrewd enough to buy well. One of the most important English jewellery collectors, her knowledge was phenomenal. Anne was as fascinated by the meaning of jewellery as she was with the skills of the people who made them. For her it was not about getting the most expensive, precious stones. It was characteristic of her taste that she preferred animal jewellery. In her view, diamonds were 'for call girls and dumb rich wives'. Cameos, silver jewellery and smaller trinkets were all valuable to her.

Anne Hull Grundy began collecting at the age of eleven. Noticing that the British Museum's collection of jewels stopped at the seventeenth century, she decided to focus on the eighteenth and nineteenth centuries. Well known among London jewellers in her early buying years, she often drove from shop to shop in a chauffeur-driven car. In later life, she bought many items by post as illness saw her bedridden and housebound. All through her life she had a reputation for buying pieces that were not in fashion.

Towards the end of her life, Anne divided her collection between a number of museums. Because of this split, she is not nearly as famous as she ought to be outside of the scene populated by jewellery experts. Hers were significant gifts. At the Higgins Gallery in Bedford, where Anne donated more than 120 pieces, her bequests make up the majority of the jewellery on show. The British Museum received an important bequest of its own from Anne and her husband in 1978, which inspired others to donate their own jewellery.

In Glasgow, there were another 1,000 pieces for the Kelvingrove Art Gallery and Museum. She also gave generously to Bristol's Museum of Costume after learning it had hardly any jewels to match its wonderful collection of clothes. Over sixty museums benefited from her donations in all, including the Fitzwilliam Museum in Cambridge. Though she is relatively unsung, she did receive the rare accolade of an obituary in *The Times*, which is an exceptional tribute considering this was in the 1980s, when almost all obituaries celebrated men's rather than women's achievements.

Anne Hull Grundy gave away a fortune as well as sharing her extensive knowledge about jewellery. But she could also be acerbic and decidedly prickly, even threatening litigation if seriously annoyed. She hated any apparent lack of courtesy, especially if people were not as appreciative or as quick to thank her as expected. She even threatened to come back and haunt the British Museum if it did not publish a catalogue of her collection – a catalogue was duly published.

Anne Hull Grundy did not wish for any religious ceremony when she died in 1984, but asked that when her dog and one-eyed cat died they should be buried with her.

We now encounter a very different Emily, born in Victorian times when domestic service was the most common job for women. In the first census of 1841, there were 1 million domestic servants in a population of just over 18 million.

Emily Green, Servant and Beloved Granny

At the age of thirteen, Emily Green left school. Like so many girls of her class, she then worked as a servant. Her father was a coachman while her mother and grandmother made the straw plait used in the straw hat industry. At that time, everyone wore straw hats. For men they took the form of boaters (still worn these days at the Henley Regatta), and there were even straw helmets for the police in Luton. Straw plaiting was a cottage industry found all across the Chiltern Hills, in the villages and towns of Bedfordshire, Buckinghamshire and over into Hertfordshire.

Emily's first job as a servant was with a farming family just a few miles away. Her mother chose a nearby employer so Emily could get home on her one day off each week. Another important reason was that the family gave their servants the same food that they ate. Some employers bought cheaper food for their servants and some didn't provide meat. Parsimony was only part of the logic here; the contrast also reinforced to the servants that they were socially inferior to the family paying their wage.

Leaving home at such a young age was full of hazards for a young girl. Whether she worked in a small vicarage or a grand country house with an army of servants, it was important for a woman to protect her virtue. Emily's grandmother Kate, as a young servant, fell in love with the son of a local solicitor where she worked. He promised to marry Kate but backed out when she later became pregnant. When he married someone else a few years later, Kate took their young son to the church, holding him up at the wedding carriage before the bride and groom left, saying, 'This is your father.' She did not care what the people there would say about her, explaining to her granddaughter many years afterwards that she wanted the bride to know the kind of man she had married. Kate had no other children and did not marry.

Hatpins, Forks and Wandering Hands in Church

Many years later, Emily told her granddaughter that hatpins were especially valuable to young women of her generation. Close at hand, a hatpin was an instant defensive weapon against any man 'taking liberties'. If he was too amorous then a jab from a hatpin was a sharp reminder to stop. No wonder large, needle-sharp hatpins and hairpins were popular for so long!

Actor Roger Moore tells a story in his biography of his aunt Nellie, who always wore a hatpin. Sometime during the 1930s or 1940s, when Nellie was watching a film at a London cinema, a man sitting beside her began stroking her leg. Nellie did not speak but reached up to take out her long hatpin and plunged it hard into his thigh. Leaping up with a shout of agony, he rushed out of the cinema.

Every female generation before (and since) has faced similar problems. In Restoration London, Samuel Pepys, that determined womaniser, records in his diary that when at church the ladies took pins from their pockets and used them to stop his wandering hands. A modern example comes courtesy of a 2019 letter to *The Times* describing a house party in the 1970s where the hosts doing the seating plan for dinner considered the letter writer 'robust enough to cope ... with a fellow guest with wandering hands'. She goes on to describe how she coped: 'Fork prongs are an active discouragement, as was, in those days, carrying a hatpin in cinemas.'

Grief, Love and the Boer War

Emily Green eventually left service to work in a rope factory near Watford, where she could earn more money. Her younger sister and fiancé both worked there, although breathing problems caused by the rope fibres would lead each of them to an early death. Emily's sweetheart was a soldier in the Second Boer War of 1899. They planned to marry, but like thousands of others in that campaign he never returned from Africa; many died in battle, but even more from sickness. Emily kept his letters and presents of Zulu beadwork all her life. She never told the story to her children, but in later life she did tell her granddaughter Gillian, who was shown the beadwork, kept in Emily's box of treasures.

The grief for many families during the Boer Wars was a precursor to the great slaughter of young men during the First World War. The grammar school in the small town of Dunstable where Emily grew up built a library in memory of sixty-two of their former pupils who did not return from the South African campaign.

A happier love story belongs to Jane Drake. Her brother was badly wounded near enemy lines during the First Boer War in 1881 and his life was only saved because another soldier, a stranger, took him upon his back and carried him to safety. After the war, the men decided to meet in England and so Jane met Daniel Wilson, the Good Samaritan who saved her brother. They fell in love and married in 1909. Much later, in the 1930s, their son Daniel fell in love with Emily Green's daughter Susan. It was love at first sight for Dan, who already knew he would marry her after their first meeting at the tennis club. He promptly offered to walk her home.

Who Stole That Leg of Ham?

Emily Green's father was once accused of stealing a leg of ham from Luton Hoo, the most important stately home in the area. There was no actual proof, no bone was found, but still he was banned. This was a disaster, as it meant no one would employ him as coachman.

It was time for the family to move. Fortunately, they found a newspaper advert offering jobs plus modern housing at Deanston Cotton Mill in Stirling, Scotland. This was well paid work, and Emily supplemented the household income through her work at an Edinburgh laundry. The other women were friendly to the young Englishwoman, and one of the older workers, Maggie, even invited her home for tea. There she met Maggie's son, the man she would marry. On their wedding day he gave Emily a little brown lustre jug filled with half-sovereigns as a token of his love.

Many years later, and now with four children, Emily was on the move again. As her husband said about Scotland, 'It is beautiful but you can't eat the scenery.' Their two eldest children had gone south to find work when her husband lost his job as a coalminer. After damaging his knee in a mining accident, he represented the other men asking for better pay and conditions. As a result, all the local mine owners blacklisted him. Concerted efforts by trade unions would only make their mark some years later.

The family could no longer afford even the few pence to pay for their church pew on Sunday. Emily took up evening dressmaking classes in Glasgow as it cost too much to buy new clothes for the children. She was talented, and in one family photo their youngest son, John, wears a smart brown velvet suit as good as any by a professional tailor or dressmaker.

As Hard as Charity

Emily was also determined her children should not wear the charity shoes given to the poorest families. One of her daughters remembers that many schoolchildren wore these shoes, each one marked with a large cross on the front so they could not be taken to the pawn shop. This had the side effect of loudly announcing to everyone the family's destitution. With little social welfare or parish help (such as workhouses), and so much desperate poverty, it was hard to keep bread on the table. Even today, almost every town needs a food bank to help those who cannot afford to buy their own food.

Free medical care was only available much later, starting in 1948 when the National Health Service was launched. Every doctor's visit involved a fee (even middle-class families had to save up to afford the doctor's fee at childbirth). Many doctors organised free surgeries for the poor, including Emily Tinne's husband, who used the fees paid by richer patients to fund such charity work in Liverpool.

Although she left school at such an early age – or perhaps because of this – Emily Green was a great believer in the power of education. She held weekly reading classes with her grandchildren when the oldest were allowed into the parlour – after they carefully washed their hands! In every respectable working-class home, the parlour (or front room) was kept spotless and reserved for important visitors such as the vicar. Gillian, Emily's granddaughter, explains that they all loved this special treat, sitting down to read with grandma. Emily was a passionate reader and had read, and owned, all Charles Dickens' novels. She bequeathed them to her eldest daughter, who later gave them to a small local library. Emily had little else to leave. One granddaughter has a marcasite cross on a silver chain together with the brown lustre jug Emily received on her wedding day.

Perhaps, though, her legacy to her children and grandchildren is something far greater, because like so many other mothers and grandmothers across the ages, Emily Green inspired them all with a love of education, of learning, and of books.

What's in a Name?

Emily had become an old-fashioned Victorian name, quite passé, until a recent renaissance along with some other names from the same era. It is fascinating to discover that many girls' names from earlier centuries are once again fashionable, among them Maud, Cicely, Charlotte, Edith, Florence, Victoria and Matilda. This reads like the roll call of a Victorian or Edwardian classroom. Florence was once widely used in honour of Florence Nightingale, heroine of the Crimean War.

The name Victoria was of course a popular name in honour of the queen who reigned for sixty-three years. She had been named after her mother at a time when the name was considered foreign and un-English. Her uncle William IV wanted her to be renamed

Elizabeth, with Victoria kept only as a middle name. But when she came to the throne in 1837, it was as Queen Victoria.

Family traditions for children's names exist in many families, as with the descendants of Lord Horatio Nelson and his mistress Emma, Lady Hamilton. Their daughter was named Horatia in a tradition which continued through to their great-great-great-granddaughter Anna Millicent Horatia Fitzroy Somerset, who died in 2020. Princess Diana, meanwhile, lives on in the names of her granddaughters Lilibet Diana Mountbatten-Windsor and Princess Charlotte Elizabeth Diana. Princess Diana was in turn named after her mother, while in her father's family the first Lady Di Spencer married the Duke of Bedford back in the early 1700s.

There were also names chosen first by the strict Puritans in the 1600s, biblical names as well as qualities like Chastity, Patience, Virtue, Faith, Hope and Charity. A few of these names have again become fashionable, as have others. For instance, wills from Tudor Bristol turn up names such as Agnes, Elizabeth, Joan, Jane, Alice, Helen, Anne, Gillian, Katherine, Margaret, Mary, Constance, Cicely, Margery, Edith and Maud. If we go further back still, to the end of the 1400s, we find familiar names in wills from St Albans: Margaret, Elizabeth, Alice, Emma, Joan, Isabella, Jane and Eleanor.

12

1,000 YEARS OF WOMEN'S LIVES AND WOMEN'S WILLS

'to niece Mary John my best Hatt...'

Some things can only – or should only – be inherited in the female line. One of the earliest doll's houses was a family heirloom, passed down the female line for 300 years until there were three sons and no daughters left to inherit. Made in 1705 by carpenters on London's Isle of Dogs for Miss E. Westbrook, it was hardly altered apart from the addition of some new dolls. When the dolls (not the house) arrived at the Tewkesbury Antiques Roadshow in 2016, expert Fergus Gambon immediately recognised their rarity, setting off to visit the owners. It was, he said, the best find of his career, estimated to be worth between £150,000 and £200,000.[1]

In almost every century a few women did wield power and influence, such as those from thirteenth-century Lincolnshire featured in Louise Wilkinson's book.[2] Nichola de la Haye or Haie (d. 1230) was Sheriff of Lincoln Castle and in 1217 successfully defended it for three months against the French. Her granddaughter Idonea inherited her lands in Lincolnshire.

While in Wiltshire, Ela, Countess of Salisbury (d. 1261) succeeded her husband as sheriff. Together they founded Lacock Abbey and set the first stones for Salisbury Cathedral. In 2020, a metal detectorist found a silver seal matrix belonging to Matilda de Cornhill, who in the early 1200s was married to the High Sheriff of Kent. Found in Hollingbourne in that county, the seal bears her name and an image of her before the Virgin holding Jesus.

In the 1690s, women played a key role in founding the Bank of England. The first stockholders included 151 women – 12 per cent of the group – keen to make a solid, safe investment. When it first opened, the bank was a modest affair with only seventeen clerks and two porters. Recent research by King's College London has discovered women were also keen investors in one of the early London theatres, The Fortune, between the 1620s and the 1640s; at times they even owned the majority of the shares. Of seventy-one investors involved, twenty-four were women, including a servant named Elizabeth Pierpoint who had been left two half-shares by her widowed mistress. Another widow left her shares to her brother. Most of them belonged to trading, merchant or acting families with sufficient cash to afford shares, and theirs was likely to be a sound investment as theatres were popular and provided excellent returns.[2] It's interesting to see that half shares were available, implying as it does that there was keen competition for them.

For the most part, however, a wife (even a rich heiress) was simply given an allowance by her husband. This was often known as 'pin money', a phrase used from the fourteenth century. By Tudor times it was common for a husband to give his wife and daughters an allowance to buy pins, which were essential to fasten together clothes and fix jewels onto rich silks and velvet garments. There were no zips, press studs, elastic or modern safety pins; everything was fastened with pins, ties and ribbons. Poor folk had brass pins, the wealthy had silver and some could even afford gold. To give an idea of the scarcity of such luxuries, however, an examination of Tudor wills from Bristol comes up with just one mention of a silver pin.

Butcher, Baker, Candlestick Maker

From goldsmiths and silversmiths through to maltsters, brothel keepers and brewers, the occupations taken up by women through the ages show surprising diversity. Susan James's detailed study of Tudor wills identifies many trades: blacksmiths, victuallers (sellers of food or other provisions), tanners, booksellers and printers, butchers, bakers and fishmongers, servants, drapers (who sold silk, linen and cloth), candle and soap makers, innkeepers, owners of coal mines, salt dealers and hoopers (makers of the hoops which bound wooden casks and barrels), millers, jewellers, mercers and pewterers.

Women's work is also clear from surnames ending with '-ster', which denotes a female occupation, hence Brewster for brewers, Baxter for bakers and Webster for weavers. Invariably, though, the status of women remained unequal. Marjorie Filbee's book *A Woman's Place*[2] highlights this constant thread as every new generation of daughters, wives and mothers took on the role of the modest and virtuous homemaker, decorative and dutiful.

We know of female silversmiths in Norwich, Hull and Newcastle, while in London one Hester Bateman (d. 1794) inherited her husband's business and ran it successfully for some thirty years under her own silver mark before passing the firm to their children. She was known as the queen of English silversmiths for her fine work, including knives and forks, teapots and coffee pots, pepper and mustard pots as well as everything else stocked by any fashionable silversmith in Georgian times.

On the subject of silver, the saying that someone was 'born with a silver spoon in his mouth', meaning born into wealth and privilege, comes from these times. A set of twelve apostle silver spoons, one for each disciple, might be mentioned in a wealthy will; occasionally there were thirteen, the extra spoon representing Jesus as the master spoon. Isabel Carew of Cowick, Devon, left six spoons to each of her grandsons.[3] But single spoons also featured in so many medieval and Tudor wills. Not only important religious symbols, they were also portable and easy to sell (or pawn) when ready cash was required.

A single silver spoon was a typical christening present, but it seems there might be certain expectations put upon a godmother or father. Samuel Pepys, for instance, was only willing to give a silver spoon if the baby was named after him. On one occasion when he was disappointed, he took his spoon back home with him.[3] Women's wills include many bequests to godchildren, and silver spoons are predictably popular in later years. In Tudor times, however, bequests tended to be more modest, as in the case of the widow Alys Clay of Sandy, Bedfordshire, who in 1532 left 'to every godchild 2 pence'.[4] In sharp contrast to this, in 1536 the St George's Day banquet was held by Henry VIII at a cost of £19 13s. Though it was a banquet, this represented just one meal in the royal household.

Chantries and Prayers

Deeply pious belief is evident in records from medieval towns all over the country. In thirteenth-century Cambridge, for instance, the founding of various colleges and chantries to pray for the dead started a property boom. The town records of 1279, recently analysed, reveal an amazing level of philanthropy, as newly wealthy families gave away more than half of the wealth made from their property investments[5] either to church or charity. While this was no doubt a pious gift to God, in a small town it had that added value of advertising the donor's impressive wealth.

Curtains, Clothes and Some Bees

Clothes and linen have been important for a very long time. Richer folk had more to leave, but linen and items of clothing were bequests at every social level. In a Suffolk will of 1626, Elizabeth Alldous of Stradbroke left her 'wearing apparel' to her three youngest daughters, who were unmarried, while the household linen was to be divided equally between all six of her daughters.[5]

Welsh wills, as quoted below, involve clothes, bees, curtains, linen and a feather pillow as bequests. Elizabeth David mentions her sister and niece (who receives the 'best hatt'), but we have no information about Ann Edwards, who was single. What family connection, if any, exists between her and the women named in the will is unclear; perhaps they were friends or neighbours. Five shillings goes to 'ye nurse', who is unnamed, presumably as everyone involved would know who she was. A likely explanation is that she was the woman who nursed Ann during her final illness.

> My boxes & Linnen & woollen & wrought Curtains I give to Ann Thomas that is att m^r [Lewis] Cox & to Charity Gibbon all my Brass And to m^{rs} [Anne] Cox all my peawter [pewter] & Irons And to Eleanor Jenkins & Mary Thomas tenn Shillings Each & to ye nurse five Shillings.
>
> Ann Edwards, of Cardiffe, spinster, 19 September 1696

> To sister Christian David ye Summ of tenn Shillings and ye halfe of ye Bees that is now by David Edward house. To niece Mary John my best Hatt & black Napkin & a feather Pillow and all ye Bees that is between She & I.
>
> Elizabeth David, of Llanedarne, 1707 21 September[6]

Poorer women may have had less to leave, but their wills are nonetheless often detailed, carefully setting out their bequests. This could be a pot or kettle, a cauldron, brewing or baking paraphernalia – the dairy or items used in household preserving such as salting troughs. An old petticoat, a pair of flaxen or hempen sheets, napkins, towels or an apron are still worth passing on to friends, neighbours or relatives. This same careful detail is mentioned by Asa Briggs in his book *Victorian Things*, noting how Seebohm Rowntree found in York that 'working class wills, with few objects to dispose of, were just as carefully drafted as middle-class wills.'

A Life Less Equal
Women lived a life of less freedom compared to men, as highlighted by Amy Louise Erickson, who surveyed over twenty

collections of wills from the fourteenth to the eighteenth century, finding that women were far less likely to write a will than men, making up just 30 per cent of the total sampled.[7]

But in every century there are the strong family bonds between a mother and her children or a grandmother and her grandchildren. One example from eighteenth-century London is the will of a wealthy widow named Frances Barraud, who gifts her daughters-in-law sums of money, china and 'a green silk damask gown'.[7]

Women were of course among the first settlers to New England in America and would also travel to different parts of the British Empire. Joanne Trollope's book *Britannia's Daughters* reveals much about those women who lived (and so many who died) in the tough early years of British colonies such as Canada, Australia and India.

Women were always restricted, expected to stay home looking after the children and attending to domestic and household matters. However, in every age a careful search reveals some who gained a little more independence. Some born into gentry families enjoyed hunting, horse riding and adventuring just as much as their menfolk. In 1818, Dorothy Wordsworth and her friend Mary Barker made the ascent of Scafell Pike in the Lake District with Mary's maid, a porter and a shepherd acting as a guide. Celia Fiennes – mentioned later in this chapter – travelled widely centuries before, in the 1600s after the Civil War, while the Ladies of Llangollen were a *cause célèbre* for their romantic elopement and friendship. A number of women also made their names in the realm of science between the seventeenth and nineteenth centuries, as revealed at Cambridge in the Whipple Museum's exhibition 'Craftswomen'.

Cycling, Tennis, Travel and Trains

Major changes in Victorian and Edwardian times provided women with far more freedom and independence, offering new and exciting horizons. Sport had much to offer. Along with the craze for cycling there was flourishing interest in punting, badminton, sailing, croquet and tennis. The first women's golf clubs were founded in the 1860s, though many disapproved, considering it an 'unbecoming' sport for a lady. In 1893, Lady Margaret Scott won the first Ladies' British Open Amateur Championship, held at Lytham St Anne's, Blackpool. Convention, however, said women should not speak in public, so Margaret's father made her acceptance speech.

Tennis at Wimbledon began back in 1877, initially to raise money so that the Croquet Club could afford to repair its grass rollers! It has come a long way since. Within a few years, in 1884, women were admitted to tennis competitions and so began the ladies' singles event. Local ladies' tennis clubs were soon found everywhere.

Skiing and climbing were popular from late Victorian times, and in the photos and postcards sent home from holidays in the Alps we see ladies in long, heavy skirts who are just as keen as the men to travel and explore. Women's involvement in archery, however, goes back much further, to the Regency when women were encouraged to take up what was considered to be a 'ladylike' sport. By the 1830s there was quite a fashion for families to arrange archery days and invite friends and neighbours.

There exists a painting from 1822 depicting a meeting of the Royal British Bowmen, showing both men and women as club members. The women wear dark green dresses with smart, bright yellow borders at the bottom of their skirts. Très chic. Just a few years later, the young Princess Victoria was invited to become patron of the St Leonards Archers, near Hastings on the south coast. After Victoria became queen in 1837, the club took the opportunity to become the Queen's Royal St Leonards Archers. Archery was in fact the only event open to women in the 1908 London Olympics. The British team included twenty-five women (of forty-one entrants) who put in a stellar performance, winning gold, silver and bronze medals. Women gymnasts, whom one might expect to see early in the competition's history, were not allowed to compete until 1928.

The railway age broadened opportunities for ordinary people to travel, not least with the first railway bridge into Cornwall in 1859, across the Tamar River, which made domestic tourism more affordable. In 1904, the arrival of the first express train helped promote the county as the Cornish Riviera in an attempt to capture the same glamorous allure that the French Riviera held for the wealthiest Victorians.

Travelling abroad had always been the preserve of the rich, but now it was available to those further down the social scale. You still needed sufficient money and leisure time to travel for a few weeks or a few months, of course. But as early as 1863, when a certain Thomas Cook made his first trip to the Swiss Alps, ladies were also in the mountaineering party, among them Miss Jemima Morrell from Selby. (We know a good deal about the journey as Miss Morrell kept an account, published in 1962; see Bibliography.) By the end of the decade, Thomas Cook was taking trips as far as the Holy Land.

Maud Berkeley and the Adventure of Cycling

Soon after the Enfield Cycle Company of Redditch advertised a ladies' bicycle, they met with success. Enterprising firms such as Raleigh, one of the earliest cycle makers from 1887, were quick to appeal to this new generation of adventurous women as potential customers. The first edition of *Country Life*, which came a few years later in January 1897, featured an advert from Osmond Cycles extolling the qualities of a ladies' bicycle, while the same year a bicycle gymkhana was held at Peover Hall, Cheshire.

By October 1919, among adverts for Sunlight soap and Fordson farm tractors, Cambridge newspapers included a delightful drawing of 'The Raleigh Girl'. Gaily waving to the reader, she stands alongside the latest modern, all-steel bicycle. More than a decade earlier, in 1902, an advert in a Hitchin newspaper featured the cycles of John T. Chalkley of Brand Street with that magical royal seal of approval: 'As ridden by ... The Princess of Wales and The Duchess of Fife, Princess Victoria.' Surely this must have inspired many young women to take up cycling and ignore those naysayers who claimed it was so dangerous that it might stop them ever having children.

Almost every county had cycling clubs. In some places there were even dedicated ladies' cycling clubs, as at Lincoln, which boasted a 100-mile club and medals for long-distance cycling. Cycling was both competitive and great fun, and bicycles quickly became popular, though some hotels took a stance and refused to serve lady cyclists. In 1912, Sidmouth town crier Theo Mortimer went around town on a tricycle, managing all the while to retain the gravitas of his office with a splendid uniform, knee breeches, buckled shoes and the customary handbell.

Even the aristocracy shared in this national craze for cycling. Duchess Millicent of Sutherland was such a keen cyclist that in the 1890s she invited lady guests staying at Trentham Hall to bring a bicycle, as well 'as a footman to clean it'.[8] Maud Berkeley, with her friends in the late 1880s and 1890s, revelled in this exhilarating new sport on the Isle of Wight. We know this because Maud kept a delightful diary, which includes her own drawings complete with records of accidents and achievements. One of the best stories of a woman with a passion for cycling was told by Beatrice Joynson, who wrote to *Country Life* in 2017:

> ... my three aunts ... were bought bicycles in 1900, just as soon as the machines arrived in Colne [in Lancashire], where the family lived. The roads thereabouts were very steep, but the middle sister, Nora, swore she would never let a hill defeat her and gallantly rode up the lot. She lived to be 95.

Car adverts around this time also cleverly conveyed a glamorous lifestyle to entice the ladies. A 1908 postcard advertising the book *The British Motor Tourist's A. B. C.* features an elegant Edwardian lady motorist. She seems to be impossibly tall, but the image is realistic and enticing. Her coat reaches the ground (for protection from the clouds of dust of unsurfaced roads, no doubt) and even with hefty leather gauntlets she appears to be effortlessly tying a long blue scarf around a fashionably large hat. In the background is the car she will drive away on her own – a rather daring approach for those times. Queen Alexandra, who was extremely popular at the time, was photographed at Sandringham in the early 1900s at the wheel of a car, which did much to inspire other women to be just as daring as their queen.

Ladies in the provinces were always keen to keep up with the latest fashions. In 1851, the *Harrogate Herald* reported young ladies in the town were wearing the daring Turkish-style harem trousers so popular at the time.[8] While these trousers were seen – and much ridiculed – in London, the fact that they simultaneously appeared in Yorkshire demonstrates the nationwide importance of staying on trend.

Hot Tennis!

Soon there were special clothes for lady cyclists – divided skirts instead of the heavy, stiff, long skirts worn typically – but such accommodations were seemingly less important when it came to the sport of tennis. One tennis dress from the 1880s, exhibited in 2019 at Cambridge University Library, showed how adaptable women had to be. The wool dress made no concession to any athletic activity; indeed, it hardly differs at all from the formal day dresses of the time. In a dark green colour, as might suit an outdoor sport, the dress reaches the ground and even has a small bustle at the back, as was fashionable in both day and evening dresses. It might look smart, but on a summer's day it would have been like wearing a hot-water bottle. Playing in these circumstances sounds similar to the modern trend for hot yoga!

Most importantly for the moral climate of those years, this approach would have satisfied even the fussiest mother's concern for modesty as no bare arms or legs were revealed. Perhaps wearing this weighty outfit was a price worth paying for the chance to play tennis, to dispense with a chaperone and mix with young men. Most well-off families insisted upon young and unmarried daughters being chaperoned, if not officially then through the constant accompaniment of a cousin or sister. Archery, croquet and cycling also represented escapes from the chaperone and opportunities for flirtation.

There were strict conventions to preserve modesty when it came to sea bathing as well. In Victorian times, men and women were permitted to swim only at separate times, and into Edwardian times there was a well-known ladies' cove (Beacon Cove) at Torquay in Devon. Cromer in Norfolk was definitely ahead of the times in advertising a 'mixed bathing ground' as early as 1898 alongside the typical segregated bathing options.

The Right to Equal Education

The 'Votes for Women' campaign, which began in Victorian times, came alongside the battle for women to be allowed to attend university. Women might make up half the graduate intake at universities today, but until the late nineteenth century they were entirely excluded.

Girton College was one of the first women's colleges, set up at Cambridge in 1869. It had originally been started in the small town of Hitchin in Hertfordshire as the College for Women at Benslow House. Newnham College, which charged lower fees and had more middle-class appeal, opened a couple of years later. Attitudes and behaviours took longer to change, though, and even in the 1920s the misogynist feeling at Cambridge was so strong that a mob of male undergraduates took a handcart to break down the college gates at Newnham. At Oxford, the women who became tutors were not full members of the university until 1920. A quota was introduced at Oxford in 1927 which restricted women students to 840 – about a sixth of the total number – and, though altered over the years, was only repealed in 1957.

The general view of many was that a university education was unnecessary for girls. Author Molly Keane, who grew up in Ireland in the early 1910s, said that in most families while the boys were educated 'the girls counted for nothing.' Families who educated their daughters as well as their sons were unusual, in Ireland and elsewhere. In Molly's case, she was educated at home by a governess.

Deliberately, diplomatically, Girton College was placed at a distance, some 2 miles outside of Cambridge; it is still on the outskirts of town. It began its first year with only thirteen students. From the beginning students were taught independence, even going so far as to establish and train their own fire brigade. Private fire engines were essential at this time, as until 1941 there was no national fire brigade. Some large country houses, as at Felbrigg, wisely kept their own, while the latest steam-driven fire engines at Dunrobin Castle in Scotland and Blenheim Palace near Oxford meant they were especially well prepared for any such disasters.

An Independent College for Women

Jane Catherine Gamble, who died in 1885, left a major legacy to Girton College of £19,000 (equivalent to more than £1 million today), which was used to buy land around the college and some buildings. More recent gifts at Newnham include the Margaret Anstee Centre for Global Studies in 2018, arising from a legacy of £4.5 million. Anstee (d. 2016) had a remarkable career and in 1987 was appointed the first woman Under-Secretary General at the United Nations (UN). Her autobiography, *Never Learn to Type*, recalls her experiences, including how even in a senior role at the UN she would be mistaken for the typist or secretary. Earlier, in the 1950s, she had been compelled to retire from the Civil Service when she married – a widespread rule in many organisations.

There were some benevolent office managers in the 1940s, and a wedding might be tactfully ignored. But a pregnancy could not be hidden, meaning at least one typist at Vauxhall Motors in Luton was asked to 'retire'. The marriage bar in the Foreign Office did not officially end until the early 1970s, and wives were not taxed independently of their husbands until 1990.

Women's Colleges in the Nineteenth Century

1869 Girton College, Cambridge begins in Hitchin at Benslow House

1871 Newnham College, Cambridge opens with five students

1879 Lady Margaret Hall opens as the first women's college in Oxford with nine students
St Anne's College, Oxford opens
Somerville College, Oxford opens, named for Mary Somerville, scientist, mathematician and supporter of women's education and suffrage

1885 Hughes Hall, Cambridge opens, named for Elizabeth Phillips Hughes, with fourteen students. She was also a keen mountain climber who in 1899 aged forty-eight climbed the Matterhorn.

1886 St Hugh's, Oxford, opens

1893 St Hilda's, Oxford, opens, named after the Saxon Saint Hilda of Whitby. In 1868, the University of London became the first university to accept women as well as men as students. Nine were admitted.

Women were not awarded degrees by Oxford University until 1920, and a quota limited the total number of women until 1957. They were not awarded degrees at Cambridge until 1948, when the Queen Mother received an honorary degree. The following month, more than 800 women were finally awarded degrees.

Over the Alps

Lucy Walker (d. 1916), from Liverpool, was the first woman to climb the Matterhorn in 1871. *Punch* magazine was sufficiently impressed to publish a poem celebrating 'the intrepid

Miss Walker'. Some years earlier, in 1862, she had climbed Mont Blanc. In total, she made ninety-eight climbing expeditions. A fine example of English eccentricity with an added dash and fizz of glamour, she apparently lived on a diet of sponge cake and champagne!

The St Moritz Tobogganing Club, founded in 1887 by British military officers, was open for four decades to men and women alike to compete on the Cresta Run. Then, in 1929, women were banned. They could only take part on an annual 'Ladies Day', which started lower down the run. The ban was not lifted until 2018.

I Saved a Castle

Leeds Castle in Kent and Mey Castle near John O'Groats are two castles that were saved by determined women. On a clear day, from Mey Castle you can see Orkney. Built in elegant local stone with a walled garden, Mey is now in fine condition but back in 1952 it was in such disrepair that the owners were considering abandoning it. Tiles were missing from the main roof, and many of the windows were gone.[8]

The Queen Mother was just the right woman to save Mey, which was then known as Barrogill Castle. It became the only house she ever owned, and with her Scottish family roots – she was daughter of the Earl of Strathmore – there was an instant attraction. Within a few months of seeing Mey, the widowed Queen Mother owned a dilapidated castle with mildew and leaky walls. Bringing it back to life became her absorbing passion for the next fifty years.[8] A few years later, when the farm next-door came on the market, that was also purchased.

The castle became a regular feature of the Queen Mother's itinerary, providing a refuge far from her royal responsibilities in London. Visitors, household staff and ladies-in-waiting quickly discovered they had to be the hardy sort; regardless of rain or the dreaded midges, the Queen Mother preferred life in the great outdoors. Staying home was not an option. Fishing and hillwalking with picnic lunches were invariably the order of the day, even if the weather was chilly. Well prepared, the Queen Mother was known on occasion to wear two headscarves, four jumpers and a raincoat lined with camel hair.

Evenings at Mey, however, more than compensated for any difficult days outside, as the food and wine were invariably excellent. Proceedings began at six o'clock, with a touch of glamour at cocktail hour. Her own favourite was gin and Dubonnet, and she had been known to bring them along for lengthy journeys.

The charm of the Queen Mother was legendary, so much so she almost converted a staunch French republican into a royalist. After a long and delicious lunch at Raymond Blanc's restaurant Le Manoir aux Quat'Saisons, the Queen Mother led her party of guests in singing the French national anthem, *La Marseillaise*. The famous chef was charmed.

Setting out to repair and then furnish a sixteenth-century castle must have been both fascinating and daunting. The Queen Mother was well known in Caithness, where she searched out furniture suitable for her grand project. She did not believe in wasting money, and the castle bathrooms from the 1950s remained the same. There is a story told by her staff about a huge refrigerator in the kitchen from the 1950s. Asked if it could be replaced with something modern, she would simply ask, 'Is it still working?'

In 1996, the Queen Mother (d. 2002) assured her beloved castle's future by setting up a trust.

Far away in the south of England, another castle was similarly fortunate to find a dedicated champion. Lady Olive Cecilia Baillie (d. 1974) was an heiress who had inherited a fortune from her mother. Picture a delightful, small-scale Windsor Castle set upon a wide moat, and then you have some idea of the beauty of Leeds Castle in Kent.

The castle dates from Norman times and has been both a military fortress and an important royal palace, belonging to Edward I and Eleanor of Castile. By tradition it became part of the dower given to six medieval queens of England, including Isabella of France. However, by the 1920s Leeds Castle was in desperate need of restoration, and this could only be remedied by someone with determination and deep pockets. Lady Baillie had both, and she bought the castle in 1926 when the owners were forced to sell it to pay death duties. At that time there were no bathrooms in the castle, but it still cost the considerable sum of £180,000. Even though it did contain twenty sizeable bedrooms, the renovations required would cost far more than the asking price.

Leeds Castle was transformed by Lady Baillie under the guiding principle to restore it to its medieval glory, albeit with the delights of modern plumbing and underfloor heating (most innovative then). The blue bedroom for Lady Baillie is a rare survivor of the famous Stéphane Boudin's work in the 1930s; he was also commissioned by the Duke and Duchess of Windsor in Paris. The banqueting hall was returned to its original size. It was the perfect setting for country house parties in the 1930s.

During her final illness in the 1970s, Lady Baillie set up a trust, leaving Leeds Castle to the nation. Her estate was valued at just over £4 million, and £1.4 million was used to endow the castle. The castle's royal connections continued into modern times; when Queen Elizabeth II visited in 1981, she was presented with the key to the castle by Lady Baillie's daughters and granddaughter.

A Doll's House

The doll's house mentioned at the start of this chapter highlights the importance of small, domestic items as family heirlooms. They do not have to be of great financial value, only sentimental weight. By Victorian times, doll's houses were popular among the middle-classes. The five daughters of the Quaker Seebohm family in Hitchin, for instance, had one dating from around 1860–1880. One of the most important is the Tate Baby House, now part of the Victoria and Albert Museum's 100-strong collection. It is imposing, to say the least, at just over 7 feet tall, 5 feet wide and with a depth of 3½ feet. Named for the last owner, Mrs Walter Tate (d. 1929), it is the miniature of a smart Georgian townhouse of the 1750s with silk curtains, four-poster beds, exquisite furniture and even painted fire screens.

Made in Dorset, it was passed down from mother to daughter until it reached Flora, born in 1866. She would become Mrs Tate, but at the end of her life there were no daughters to inherit. The doll's house was already on loan to the V&A and was therefore purchased from the family.

A Stitch in Time

From early Tudor times, needlework samplers were a way for the daughters of well-off families to flaunt their domestic skills. In large households, the ladies of the family would often sew shirts, handkerchiefs and fine clothes. Skill in embroidery was likewise celebrated. Samplers are sometimes mentioned in wills, the word 'sample' coming from Old French meaning 'example', specifically of sewing. A sampler might be a row of numbers and alphabet letters, but equally it could be far more intricate.

A rare sampler kept at Eltham Palace was made by Mary Body in 1669 at the age of eleven. When she married, she kept the sampler and as Mary Corbett left it to her sister-in-law in her will of 1732. Together with her handwritten cookery book and an embroidered workbox, the items passed down the generations. Now, nearly 300 years later, they belong to her five-times great-grandson.

Divorce: A Rare and Unequal Affair

In earlier centuries, any divorce required annulment either by the Pope (before the Reformation) or by a private Act of Parliament. It was therefore only available to the elite. It could also be a lengthy business, as evidenced by documents in the National Archives concerning a thirteenth-century divorce between Gilbert, Earl of Gloucester and Hereford, and his wife Alice. The couple separated in 1267, with the countess appealing for divorce in

1271, but the marriage was not annulled until another fourteen years had passed, in 1285.[9]

Even into the mid-twentieth century, divorce was rare. In 1857 the Matrimonial Causes Act allowed divorce, although the conditions were more stringent for wives than for husbands. A husband could claim adultery, but his wife had to prove bigamy, incest, desertion or cruelty. This requirement did not change until 1923. A young wife during the Second World War planned to leave her husband after he lost his temper and hit her. Many years later, she remarked that in the 1940s a woman might as well have murdered someone rather than be a divorcée, as people considered you little better than a hussy, a scarlet woman. Men in such circumstances were not judged in the same harsh way, although people still might disapprove.

Celia Fiennes, Traveller Extraordinaire

As we have seen, in each and every century there are pioneers. One such is Celia Fiennes (1662–1741). Her descendant Sir Ranulph Fiennes is famous as an explorer these days, but they both shared that wandering spirit which craves travel. Broughton Castle, just beyond Banbury, is still home to the Fiennes family, just as it was when Celia began travelling after the upheaval of the Civil War. Her father had been one of Oliver Cromwell's colonels.

At first, riding side-saddle around England was a way for Celia to regain her health. But it would eventually become an important part of her life, as she travelled ever further with relatives or servants. By the end of her life, Celia Fiennes had visited every county in England, using William Camden's *Britannia* (1610) as her reference point. Travelling past Stonehenge in Wiltshire, she commented,

> It is reckon'd one of the wonders of England how such prodigeous [*sic*] stone should be brought there, as no such Stone is seen in ye Country nearer than 20 mile.

In 1698, Celia began her 'Great Journey', which took her as far north as Newcastle and as far south as Cornwall. In total her travels took her over some 5,000 miles. It would still be an achievement today to visit every county, never mind in the seventeenth century with poor roads, rough and ready inns, highway robbers and so much else to vex travellers. Local roads in more rural places were rarely signposted, making a local guide indispensable, and inns might or might not have clean bedlinen.

Twenty years later, Daniel Defoe published his own travels in England and received most of the glory that should have been hers (he also witnessed her will). Celia's journals were kept by the family until 1888 at which point they were published as *Through England on a Side-Saddle in the Time of William and Mary*. Transcribed appropriately by Emily Griffiths (*née* Fiennes), the book has remained in print ever since.

Blessed with a curious mind, Celia Fiennes was a keen observer and painted a fascinating picture of life just after the Civil War, including footmen running races and the luxury of a thermal spa at Bath. Then as now, it seems, we yearned to go abroad instead of appreciating what we have on our doorstep:

> ... all persons, both Ladies, much more Gentlemen, [should] spend some of their tyme in Journeys to visit their native Land, and be curious to inform themselves and make observations of the pleasant prospects, good buildings, different produces and manufactures of each place ...

Celia Fiennes made her will the summer before she died, but there is no mention of her travel journals. She bequeathed a 20-shilling annuity for ten years, together with a tablecloth and pewter plate, to the Nonconformist church in Barnet. This was a well-known meeting place for dissenters like Celia who wanted more freedom of religious worship. Puritans, Methodists and Baptists all represented this broader church, which the government would only reluctantly accept. But apart from religion, Celia Fiennes was most respectable. Christopher Morris, editor of her journals, describes her as a model of propriety.

Celia, who never married, died in Hackney in 1741. She requested a simple funeral with 'no obsequies', to 'be as private as can be ... to go out early in the morning and goe the backside of the Town to the Western roade'. Her niece Jane was executrix, and in the will Celia reminds her nieces of gifts given to them in wealthier times – of expensive jewels of 'a diamond necklace of 48 large diamonds'. There are clothes, a repeating clock, books, a coffee pot, linen and cushions, paintings of her grandfather Lord Say and Sele, together with '2 silver spoons with C. F.', her initials, and a sable fur muff 'to be made up'. Bequests were made to her female servants, including a request to 'let my washer woman have my cotton night gown.'

The Lady with the Lamp

Florence Nightingale (1820–1910) became a national heroine in Victorian Britain for her nursing work during the Crimean War. The soldiers called her the 'lady with the lamp', as she toured the wards of the hospital each evening holding a lantern. But there is another, far tougher side to Miss Nightingale which is just as appealing. Indeed, she was also known as the 'lady with the hammer'. This was due to her determination to break into locked supplies when officials proved reluctant to share the contents.[10] Being a very practical soul, she carried her own set of tools, all wrapped in a soft leather cover. Each tool fitted into a single slot, so it was an ideal travelling set. It was kept and passed down through her sister's family, the Verneys of Claydon House.

Florence's early ambition to nurse was not accepted by her family. Her parents at one time sent her off for a cruise up the Nile, hoping it would distract her from her ambition. It did not have the desired effect. Finally, her determination meant she was allowed to train in Germany. She believed this was her vocation, that God had called her to be a nurse.

Miss Nightingale took thirty-eight volunteer nurses to the Crimea, carefully selected from a long list of women writing to the Foreign Office offering their services. Those unlikely to have the stamina for such demanding work were rejected, as were those considered too young and flighty. Older, more matronly women were less likely to be involved in any impropriety or flirtations. Respectability was essential.

The war was brutal. In Haidar Pasha Cemetery in Istanbul, there are perhaps as many as 8,000 men buried in mass graves from the conflict. Despite continuing opposition from the military men in charge of the campaign, Florence transformed the Scutari Hospital. It had been built over an open sewer and rats were a constant problem. Hygiene and fresh air were among her obsessions, and the focus on these elements was just as vital as the professional nursing attentions in saving so many lives.

It was not only Florence Nightingale's practical and invaluable medical knowledge but her organising genius and love of statistical data which transformed nursing practice. She changed the course of nursing, but most importantly she also showed that a respectable woman could be a nurse, which was not the case before she gained her fame.

When Florence returned to England from the Crimea, she was unhappy with her newfound fame. She had even journeyed back incognito as 'Miss Smith' in a bid to avoid the waiting crowds of admirers. Biographer Mark Bostridge comments that Florence's sister and mother were far less modest and rather enjoyed the celebrity status. When asked in later years for permission to sell her photograph in America, she said no.

She did, however, accept Queen Victoria and Prince Albert's invitation to Balmoral in 1856, providing them with a first-hand account of the Crimean campaign. Her account was very well received, and she used it to outline ways in which nursing could and should be improved. In 1860, the first training school for nurses opened at St Thomas's in London, funded from public donations that totalled more than £44,000.

Florence's time in the Crimea had weakened her. Indeed, she was so ill that she was expected to die. By the end of 1857 she had written her will and settled the funeral details. Fortunately, this proved unnecessary and she lived another fifty years. Her health thereafter was nonetheless poor, with some even accusing her of malingering. The truth was only discovered in 1995, when David Young of the Wellcome Foundation found that Crimea fever contracted from contaminated milk was the real reason for her chronic illness.

Ill health did not stop Florence's work, however, nor did it stop her prodigious writing of books, articles and letters. Even by Victorian standards she was a dedicated letter writer. Some 14,000 exist today, and likely there are more to be brought to light. She also wrote roughly two hundred books, including *Notes on Nursing*, which remains in print. Her last work, written when she was seventy-four, was *Rural Hygiene*.

For the rest of her life, Florence Nightingale worked as a health reformer, investigating army hospital conditions in England and India. Always interested in modernising nursing, she was unquestionably a genius when it came to statistical analysis. Always called upon to advise on health, nursing and hospital projects, Florence Nightingale was the grand dame with influence across the British Empire, from Canada to Australia.

In asserting her influence, she often prompted her brother-in-law Sir Harry Verney, MP for Buckingham and Bedford, to ask questions in the House of Commons. As a result, he became known as 'The Member for Miss Nightingale'.

My Body for Medical Dissection

Florence Nightingale died of heart failure at the age of ninety, in 1910. She never married. Her estate, worth the princely sum of £36,127, with a house in Mayfair, mostly went to her cousins and their children. So far, so conventional – but one of her dying wishes was not at all ordinary.

Florence wanted her body to be donated to science for medical dissection. Her relations strongly disagreed, as such a move would have shocked and scandalised society. She was, of course, way ahead of her time; it is only in recent decades that more people have begun opting to leave their body to medical science.

There could have been a state funeral at Westminster Abbey – the invitation was graciously made – but Florence preferred the village church at East Wellow, near the family home in Hampshire and where her parents were buried. A special train from London took the coffin down to Romsey and then a glass-sided carriage continued for the last few miles down the country lanes. The funeral procession was escorted by those regiments that had served in the Crimea, and six soldiers carried her coffin into the church.

The grave at East Willow was covered with flowers and wreaths. Postcards bearing photographs of the grave were quickly printed, and a few weeks later one of these was posted to Miss Jackson in Boldre, Hampshire from her friend who also lived locally. These were places that Florence Nightingale would have known well when she was young.

Attitudes about women were painfully slow to change in Victorian and Edwardian times. One illustration of this comes from the will of author Samuel Smiles (famous for his book *Self-Help*). He was a wealthy man when he died in 1904, and named his wife Sarah Anne as executrix together with their two sons. However, the bequests of furniture and household items Mrs Smiles received were only hers as long as she remained a widow.[10] Similarly, when Edward VII created the new Order of Merit in 1902 he refused at first to include Florence Nightingale, insisting 'women are not eligible.' Only after a lecture from his Prime Minister, Henry Campbell-Bannerman, about Miss Nightingale's achievements did the king relent five years later.

Brave Mrs Seacole

Two other brave women surely changed history during the nineteenth century. First, we must return to the Crimean War in the company of Mary Seacole, another nursing pioneer who was there amid the blood and battles. Born in Jamaica, Mary Seacole (*née* Grant, d. 1881), who was the daughter of a nurse, hoped to travel from London with Florence Nightingale's volunteer nurses. Having been rejected twice, Mary decided to make her own way out to the Crimea.

When British troops entered Sebastopol after its successful siege, Mrs Seacole was close behind with a mule-train containing medical equipment, food and wine. Her frontline canteen sounds glorious with its supply of tinned lobsters and oysters and plenty of wine. Mary was also present earlier at Balaclava, building a hotel in Kodikoi from her own funds and holding outpatient clinics for the soldiers.

Conditions in the Crimea were nothing less than appalling, and Mrs Seacole's bravery so close to the fighting was widely admired; less so her talent for self-promotion. And while it was true that her clinics helped more officers (who could pay) than ordinary soldiers (who could not), she nonetheless achieved a great deal and saved many lives. She also wished to help the nation, and said in her autobiography, 'Wherever the need arises on whatever distant shore, I ask no greater or higher privilege than to minister to it.'

'Mother Seacole', as the soldiers called her, was declared bankrupt on her return to London and a 'Seacole Fund' rather like the 'Nightingale Fund' was started. Supported by *The Times* and *Punch*, it was partly intended to repay her personal expenses but also to reward exceptional service to the nation, the navy and the army. The Prince of Wales as one of the fund's patrons ensured enough money was raised for Mrs Seacole to live in reasonable comfort. There was a four-day fundraising event held beside the Thames which was so popular that thousands of people attended.

Mary Seacole's autobiography in 1857 was hugely popular, but later generations quickly forgot her heroism. She lived a long life, dying in 1881 aged seventy-six. Her estate was valued for probate at £2,615 11s and 7d. Her sister Louisa was the main beneficiary. Both *The Times* and *The Manchester Guardian* published her obituary. Buried in St Mary's Catholic Cemetery in Kensal Green, London, Mary's gravestone was later restored in 1973 after funds were raised by the Jamaican Nurses' Association.

Elizabeth Fry, Convicts and the Rajah Quilt

Another heroine of a similar nature was Elizabeth Fry (1780–1845), born into the well-off Gurney family of Quakers from Norwich. Her social conscience prompted her to work for prison reform, in which field she highlighted and criticised the cruel mistreatment of prisoners. The typical regime of the time was brutal. One of her first innovations was to set up a school at Newgate for the children imprisoned along with their mothers. Having been invited to advise on prisons, in 1818 she became one the first women to appear as an expert before politicians at the Houses of Parliament.

One of Mrs Fry's achievements was to get matrons (female prison warders) into women's prisons. Before her intervention, there had only ever been male warders. A ladies' group was also set up to help women prisoners awaiting transportation to the colonies. Skills such as knitting and sewing were taught, as these might provide employment and an income to the women once arrived. When in 1841 the *Rajah* sailed to Australia with 180 female convicts on board, twenty-nine of them spent the long voyage making a large quilt. As well as being a delight to look at, the *Rajah* quilt is both technically complex and exquisitely designed, with flowers and birds on cotton chintz.

A few years later, the quilt returned to England so that Mrs Fry could see what the prisoners had achieved. Its whereabouts afterwards are shrouded in mystery until 1987, when it was discovered in the attic of an Edinburgh house owned by Mrs Fry's descendants. Now returned to Australia, the *Rajah* quilt is one of the most treasured objects in the National Gallery of Australia. It is so fragile that it is only exhibited once a year.[11]

Elizabeth Fry was most definitely on the side of the angels. Her brave and passionate campaigning ultimately did much to improve social problems and foster more liberal attitudes, reforming what was a brutal system of crime and punishment. Her reforms were unpopular at the time, as most people were conditioned to believe that corporal (or even capital) punishment and hard labour were the best way to reform criminals.

Later generations have sometimes harshly criticised Elizabeth Fry for amateurish efforts, but surely that misses the point. Her spirit, goodness, zeal and energy were important in making life better for prisoners; she was also one of the first brave enough to step forward and take a stand against inhumane treatment in prisons.

However, prison wasn't her only focus. Her campaign to abolish slavery required even more determination. So many rich families had slavery connections, if not directly owning plantations then in more subtle ways, such as the fashion to keep a black servant as a pageboy. So many people financially profited from the trade that the MP Alan Johnson is probably correct in suggesting that the scale of economic implications meant its deconstruction would be financially comparable to abolishing the automotive industry today.

Supporters of slavery were close to the seat of power and skilled at lobbying Parliament (long before the term 'lobbying' became part of modern political life), which blocked progress for many years. Some MPs, including those from Bristol, were slave owners and so deeply opposed reform. It may be hard for us, living in modern times, to understand why the campaign took so long to succeed. How, for instance, did the many devoted Christians of the era reconcile their faith with the cruelty and inhumanity involved in slavery?

The answer is all too obvious: the profits were enormous for those who held power. Additionally, they either could not or would not see that slaves had the same rights and refused to acknowledge any cruelty. The first bank in Liverpool was founded by merchants involved in the slave trade, while in London William Beckford, twice Lord Mayor in the 1760s, became very rich through his sugar plantation in Jamaica with 3,000 slaves. Many stately homes have connections with the slave trade. The Lascelles family, who built Harewood House near Leeds, owned six plantations in the Caribbean. Along with African chattel slaves, Jacobite Scottish prisoners from the Battle of Culloden were transported by the government to plantations in the West Indies as indentured servants.

Sea captains from the slave ports of Bristol, Liverpool and London made considerable profits from slavery. People rarely talked about the 'slave trade' then, using instead more obscure phrases like 'the African trade' or 'Guinea trade', as the coast of Guinea was where most ships loaded their human cargo. It was even possible to insure slaves, allowing claims to be made for the common occurrence of lives lost at sea. In 1783, on the slave ship *Zong*, more than 100 people were thrown overboard because they were worth more dead than alive once an insurance claim was made. This resulted in a notorious court case that highlighted the immorality and brutality of slavery. There was also an important American legal decision in 1841, when the US navy seized the Spanish schooner *Amistad* near New York after the slaves on board, destined for plantations in Cuba, mutinied and changed course. The US Supreme Court ruled the that enslaved Africans had the right to mutiny.

The Ladies Anti-slavery Associations

The involvement of women in the abolition of slavery is rarely mentioned in history books, but many played a crucial role through ladies' anti-slavery associations in Bristol and elsewhere. These local groups would help turn public attitudes away from acceptance or approval and towards abolition. Many of these women came from Nonconformist, dissenter backgrounds, being Quakers or Methodists.[12] Others, like Mary Ann McCracken in Belfast, were fervent reformers for many social causes. Mary Ann

McCracken was one of those who refused sugar because it was produced in the Caribbean through slavery. Even in her eighties, during the 1850s, she distributed anti-slavery leaflets in Belfast among people emigrating to America.

One initiative by the abolitionists in the early 1830s raised funds to educate and supply clothes for slaves in the Caribbean. London, Norwich, Chelmsford, Newcastle, Edinburgh, Birmingham and Leicester all had such campaigns. All the while, women were learning how to win national support and change public opinion; it was exactly this kind of local, energetic, grassroots campaigning that would prove so powerful in the later battle for 'Votes for Women'.

In 1853, the Glasgow Ladies' Anti-slavery Society funded a tour by American author Harriet Beecher Stowe, whose recent book dealing with slavery, *Uncle Tom's Cabin*, was proving highly popular. This soon became a celebrity tour, with large crowds turning out everywhere to greet her; there is a fascinating painting by William Henry Fisk of a grand event held in her honour in London. The large assembly room is packed with all the great and good, suggesting it must have been one of the major events of the social calendar. The headline in *The Illustrated London News* for 25 June 1853 ran, 'Harriet Beecher Stowe takes London by storm.' She met the Lord Mayor and stayed at Stafford House, home of the Duchess of Sutherland, who was one of the most important women in polite society. Mrs Stowe only spoke at smaller meetings of women; at larger public meetings, her brother or father read her speech as social convention dictated.

The local anti-slavery associations promoted their message in many ingenious ways. A silk bag made in 1825 for the Birmingham society depicts a black slave with her baby and a whip-brandishing overseer close by. This menacing picture goes straight to the heart even now. Such bags were sent to influential society women, who would wear them and thereby advertise the cause. One of these bags – or reticules, as they were called – was included in the 2021/2 Victoria and Albert exhibition 'Bags: Inside and Out'. Modern bags in that exhibition had used campaign statements to sway public opinion, as with Anya Hindmarch's 'I am a plastic bag.'

Slavery was finally abolished in Britain in 1833, forty-two years after the first bill was defeated by a large majority in 1791. Next came compensation. But this was not compensation for the slaves; on the contrary, some 46,000 slave owners were eligible for payments to account for their loss of earnings. This turned out to be a most expensive concession by the government, as it meant borrowing £20 million. To explain the scale of this debt, only in 2015 was it finally repaid by the Treasury.

Some claims for compensation were made by owners of large estates with hundreds of slaves. John Gladstone, father of Prime Minister William Gladstone, received £10,000, but payments also reached down to far more modest levels of society. A surprisingly high proportion of the claimants for 'loss of property' were women: 41 per cent.[12] One of these was an elderly widow named Dorothy Little, aged seventy and living in Bristol. She received £297 1s 6d for thirteen slaves in Jamaica. Two sisters from Perthshire, Martha and Agnes Montgomerie, owned a single slave in Trinidad and received £63 19s 3d in compensation.

Go to Kew!

There were countless adventurous lady travellers, one of whom was the artist Marianne North. Her beautiful gallery, crammed with 800 superb paintings of fauna and flora from all over the world, can still be seen at Kew Gardens. Some of the specimens depicted were unknown at the time, as with a pitcher plant painted in Borneo, which was named in her honour as *Nepenthes northiana*.

An intrepid traveller as well as a gifted and innovative painter,[12] she also designed the glorious light-filled gallery at Kew. The paintings are squeezed into a tiny gallery with hardly a gap between them. Though it may sound absurd to try to display so many paintings in such a small space, it is an artistic delight. Miss

North made it a condition of the gift that her paintings should be shown together and not altered. She had also wanted visitors to be offered tea or coffee, but Sir Joseph Hooker, who was in charge of Kew, refused. She managed to smuggle them in after a fashion – around the entrance are paintings of tea and coffee plants!

Travelling up the Nile

Other Victorian women played a significant, mostly forgotten role in the preservation of ancient Egypt. Marianne Brocklehurst, Mary Booth, Amelia Oldroyd and Annie Barlow brought home historical artefacts and set up local museums in which to house them. Amelia Oldroyd's museum was in Dewsbury, while one at Bolton was created by Annie Barlow. Marianne Brocklehurst founded one in Macclesfield just before her death in 1898. She left her house, Bagstones, to her dear friend Mary Booth, and they are buried together just a few miles away.

Amelia Edwards (1831–1892), a writer, also fell in love with Egypt during her first trip in 1873. The bad weather in France that year meant a change of plan and a visit to Egypt with a friend. The trip changed her life. Her account of the journey, *A Thousand Miles up the Nile*, was a bestseller. Her interest in preserving antiquities and monuments saw her become involved in the founding of the Egypt Exploration Fund. Amelia Edwards died a wealthy woman, leaving £8,446 15s 5d. One of her bequests was for £2,500 to fund a teaching chair for Egyptology, with the wish that her protégé Flinders Petrie be appointed to this role. Her collection of Egyptian items is held at the Petrie Museum.

A keen supporter of education for women and vice-president of the Bristol and West of England Society for Women's Suffrage, her bequest went to University College London rather than Oxford or Cambridge, as it awarded women degrees while the they did not. Somerville College at Oxford does, however, hold her archive of personal papers, including watercolours painted during her travels.

Suffragettes and Suffragists

Records of suffragettes, who determinedly broke the law, and the earlier suffragists, who remained strictly within the law, can be found in many counties. At the peak of the movement for universal suffrage there were more than five hundred local groups. Votes for Women chapters were set up all over the country, with meetings everywhere from Wick near the northern tip of Scotland to Penzance in Cornwall.

At Bodnant in north Wales, suffragist Laura McLaren founded the Liberal Women's Suffrage Union. Even small towns like Loughborough and Kibworth near Leicester had their own activists and campaigns. Miss Elizabeth Rowley Frisby, who was involved in burning the local Blaby railway station, would much later become the epitome of respectability as Leicester's first woman mayor (in 1941).

Women from all levels of society joined the campaign, including Queen Victoria's daughter Louise and the queen's goddaughter Princess Sophia. Lady Constance Bulwer-Lytton and her sister Betty, daughters of the Viceroy of India, were also involved.

When Emmeline Pankhurst wrote a letter to her supporters from jail, she described herself as a 'prisoner of war'. Some of the imprisoned suffragettes, having embarked upon hunger strikes, were force-fed. Constance Bulwer-Lytton went to jail four times and was subjected to this dreadful procedure, which ruined her health.

But it was Emily Davison in 1913 who made the most dramatic sacrifice when she stepped out in front of King George V's horse, Anmer, at the Epsom Derby. This fatal accident, followed by her suffragette-themed funeral (the mourners strikingly dressed in white), made her a martyr for the cause. Her earlier actions were just as brave: she had served eight prison sentences and suffered over 100 force-feedings, leaving her mouth paralysed on one side and with many teeth missing.

The fact that Emily Davison bought a return railway ticket for Derby Day has been much debated in recent years, with some suggesting that it shows she did not intend to die in the act of protest. This seems unlikely, however, as she had made a suicide attempt a year earlier in Holloway Prison, and in 1909 Emily wrote a will, leaving her estate to her mother.

In June 1913, a great suffrage march began in Devon and Cornwall with the eventual destination of Hyde Park in London. The walk began in Land's End and took six weeks to reach the nation's capital, with similar marches converging from various parts of the country. Eventually it merged into one large protest of some 50,000 people.

That same year, so great was anxiety around the country that the organisers of the Abergavenny Eisteddfod took out extra insurance, fearing that the event would be targeted by suffragettes and the pavilion set alight.

Physician Elizabeth Knight, who was involved with the London suffragettes, went to prison several times. She became treasurer of the Women's Freedom League. When she died in the 1930s (following a car accident in Brighton), she left £15,000 to her sister and another sum between £80,000 and £100,000 to her sister's daughter. The newspapers described this as a 'fortune', and indeed it was.

Women and War

During both world wars, women's work naturally included nursing. Indeed, there were 30,000 Wrens – members of the Women's Royal Naval Service. Others were recruited to make ammunitions in factories such as the huge cordite plant in Gretna, Scotland (which employed 12,000 female workers) and at George Kent Ltd in Luton. By the end of the First World War, a million women were involved making munitions; at the R101 airship site at Cardington, all twenty-one staff on the fabric department's assembly team were women. Kew Gardens recruited lady gardeners, though not everyone approved.

Hilda and Phyllis Hobson, who worked on the royal Sandringham estate in Norfolk, were encouraged 'to take the place of men'. For the first time, farming jobs everywhere became women's work along with all aspects of town maintenance such as collecting refuge. The Land Army, which existed to release men from farming, recruited 23,000 women to replace those men who went to fight.

Another major change came in 1916, when twelve women were admitted to the Proms orchestra to stand in for men absent on active service. Women had previously been excluded on the assumption that the Proms concert season would be too strenuous for them. Wrest Park, a stately home in Bedfordshire, was among the first wartime country-house hospitals, and more than 100 women served there in a nursing capacity. In 1915, Edith, Lady Londonderry founded the Women's Legion, which was a volunteer force whose members took roles as drivers and cooks for the army camps and in agriculture. At its peak, 40,000 women were involved. Another 50,000 women were employed on the railways at that time.

But as soon as the war finished, women were expected to give up their jobs and make way for the men returning home. The same happened in the Second World War. Men worked by right, and women by exception or because it was the family business.

Croix de Guerre

Over 6,000 nurses served in or close to the front during the First World War. One all-women ambulance unit was led by May Toupie Lowther, who badgered the French to let them attend Compiègne as a fighting unit. *The Times* proudly reported on 5 August 1919 that the unit had received the Croix de Guerre – the highest honour bestowed in France – with citation.

The scale of the care required to treat wounded soldiers was overwhelming. Companies such as Cadbury at Bourneville established hospitals staffed by their female workers, who volunteered to work as nurses. Many aristocratic women also stepped forward to offer help, sometimes providing accommodation at their stately homes. Mary, Duchess of Bedford built a hospital at Woburn Sands, trained as a nurse and helped with operations. Cliveden and Blenheim Palace were involved, while at Wrest Park in Bedfordshire Nan Herbert earned the nickname 'no nonsense Nan' for her organising abilities as matron. A convalescent home for officers was set up at Polesden Lacey, and at Highclere Castle the Countess of Caernarvon set up a hospital; everywhere women were volunteering as nurses.

Catherine Roy (d. 1976), one of the nurses on the Western Front, was matron-in-chief of Queen Alexandra's Nursing Corps. Trained as a nurse in 1909, she was among the first group of fifty nurses sent to France only a week after the outbreak of the First World War. After the Armistice, she bravely remained in France to help minister to the sick during the Spanish Flu epidemic. A portrait of her in her matron's uniform decorated with medals, painted by Elizabeth Mary Watt, was willed to her niece.

The Thankful Villages

Arthur Mee, writing in the 1930s, found just thirty villages where every soldier returned from the First World War. He called them the Thankful Villages. Later enquiries turned up some more: there were at least fifty in England and Wales, but this shows just how few places were spared the tragedy of the war. A heavy cost was borne by women waiting at home; a mother might lose one or more of her sons, brothers or uncles. In one family, six brothers died. Many women became widows. Few families escaped such grief and suffering.

Wives were left widowed with young children, and single women lost fiancés. Mary was one of the latter. She lived in a small Hertfordshire town with happy plans to marry, but her fiancé never came home. A housekeeper and cook for a local family, Mary was also pregnant. This meant she would likely be dismissed, and her family probably would disown her as well.

In 1913, the Mental Deficiency Act allowed unmarried mothers to be categorised as moral imbeciles. Some were sent to lunatic asylums. Even up until the 1960s and 1970s, an unmarried mother could expect to be turned out by her family as it was such a disgrace. Marriage, any marriage, was considered better than being a single mother. Alternatively, she might be expected to give up the baby for adoption.

Mary, however, was fortunate. Her two brothers, who worked in a paper mill, were single and owned the family home. Mary therefore came back to keep house for them along with baby Dorothy, who was always known to family and friends as Bubbles. Mary never married, and some fifty years later left her share in the house to Dorothy.

Surplus Women

So many men died in the First World War that there was a gender imbalance during the 1920s and 1930s, with far too few young men for the number of women of their age group. Newspapers soon labelled these two million extra unmarried women 'surplus women'. Despite this unfortunate description, the increased number of single women helped to create a major push for women's rights, providing the generation with a new sense of independence compared to earlier times.

The Spitfire Women

The Second World War brought yet more upheaval and social change. In 1941, unmarried women and young widows without children were conscripted. By the end of the war in 1945, more than 7 million women had been called up. Top-secret codebreaking work at Bletchley Park is a well-known example of women's contributions, and women were famously recruited as spies. There were also the brave 'Spitfire Women' like Eleanor Wadsworth. These female pilots were part of the Air Transport Auxiliary (ATA), flying newly manufactured military planes from the factories to the airfields so that they could be airborne as quickly as possible. There were eventually 168 such women, although to begin with there were just eight. In 1945, Lesley Cairns Murray lost her life aged twenty-eight when her Hudson aircraft crashed at Taplow. Sixteen other women were killed on active service. In 2022, Biggin Hill Museum put on an exhibition about what they called 'the hidden heroes of World War Two'.

Mary Ellis, who flew 400 Spitfires among her 1,000 deliveries, once arrived at an East Anglian airfield in a large Wellington bomber. The men searched the plane looking for the real pilot, unable to believe this slim young woman could fly such a heavy plane – it seemed incredible. In 2017, Mary celebrated her 100th birthday in the grandest style by flying a Spitfire. There was of course a co-pilot just in case any help was needed. Molly Rose was another of those 'Spitfire Women', and her 2018 obituary in *The Guardian* makes clear the danger involved in the job:

> On some days she flew three or four different types of aircraft ... they flew without radios, and many airfields were camouflaged and difficult to find.

Suffragettes, Flappers and Votes for Women

While it cannot be doubted that the militant, terrorist tactics of the suffragettes helped win the vote for women, such acts were highly controversial. Many people, women as well as men, strongly opposed their behaviour.

Politicians blew hot and cold, promising change and progress before they were elected and conveniently forgot their promises, much as they do today. One early postcard from the 1910s shows the shilly-shallying behaviour clearly, with two cartoons on a single card. In the first picture, the politician welcomes the protestor and is her friend; in the second, he turns from her as she is dragged away by a policeman.

The campaign finally succeeded in 1918 with the Representation of the People Bill, when some women – those over thirty, married or a member of the Local Government Register – were allowed the vote for the first time. There was, however, a strong prejudice against giving the vote to working-class women, and so it would be yet another decade before all women could vote on equal terms to men. Some violent methods employed by suffragettes included breaking windows in London's West End, setting fires at railways stations and hotels and flooding the organ at the Albert Hall. They even detonated bombs in Westminster Abbey (a minor explosion under the Coronation Chair) and outside the Bank of England (a bomb in a milk tin).

But they also employed clever, sophisticated techniques to promote their cause. Their dramatic use of colours – white, purple and green (from 1908) – to identify the cause was used to great effect in the popular art deco jewellery of the day. There were even cakes made using the colours to show support. This was a stroke of brilliance, an early example of branding.

Liberty and Selfridges, two of the most important London department stores, sold hat ribbons in suffragette colours as well as badges, rosettes, handbags and even belts. Derry & Toms on Kensington High Street, however, was even more daring, selling underwear in suffragette colours! A disapproving parent would never know. Shoemaker Lilley & Skinner showed support by producing slippers in suffragette colours, and Selfridges founder Harry Gordon Selfridge was a great champion for the cause, advertising in the suffragette magazines and flying their flag above the shop. Such a prominent display must have been good for business, and for the legitimacy of the cause.

Fortnum and Mason went one better in the most practical way, sending hampers to suffragettes released from Holloway Prison in 1911. Each contained beef tea to help the freed protestors regain their strength. That same year, many suffragettes boycotted the Census; some refused to supply details, but the scientist Hertha Ayrton was more direct, saying, 'I will not supply these particulars until I have my rights as a citizen. Votes for Women.'

This declaration of rights must have infuriated both politicians and the bureaucrats in the census office.

The suffragettes knew all about the value of a theatrical display, which often helped them capture public attention and sympathy. One dramatic example comes from Waverley railway station in Edinburgh, where Scottish suffragettes were about to board the train to London and imprisonment at Holloway. They boarded to the accompaniment of bagpipes played by Bessie Watson, aged eleven. No one who witnessed this scene would have forgotten it.

Equally dramatic are the photographs of suffragettes released from Holloway Prison. Now exhibited at the Museum of London, these pictures were circulated by officials so that security guards would know who to watch out for at major landmarks. Often, suffragettes leaving prison would be greeted by a welcoming group of supporters, and the government soon discovered prison was not a deterrent. Even force-feeding did not work; indeed, this brutal, barbaric act only turned public opinion against the government.

A 2015 exhibition by the Jewish Museum in London highlighted the part played by the Jewish Suffrage Campaign. Founded in 1912, their actions were mostly peaceful but occasionally not, as in 1913 when three women protestors were evicted from the West End Synagogue for creating a disturbance during the Yom Kippur ceremony.

Postcards were extremely popular at this time, and some show the suffragettes as ugly old maids, spinsters, the message being that they were simply frustrated at their inability to get a husband. Suffragette propagandists was quick to respond. One of the best posters bears the legend, 'What a Woman May Be and Not Have the Vote.' In one drawing are five women: a mother, a mayor, a nurse, a teacher (or doctor) and a factory hand. In all cases, they cannot have the vote. Then, beneath a second heading, 'What a Man May Be and Not Lose the Vote,' five men are drawn: a convict, a lunatic, a man unfit for military service, a proprietor of white slaves and a drunkard.

In 1928, a new Representation of the People Act allowed everyone over the age of twenty-one to vote. The first election held on these terms took place on 30 May 1929. The press was quick to call it the 'Flappers Election', a term used to describe the young, liberated women of the 1920s. In Italy such rebellious women there were known as *maschiette*, meaning 'young boys'. Cecil Beaton's photos of the Bright Young Things illustrate this new rebellious generation. Among the most daring were twin sisters Betty and Nancy Debenham, who raced BSA motorbikes at Brooklands and travelled around Britain.

Earlier generations of women, despite their struggles for independence, had been more conventional, dutiful and obedient. At last, things were changing.

A Fashion Revolution

Let us turn to those daring flappers, the flibbertigibbets of the 1920s and 1930s. They smoked cigarettes, not only privately but in public. Even worse, they liked decadent American jazz music and became dedicated 'bathers' and swimmers. *The Times* of 12 July 1922 took delight in reporting how much trouble the Englishwoman took over her bathing costume, 'especially if she is going abroad to such fashionable places as Deauville or the Lido, where she will find the best dressed women of France and America.'

Contemporary fashion dictated shorter skirts for women, with a dropped waist. The female shape was transformed from curves into straight lines, the slim tunic style creating an elegant silhouette which gradually gained its own gamine elegance and sex appeal. Within a few years the full skirts and trains worn by their Edwardian mothers and Victorian grandmothers had vanished. Gone, too, were low-cut décolleté evening gowns and tight corsets with impossibly tiny 18-inch waists.

The latest fashion was on show in the royal weddings of the 1920s, including those of Lady Elizabeth Bowes-Lyon, Lord Louis Mountbatten and heiress Edwina Ashley, as well as by

Princess Mary's bridesmaids in their slimline dresses. One can only imagine the comments from some of the older guests. Or did some of them think about how their own lives might have been different if this revolution had come sooner?

In the 1960s, fashion was once again turned upside down. This time Mary Quant was in the vanguard, with her fabulous miniskirts. This was just as shocking and revolutionary as the flapper movement had been decades before. When model Jean Shrimpton appeared in a miniskirt at the exclusive Goring Hotel in Knightsbridge, people turned to stare.

A few years later, one teenage bridesmaid went shopping with the bride's mother at Blundell's department store, the best in Luton. Their discussion was about exactly how short the bridesmaid's dress could be. The bride's mother, who was paying, wanted a modest, longer hemline just above the knee. The bridesmaid, who was to wear this expensive dress at her cousin's wedding in Brighton, wanted the shortest miniskirt. 'I'm not wearing anything so old-fashioned,' she protested. 'I'd rather not be bridesmaid!'

Can there a worse fate for a teenager than being made to wear something old-fashioned? The floral dress finally bought for cousin Alex's wedding was quite striking: beautiful swirls of sweet pea colours on gauze over deep pink silk, with a high neckline – but very short!

Her Crowning Glory

Dances like the Charleston, imported from America, became a craze in the 1920s, being fast, daring and as different as could be from dances of the last generation. Women drank alcohol, enjoying the new-fangled fashion for cocktails like pink gin, another insidious, appealing American import. Some women copied men in swearing loudly or cutting their hair short.

This last change was perhaps the most revolutionary, as women had worn their hair long since time immemorial, leaving it down when single and putting it up once married. One of the few reasons for cropped hair before this time was because of illness, fever or for mourning. With hair considered to be a woman's 'crowning glory', cutting it off was another way to prove you were different.

The burgeoning trend for make-up was equally novel, challenging earlier conventions. Lipstick until then was not something used by a lady; to these girls' parents and grandparents, a woman who 'painted' her face with rouge or lipstick was most likely to be 'fast' and immoral. The writer Nella Last recalled how at her marriage in 1911 she could not wear make-up, even though it was her wedding day, as no respectable woman would do so. Even into the 1920s, red lipstick was a sure sign of a Jezebel, a loose woman without morals. But these radical approaches were intoxicating, a tidal wave that could not be stopped.

Racing Drivers

Though we talk about flappers throwing off conventions observed by the women who came before, we should also acknowledge earlier Victorian rebels who defied some or all of the rules of their day. For example, when cars first arrived, so too did the women who wanted to drive them. The wealthy Ada Anne Watney (later Weguelin) was a pioneer who in 1897 drove a new 3½-hp car the 20 miles from Old Malden to London. Later, as the owner of the far more powerful 12-hp Panhard, she could be seen driving around fashionable Piccadilly and Bond Street.[13]

The Honourable Mrs Victor Bruce – born Mildred Mary Petre (d. 2021) – was an ace racing driver who also flew planes and raced speedboats. This was an age when married women took all of their husband's name. She won the Coupe des Dames at the 1927 Monte Carlo Rally, driving seventy-two hours from John O'Groats through England and down to the south of France. She had a lightning turn of speed and legendary endurance, and with precision driving this must have been exhilarating. Dorothy Levitt, a glamorous racing driver, broke the record at the Brighton Speed Trials in 1905. The following year, at Blackpool, she set a new land speed record of 90.88 mph; in her book she advised women driving alone at night to carry a small revolver.

Another winner of the Coupe de Dames was Ada, Lady Jardine (d. 1960) of Applegarth, Scotland. She owned what is known today as the Jardine Star diamond brooch, a late Victorian jewel that was left to Queen Elizabeth in 1981. Lady Jardine was described by her great-great-nephew as 'an extremely formidable woman'. Another said she was 'someone who would have commanded an armoured division with distinction', suggesting a strong woman full of spirit and energy. It should be said that her nephew had great expectations to inherit as his aunt had no children. However, Lady Ada was far more of a philanthropist than he had realised and preferred to set up a charitable trust. In this she echoed her father, a member of the Younger brewing family, who left most of his fortune to the Salvation Army.[14]

Women after the War

Involvement in both world wars changed how women thought about themselves as well as changing men's views of women and their capabilities. Gladys Eva, who died in April 2021 at the age of 100, was a sergeant in the Women's Auxiliary Air Force. An aircraft plotter during the Battle of Britain, she neatly summed up the change:

> Before the war you married and had your babies, did the cleaning, cooking and shopping, and that was life. Women didn't know what it was to go to work. After the war, because of what the girls had done, more of us went into the workforce. The world had changed.[15]

As far back as the 1920s, the newspapers noticed the streak of independence shown by many women. *The Daily Telegraph*, in a 1921 report about punting on the River Thames headlined 'Call of the River', offered the following perspective:

... punting seems to be more popular than ever ... an interesting development of the use of the punt has been noted in the past few years at Richmond and farther up the river. The modern girl has realised that a man is by no means an essential part of a happy day on the river ... inducing an increasing number of girls, many of whom toil at desk or in shop during the week, to club together to secure a punt for the season.

Over the course of the two wars, and with much reluctance, women were accepted into the professions of medicine, accountancy and the law. In the 1950s, Margaret Booth's father was advised not to steer his daughter towards the legal profession and was warned, 'There is no place for women in the law.'

Helena Normanton and Rose Heilbron were the first women appointed in 1949 as King's Counsel, but the prejudice remained. Nevertheless, Margaret Booth began a legal career and in 1976 was only the tenth woman appointed as Queen's Counsel. Three years later, she was the third woman to become a High Court judge.

Finally, in the 1970s, there was a momentous change in the Civil Service. The good news was that instead of being merely the diplomat's wife, women could now aspire to be the diplomat. One reason women had been excluded was ingrained misogyny; in Helen McCarthy's book about female diplomats, she refers to the struggle for recognition as the 'battle for the Foreign Office'. The first female ambassador was not appointed until 1976, when Anne Warburton (1927–2015) became ambassador to Denmark. Only three years earlier, women had been obliged to resign from the Civil Service if they married. They had only been allowed into diplomatic service in 1946.

Anne Warburton joined the Civil Service in 1958 but never married. The choice between a career or a family also happened for many women in business; at the time it was almost impossible to have both. *The Guardian* commented in her obituary,

Dame Anne Warburton was Britain's first female ambassador, at a time when women in the diplomatic service were often seen as mere appendages.

By 1997, women were still only a tiny minority with nine female ambassadors. The numbers have gradually improved, though. Twenty years on, in 2017, women led nearly half of the European embassies. Nevertheless, gender equality in the Civil Service remains a work in progress. A breakthrough came in 2021 when women held the senior diplomatic appointments in Rome, Paris, Moscow, Berlin, Washington, Beijing and Tokyo, plus the United Nations.

Let us close this chapter by turning from politics to art.

The Artist, His Lover, a Jealous Wife and Some Modern Art

Lady Kathleen Epstein (*née* Garman, 1901–1976) makes her mark in this book because she left the Garman Ryan art collection to the town of Walsall.[16] She had grown up in nearby Wednesbury and wanted to give something back to the Black Country. She certainly did, because her collection remains one of the most important in the country, boasting more than 360 paintings and works of art including Jacob Epstein sculptures.

It all began in rackety, raffish, bohemian London, when Jacob Epstein first saw Kathleen (Kitty) Garman in 1921 and at once asked her to sit for a portrait. Half his age at the time, Kathleen and her older sister Mary had run away from a dull, provincial life in the Midlands and were keen to sample every excitement London had to offer. The attractive Garman sisters soon had many admirers.

After becoming Jacob Epstein's model, Kitty next became the married sculptor's mistress. This was a toxic situation, and his wife Margaret was so jealous that she tried to shoot Kitty with a pearl-handled gun. Fearing the newspaper coverage would ruin Jacob's career, the Epstein family managed to hush it all up – with Kitty's cooperation.

Kitty returned home when her father was ill in 1923, but his disapproval of her London life was so severe that she received nothing in his will. She and Jacob had four children during a long affair. At first she lived with her sister in Bloomsbury while he stayed with his wife, in an arrangement intended to preserve respectability as society expected at that time. In 1955, however, they married. By now, he was the famous Sir Jacob Epstein.

Kitty was the sole beneficiary of Jacob Epstein's will when he died in 1959. Together with her friend Sally Ryan, another sculptor, she began collecting modern art. This would become an outstanding collection – indeed, perhaps the greatest British collection outside of London – with works by Picasso, Cézanne, Delacroix, van Gogh and Lucien Freud.

13

OTHER WILLS: MOLLY THE BRUISER, CHASING BUTTERFLIES AND HARVARD UNIVERSITY

'To the poor of Glasgow'

This chapter includes examples of women's wills throughout time, all of which have an interesting story to tell.

To the King
Sometime around AD 990, a noblewoman named Aethelgifu set out her will, which begins with gifts to the king and queen:

> Aethelgifu declares her will to her royal lord and to her lady and to her friends, what she wishes to render to God, what to her lord, what to her friends. Namely, to her lord the King 30 mancuses of gold and two stallions, which must be offered to him and my deer hounds; and to my lady 30 mancuses of gold.[1]

Lady Aethelgifu owned estates across Oxfordshire, Buckinghamshire, Berkshire and Hertfordshire. She mentions livestock in her will, as well as property in Somerset at Downscombe. She gave land at Watford ('Wadforda') 'to my kinswoman Leofrun, and two men and eight oxen at Weedon [in Northamptonshire] … and after her lifetime the land at Wadforda is to be given to her daughter, Godwif.'

The men are slaves, traded in the same way as 760 sheep and seventy-four oxen who are also in the will. Seventy luckier slaves were to be set free for the 'salvation of her soul'.[2] The earliest mention of the Hertfordshire village of Ashwell is also noted in this tenth-century will.

A Family Secret
Illegitimate children were a common family secret, as in the 1920s with Dorothy L Sayers (1893–1957), creator of the fictional super sleuth Lord Peter Wimsey. The unmarried writer's pregnancy would have been a dreadful scandal for her family as the child's father was already married. It would be impossible to exaggerate the shame this meant for a respectable family. Far better to keep it secret. Using an assumed name, the baby was born in a place then known as a 'mother's hospital'. So much has changed; in 2021, for the first time since records began in 1845, more babies were born out of wedlock than within marriage (51.3 per cent).

Dorothy's aunt and a favourite older cousin brought up the boy, and Dorothy kept the secret all her life, even when she later married and 'adopted' her son. Only when her will was read after her death in 1957 did friends discover that 'nephew' John Anthony (Tony) Fleming was actually Dorothy's real son and only child. In fact, the *Oxford Dictionary of National Biography* in 1971 stated incorrectly that Dorothy had no children, only an adopted son. The sole beneficiary of an estate valued at £36,276 13s 9d, her son also inherited letters and manuscripts. These were auctioned at Sotheby's, long after his death, by his wife.

Saving Lives
John Barr, a Glasgow GP, has the unusual distinction of having a lifeboat named after him. When his widow Kitty (Catherine) died in 2008, she left a legacy of £2.6 million to the Royal National Lifeboat Institution to fund a lifeboat in his memory. It was a most appropriate legacy, as Dr Barr saved lives during the Second World War, albeit in a different sphere. He served in the Royal

Army Medical Corps as lieutenant doctor, seeing active service with the 78th Division in the African campaign, as well as in Italy.

The *John Buchanan Barr*, the most advanced lifeboat in the fleet when it was launched in 2011, is based at Portpatrick, Scotland, where John and Kitty Barr spent many holidays.

An Unsuitable Boy?

Throughout the ages, disinheritance has been used by families to dissuade women from marrying the man they loved. In the 1890s in Worcestershire, this was the fate of Caroline Alice Roberts (d. 1920), who was told by her family that if the marriage went ahead she would be cut out of various family wills.

The objections to her husband were many, and all were crucially important to her family. Eight years younger than Alice, he was far beneath the Roberts in social standing. Caroline's father was a major general in the British Indian army, serving with distinction, and the Roberts were important in the area. The bridegroom was a nobody to them. Not only was his father in trade as a shopkeeper, but his family was Catholic while the Roberts were staunch Protestants. The son's profession as a poor music teacher was another obstacle; the couple had first met when Alice took piano lessons. Nothing was in his favour – except for love.

Describing her suitor as a genius, Alice ignored her family's threats and disapproval. In May 1899, the forbidden couple had a quiet Catholic wedding in London and then a three-week honeymoon on the Isle of Wight.

Well, who was the groom? It was Edward Elgar. He would later become one of the most important British composers. His engagement present to Alice was most romantic: a composition of his own, which eventually became his famous piece '*Salut d'Amour*'.

Anyone for Tea?

Until 2018, when Kate Cranston's portrait featured on the Royal Bank of Scotland's £20 note, few would have known about her. She was born in 1849, during the flourishing of the temperance movement, which believed that alcohol was at the root of a great number of the problems plaguing society at the time. The Cranston family in Glasgow all belonged to the temperance movement, and Kate's brother opened a tearoom to provide an alcohol-free meeting place. Kate followed with her own tearoom in 1878, helped with financial contributions from her aunt and uncle. It was a successful venture, attracting working-class men. Her second shop had a quiet space where respectable women could meet their friends.

Miss Cranston was widely respected, the only businesswoman of the seven women included in the 1909 *Who's Who in Glasgow*. Delightfully eccentric, she wore old-fashioned Victorian clothes but in terms of business sense she was on the cutting edge. Her success continued through until 1917, when she was widowed. She was an important patron to architect and designer team Charles Rennie and Margaret Mackintosh; one of the couple's early commissions in 1903 was to design the famous Willow Tea Shop, her fourth tearoom. Everything was very stylish and of the finest quality. Chairs were lined with purple velvet from Italy, there hung above the room a most extravagant glass chandelier, and both cutlery and waitresses' uniforms had Kate's name on them.

Kate died in 1934, leaving two-thirds of her estate (worth just over £67,000) to the poor of Glasgow. She had no children. Thanks to Celia Sinclair's fundraising efforts, the Willow Tea Shop was restored in 2018, with every detail of the 1903 interior faithfully copied to recreate that amazing Mackintosh flair.

A Simple Funeral
Queen Mary II only reigned for five years, dying of smallpox in 1694. She wished for a simple funeral, without excess expense, but instead it became a most extravagant and lavish occasion. The funeral procession was attended by the members of the House of Commons and the cost was reported to be £50,000. Other estimates place the cost far higher, at £100,000, a fortune for those times.

A Woman's Will

Victorian Celebrity Chef

In recent years, the unlikely star on social media and YouTube is Avis Crocombe (1838–1927), who has been brought back to life by English Heritage for their series *The Victorian Way*. This is an unusual development for the farmer's daughter from Devon who back in the 1880s was head cook at Audley End, a large country house near Saffron Walden.

The YouTube broadcasts used imaginary recipes until 2009, when a minor miracle occurred. When Avis's great-great-nephew Robert Stride attended an event at Audley End, he recalled a handwritten book at home, tucked away at the back of a drawer. It turned out to be her handwritten recipe book, which he donated to English Heritage. Now the recipes used are authentic, from kedgeree to saffron buns and cucumber ice cream!

Bacon and onion roly-poly pudding was a favourite in the servants' hall, and considered much improved if left to cool and then fried in lard. It seems as if everything was cooked in lard, which was not considered unhealthy at the time. Even pastry for an apple pie would use lard rather than butter, and beef dripping was immensely popular. Lard pastry (and using lard to fry chips) continued well into the 1970s.

Joan Hughes, Spitfire Pilot and MBE

Joan (1918–1993) served in the Air Transport Auxiliary during the Second World War, one of those brave women who helped deliver Spitfires and bomber planes to RAF bases during the Battle of Britain. She took her first flying lessons at the age of fifteen at a cost of £2 10s per hour. By the end of her career, she had amassed 11,800 flying hours in her logbook. When Joan Hughes died aged seventy-four, she left her wartime photos and her MBE medal to a friend.

Three Copies of My Will

Mary, Queen of Scots made her pregnancy will in 1566, when three copies were made. She kept one, a second was for her mother's family in France as beneficiaries, and the third was to be given to whoever ruled Scotland after her death. She and her baby son happily survived the pregnancy, however, and at the christening at Stirling Castle there was an elaborate three-day celebration including theatre, fireworks and a feast served on a moving mechanical stage.

The tradition of three copies of a will goes back at least as far as Saxon times, with the understandable purpose of ensuring no will was conveniently mislaid or forged. The testator had a copy, the king had another and a third went to the abbey or church receiving the largest bequest. For added protection, some Saxon wills ended with an awesome curse upon anyone who dared tamper with the document.

For the Glory of Art
In 2012, Marcia Lay made a generous gift to the National Gallery. For many years, she had been an art teacher at Lordswood Girls School in Harborne, Birmingham. A David Wilkie painting, *Young Woman Kneeling at a Prayer Desk*, was acquired as a result. Nearly a quarter of the paintings on display in the National Gallery have been acquired due to gifts made in wills.

I Will Take it With Me
In ancient pagan times people were buried with certain items, and this tradition has become popular again in recent years. A 2019 survey by the Co-operative Funeral Service reviewed 500,000 funerals over a five-year period and found that typical items included photographs, jewellery and love letters. Some are rather more unusual – mobile phones and a violin for instance – and a few are downright strange. How about a broomstick and a scone with cream and jam?

Molly the Bruiser
Mary Caryll, who died in 1809, left a field to her mistresses Lady Eleanor Butler (d. 1829) and Miss Sarah Ponsonby (d. 1831).

Usually it was the mistress who left a bequest to her maid or servants, but in this case Mary, known as Molly, used her life savings to buy the field beside their cottage. The money came from tips from visitors who came to see The Ladies of Llangollen, as the two became known.

More than twenty years before, in 1778, Lady Eleanor and Miss Ponsonby ran away from their families. Both were desperate to escape. Eleanor was to be hidden away in a French Catholic convent so her family could reinvent themselves as loyal Protestants to the English Crown. Sarah's fate was possibly even worse, as her guardian intended to marry her just as soon as his wife died. In their first dash for freedom, the two were caught heading for the Waterford ferry. Lady Eleanor then ran away again, hiding in Sarah's room while Molly, her maid, smuggled in food. This time, Eleanor's family did not want her back and Sarah was also allowed to leave.

While touring around Wales, they found a small cottage called Plas Newydd in Llangollen. They sent back for Molly to join them, and she stayed for the rest of her life. Known as Molly the Bruiser for her rough, argumentative ways, she was the ideal guardian for two genteel, poverty-stricken ladies. The elopement created a scandal at first, and visitors came out of curiosity, though in time there was friendship from the Duke of Wellington, Anna Sewell (the author of *Black Beauty*) and Sir Walter Scott. William Wordsworth even honoured them with a poem composed in their garden.

When Molly died, while her employers got the field, her siblings back in Ireland were pointedly left only a shilling each. Furthermore, to claim it they had to travel to Wales. Molly was buried in the local churchyard, where Lady Eleanor and Miss Sarah were later buried as well. Their cottage is a museum today.

The Man I Could not Marry
Despite family opposition, Beatrix Potter planned to marry Norman Warne. Just weeks after their secret engagement, however, in 1905, he tragically died of pernicious anaemia. His

family's firm, Frederick Warne, had published the first of her bestselling books in 1902; Norman had been the editor. Twenty-three more books would follow, and international fame with them. Many were translated into other languages, including Japanese, in which language she has remained immensely popular.

Beatrix did marry much later in life, though she always remained close to Norman's family. In her will she gave the copyright to all her published works to Norman's nephew, Frederick Warne Stephens.

To the National Trust

Elizabeth Mackintosh (1896–1952) was one of three daughters who began her writing career in her late twenties. Known as Beth, she returned to her family home in Inverness in 1923 to look after her sick mother and then stayed to keep house for her father. Thereafter she wrote some brilliant plays, poems and novels. She never married, and under the *nom de plume* Josephine Tey she wrote mystery stories including *Brat Farrar* and, perhaps her most famous nowadays, *The Daughter of Time*. Under the name Gordon Daviot she was a poet and playwright with a 1930s West End hit, *Richard of Bordeaux*, starring John Gielgud.

Beth died from liver cancer in 1952, leaving almost her entire estate and her royalties to the National Trust. Her plays were all to be published and her ashes to be scattered at the village of Daviot, where the family once spent holidays – this explains the surname Daviot in her playwright pseudonym.

A Single Chess Piece

One man inherited a small walrus ivory carving from his mother but was uncertain if it had any value – 'she thought perhaps it could have some magical significance,' he said – and never displayed it. Her own father had paid £5 for the 3½-inch piece at an Edinburgh antique shop in 1964. When it arrived at Sotheby's – items brought into the front desk are rarely valuable – an expert was quickly called to take a look. Immediately,

Alexander Kader realised this was a lost 'warder' (one of four) from the famous Lewis chessmen. Most of the set was found on Lewis after a storm in 1831 and later cleaned to a pale walrus-ivory colour; they dated all the way back to the twelfth century.

Auctioned in 2019 by Sotheby's for the astronomical sum of £735,000, this proved to be a rather good return on that original £5!

According to the Law
National law (plus some regional differences) dictates matters of inheritance. Children in Belgium are entitled to a fixed proportion of their parents' estate, for instance, while in France children are protected heirs with certain rights of equal distribution. Children in Scotland also have legal rights.

Beware, however, the enduring British myth that common-law partners have inheritance rights if there is no will. As of writing, they have none. There is no such legal term as a 'common law' partner, as highlighted in the view below from a financial adviser:

> Better to rewrite your will as soon as you separate. I had one client who didn't and who died suddenly. Everything went to his estranged wife, who gratefully accepted the lot, leaving his second partner, with whom he had been living for some years, with just one keepsake – their dog.

Chasing Butterflies
Somebody who is not of sound mind cannot make a will, and it was for this reason that in the early 1700s Eleanor Glanville's husband and son challenged her will, claiming she was mad for chasing butterflies.

Eleanor Glanville (née Goodricke, 1654–1709) was the first female entomologist, though few probably recognise her name. Born just before the Civil War, she was brought up in the West Country. Her father had been a Parliamentarian officer in

Cromwell's army and from her mother she inherited considerable property. In 1703, she took her butterfly collection to London. One collector described it as outstanding, saying it 'has sham'ed us all'. Two butterflies, including the Glanville fritillary, are named after Eleanor, and a few of her butterfly specimens were among early exhibits in the Natural History Museum.

Eleanor separated from her second husband, who was a violent man. She decided to leave most of her wealth and property to a cousin, but her son and second husband challenged the will three years after her death. The court case was a determined character assassination, with 100 witnesses called to show Eleanor Glanville was mad. Tragically, the court set her will aside in the belief that nobody 'not deprived of their senses should go in pursuit of Butterflyes'.

Miss Eliza's Wedding Dress
A veil made of Honiton lace, a wedding dress of silk satin and a pair of dainty leather boots trimmed with silk were worn in 1865 by the wealthy Eliza Clay when she married Joseph Bright. After a smart wedding at St James's, Piccadilly, the dress, veil and boots were carefully preserved and in 1947 given by her daughter to the Victoria & Albert Museum.

Thomasine Bonaventure
By her will, Thomasine Bonaventure (*c.* 1470–*c.* 1530) founded a college in the Cornish village where she was born, this college being both a place of learning and a chantry offering prayers for her soul. Her third husband, Sir John Perceval, Mayor of London, had founded a school in his hometown of Macclesfield in 1498, and Thomasine was similarly generous to her home village of St Mary Wycke, now Week St Mary. Her cousin John was asked to supervise:

> And as for all thinges concernyng my Chauntry and gramer scole at saint Mary Wike in the Countie of Cornewall I comitte only to the discretion of my said cosyn John Dynham requiringe hym to

see every thinge concernynge the same to be parfite [perfect] and sure as nygh as he can accordyng as he knoweth my mynde and as I have putt my confidence and trust oonly in him therein.

Only a few decades later, during the Reformation, chantries were banned. However, Thomasine's college remained because it was also a school. Even today, walk down a village lane and there it stands, now looked after by the Landmark Trust.

Beating the French
Jemima Nicholas (d. 1832) in 1797 singlehandedly captured twelve French soldiers with the aid of a pitchfork and locked them in the local church of Llanwnda in Pembrokeshire. Such brio and heroism earned her a life pension of £50 a year from a grateful government. The soldiers were part of a French invasion which fortunately turned out to be a storm in a teacup, fizzling out after a couple of days. But all might well have been disaster. Indeed, when news of the invasion first reached London it created such panic there was a run on the Bank of England.

Constant fear of a French invasion by Napoleon meant each county had to raise a local militia and find officers to organise and train its soldiers. By 1803, some 400,000 men were ready to fight. In Hitchin, Hertfordshire, the men of the Loyal Volunteers were billeted in one of the town's pubs. Those in Harwich, Ipswich and Colchester were so well organised that they had buttons made for their uniforms.

Jemima Nicholas's distinctive tall, black Welsh hat became a family heirloom after it was bequeathed to her brother and his descendants. In 2019 it was put up for sale to raise funds for the local church. It did stay in the family even after this, as distant relative Denise Hutton travelled from Australia to make the winning offer of £5,000.

My Children Will Not Approve
During the last years of her life, Queen Victoria wrote out instructions for her death. The document was a secret known only

to Sir James Reid, her doctor, and to her head dresser, Mrs Selina Tuck. She carried it with her at all times, and her confidantes were told in no uncertain terms that it must not be shared with her children as they would never have approved of her plans.

Victoria wished to be buried with numerous items, including a plaster cast of Prince Albert's hand and his dressing gown, her wedding veil and small keepsakes such as a sprig of heather from her beloved Scottish home at Balmoral. So far, so good. Far more controversial, however, was the inclusion of a lock of hair from John Brown, her most beloved servant, a photograph of him, and his mother's wedding ring. All of this was to be hidden from sight, as the family would visit the open coffin. The story was only discovered many years later from information found among Dr Reid's papers.

Mrs Fillis, Mrs Fortescue and William Shakespeare's First Folio
Ann Fortescue and Elizabeth Fillis (*née* Herbert) were sisters who in 1829 donated a copy of Shakespeare's First Folio to the public library in their home town of Plymouth. These were the early days of public libraries in Britain, and for the first few years the folio could even be borrowed. Cassandra and Jane Austen in 1798 were among the subscribers to Mrs Martin's library in Basingstoke, and Bath had a lending library a few years earlier. The idea of book donations was well known, and when the London Lending Library opened in 1841 Prince Albert gave books for its collection. Sadly, public libraries are now fast disappearing due to a lack of government funding.

The First Folio was possibly inherited, as a collection of books is mentioned in the 1826 will of Ann and Elizabeth's father. He also expected his daughters might disagree about who would have what, and stated that if necessary the book titles should be placed in a bag and beginning with the eldest sister they would in turn select slips from the bag. This First Folio now belongs to the American Folger Library as Folio 59. Folger's is the largest collection, with eighty-two of the 230 First Folios known to exist. By comparison, the British Library has only five, and the Victoria & Albert Museum three. In

1913, Henry and Emily Folger paid $255 for the folio – the same price one would pay for a Ford Model T car.

In the twenty-first century, First Folios are of course vastly more expensive. In 2006, a First Folio sold for £2.5 million.

Lennoxlove House

Frances Teresa Stuart (1649–1702) preferred to marry the Duke of Richmond and Lennox rather than become a mistress of her cousin Charles II. Frances was such a beauty that she was the model for Britannia, the portrait used on all our coins until decimalisation in 1971. The likeness can still be found on the reverse of some traditional 50 pence coins.

Duchess Frances died in 1702 without children. Her ladies were requested to look after her cats and most of her estate went to her 'neare and deare kinsman the said Walter Stuart', Lord Blantyre. The executors bought Lethington Castle in Scotland for him, and the duchess requested this be called 'Lennox's Love to Blantyre' – or, as it is now known, Lennoxlove.

My Imprudent Sons

In 1797, Margery Williams of Baydon in Wiltshire added a codicil to her will in an attempt to protect her two sons:

> Whereas it is the Misfortune of my sons Benjamin and Joseph to be very indiscreet and imprudent and as they have expended their Fortunes and I am extremely apprehensive any Other Property would be in like Manner Wasted and Yet unwilling that they should be left intirely Destitute...[3]

Her third son, Francis Williams, would instead pay them 2 shillings a week for life.

Miss Fairfax's Trousseau

Ann Fairfax died aged sixty-nine in 1793. Her family was one of the most prominent among the wealthy Yorkshire Catholic families, and their smart Georgian townhouse in York is now a museum. In her will Ann left the considerable sum of £500, as well as her trousseau – which had been purchased for the wedding she never had – to the English nuns in Cambrai, northern France, where she had stayed several times.

Sons and Daughters
When John Vivian died in Padstow, Cornwall, in 1506 he left £20 to be equally divided between his son John and his daughters Margaret and Joan. If any of them died before they came of age, the money was to be shared among the others. Joan was a name across three generations of Vivians. The executrixes named in John Vivian's will included his wife Joan, his mother Joan and his daughter Joan.

The Good Solicitor
Stradey Castle in Llanelli, Wales, was left by Mary Ann Mansel in 1808 to the solicitor Thomas Lewis. In the 1770s he had helped to obtain her father's release from the dreaded Fleet, a debtors' prison in London. Debtors' prisons were not abolished until 1869, until which point anybody could be sent to jail by debtors. Mary Ann had no children, and so left the castle and 3,000 acres to Thomas Lewis, who acknowledged his good fortune by adding 'Mansel' to his surname. In fact, he was so grateful that his new surname came before 'Lewis'. His descendants still live at Stradey Castle.

A Rich Widow and Mr Austen's daughters
Mrs Lillingston (d. 1806), a rich widow from Bath, had quarrelled with her close family and so left bequests to her servants, more distant relatives and many of her friends such as Jane Austen's aunt, whose husband was chief executor of the will. The Austen family, Jane and her sister Cassandra, were living in Bath at this time and were part of the same social circle as the wealthy Mrs Lillingston. The sisters were left the most welcome inheritance of

£50 each, which family letters reveal was more than sufficient to pay Jane's living expenses for the following year.

The Key to Napoleon's Bedroom
Emperor Napoleon died on St Helena in 1822, and a year later General Charles Richard Fox visited his prison on the island. When he left, he took as a souvenir the key to Napoleon's bedroom door and gifted it to his mother, Baroness Elizabeth Holland. The baroness had worshipped Napoleon since their first meeting in 1802, and corresponded with him during his earlier imprisonment on Elba, sending food and books. Recently rediscovered in a Scottish attic, the key had remained in the family and was expected to sell for £5,000. The final auction price was much higher, however, at a staggering £81,900.

Mrs Luffman and Handsome Mr Darcy
Writing about the National Trust, Merlin Waterston tells a fascinating story about a certain Mrs Luffman. After watching a famous scene in the BBC's 1990 adaptation of *Pride and Prejudice* when Mr Darcy (Colin Firth) dives into the pool at Pemberley (staged at Lyme Park), Mrs Luffman made a special provision in her will. A bequest of £100,000 was given to Lyme Park in Cheshire. Was this out of appreciation for the delightful house, or the BBC's stellar adaptation? Perhaps it was simply the delightful Mr Darcy. He certainly captivated almost every other female viewer.

Mary, Queen of Scots
When she was escorted to her site of execution at Fotheringay Castle on 8 February 1587, Mary, Queen of Scots carried a rosary with her. The gold and enamel beads were left to Anne Howard, Countess of Arundel, who also was a Catholic. That rosary, together with the queen's Bible, remained with the Howard family until summer 2021 when they were stolen.

Other Wills

Shakespeare's Granddaughter
New Place in Stratford-upon-Avon was purchased by William Shakespeare in 1597 for £120, and he died there in 1616. Built a century before, it was one of the largest houses in Stratford with ten hearths, suggesting it had as many as twenty rooms. Lady Elizabeth Barnard inherited the house from her mother Susannah Hall, who was Shakespeare's daughter. Twice married but childless, Lady Elizabeth died in 1670 and left instructions in her will for New Place to be sold and the money to be distributed as legacies to friends and relatives.

Coombe Abbey
Elizabeth Craven was particularly wealthy. Her husband, William, was Mayor of London in 1610–1611. One of the richest men in London, he had been knighted in 1603. By 1622, his widow Lady Elizabeth could afford to buy Coombe Abbey near Coventry for what was then the immense sum of £36,000. It stayed within the Craven family for the next 300 years. By 1964, Coombe Abbey was bought by Coventry Council and in 1995 it opened as a hotel.

A Lady's Fan
From the sixteenth century, fans were essential fashion accessories. In Victorian times Queen Mary received bequests of fans from her mother and grandmother. Queen Victoria similarly inherited some of her mother's fans. Their history goes back to Ancient Egypt, with an ostrich fan (among others) being discovered in Tutankhamun's tomb. Fans were popular presents for brides and both men and women collected them. Indeed, Queen Victoria gifted thirty favourite fans to her son Edward VII, and a list compiled just before her death records eighty-five fans.

Jewels from Mesopotamia
A portrait of Lady Enid Layard from 1870 shows her wearing Mesopotamian jewellery dating from the nineteenth and eighteenth centuries BC. These had been reset as part of a

wedding gift in 1869 from her husband, the archaeologist Sir Austen Henry Layard. Sir Austen discovered the jewels during excavations of the ancient Assyrian cities Nimrud and Nineveh. Sir Austen and Lady Enid had no children, and in 1913 Lady Enid bequeathed the jewels to the British Museum.

The Wallace Art Collection
In 1897, just as he had wished, Lady Wallace left her husband Sir Richard Wallace's art collection to the nation, together with Hertford House, a grand London town house close by Oxford Street. The collection is the largest single bequest given to the nation, with some 5,000 works of art including Frans Hals' *The Laughing Cavalier*.

Lady Wallace's will clearly stipulated that no object could ever leave the collection. This was noted in Hansard in 1897, when the bequest was debated in Parliament:

> I bequeath to the British nation my pictures, porcelain, bronzes, artistic furniture, armour, miniatures, snuff boxes, and works of art which are placed on the ground and first floors and in the galleries at Hertford House, on the express condition that the Government for the time being shall agree to give a site in a central part of London and build thereon a special museum to contain the said collection, which shall always be kept together unmixed with other objects of arts and shall be styled 'The Wallace Collection' ...

However, after 122 years, the trustees did make a loan in 2019, sending Titian's *Perseus and Andromeda* a short distance across London to the National Gallery. This special reunion saw the seven mythological paintings by Titian created for King Philip II of Spain displayed as they were first intended in the sixteenth century.

A Gift to the Welsh Nation
Margaret (d. 1963) and Gwendoline (d. 1951) Davies were sisters from a strict Calvinist family. Their grandfather's wealth came

from building railways around Cardiff just as the coal industry grew. In the First World War, when the sisters were helping at a Red Cross canteen in Troyes, France, they were already buying modern French paintings. Each sister had received the enormous sum of £500,000 and could afford to purchase the works of modern artists such as Renoir, Monet, Manet and van Gogh. Neither Gwendoline nor Margaret married. Their interests in art and music developed at Gregynog Hall, Powys, where they set up and took part in a choir with estate workers and developed an annual music festival. When advertising for an under-housemaid, they made the unique stipulation that 'a soprano was preferred'.

This sounds quirky and delightful, but life with the Davies sisters at Gregynog Hall involved observing a teetotal lifestyle according to Calvinist principles. An exception was made for Prime Minister Stanley Baldwin, who came to stay in the 1930s. A hamper was ordered – including wine – from Fortnum & Mason, although the sisters sensibly asked for this on a 'sale or return' basis.

Gregynog Hall was left to the University of Wales, and 260 paintings went to the Welsh national collection. The art bequest was especially important in helping reinforce Cardiff's claim in the 1950s to be the Welsh capital.

All My Cookery Books
Elizabeth David (d. 1992) did much to introduce the British to the many delights of Mediterranean cooking. Her 1955 book *An Omelette and a Glass of Wine* is still an enjoyable read, and another work, *Summer Cooking*, remains in print to this day. But she also was a collector of cookbooks authored by others, and these she left to the London Guildhall Library. These days, a first edition of her 1950 work *A Book of Mediterranean Food* is likely to fetch upwards of £1,500.

Of Women and Books
The famous relationship between women and books is to be found as far back as in medieval wills, in which many bequests of

devotional and religious books were made. One wealthy Norwich widow named Margaret Purdens gave money in 1481 to eight of the eleven nunneries in East Anglia, with books to three of these including Thetford, whose Benedictine nuns she hoped would enjoy the bequest.

The Tobermory Clock
The prominent clocktower on Main Street in the Scottish town of Tobermory exists thanks to the generosity of the traveller, explorer and early photographer Isabella Bird. The first woman to join the Royal Scottish Geographical Society, she travelled an arduous route through the Rockies and in 1879 published a book of her travels called *A Lady's Life in the Rocky Mountains*. This travel journal based on letters home to her sister proved to be immensely popular.

When she died in 1904, Isabella left money for a clock in Tobermory on the Isle of Mull, where the family used to spend holidays. Designed by a family friend Charles Whymper, the clock tower was built in 1905 in memory of Isabella's beloved sister Henrietta Amelia Bird, who had died of typhoid in Tobermory in 1880.

Murder Most Foul
Helen Bailey (d. 2016) was a successful children's author who after the death of her husband had the great misfortune to meet Ian Stewart. In 2014 she changed her will, leaving most of her multimillion-pound fortune to Ian Stewart, then her fiancé. Two years later, Helen and her dog were reported missing. The police had already searched the house and gardens when by chance neighbours mentioned a hidden cesspit, where they found Helen's body together with that of Boris, her pet dachshund. Stewart used his own medication to drug Helen, suffocated her and threw her body into the cesspit. Charged with her murder, he was sentenced to serve at least thirty-four years. In 2022, he was accused and found guilty of earlier murdering his wife Diane. Both murdered by the man they loved.

The Butler and a Rolls-Royce

Countess Raine Spencer was for many years resented and considered a wicked stepmother by Princess Diana and her other Spencer stepchildren. When the countess died in 2016 at the age of eighty-seven, unsurprisingly, she left most of her £8.7 million estate to her four children from an earlier marriage. But to her 'devoted' butler Brian Davis, who had worked for the countess for more than thirty years, she left £75,000 and whichever car she owned when she died. Fortunately for him, it was a Rolls-Royce Silver Cloud.

Dervorguilla and Balliol College

Dervorguilla of Galloway (d. 1290) was a wealthy heiress who married John de Balliol, an English nobleman, with whom she had a son who would become John, King of Scotland. John de Balliol founded Balliol College, Oxford in 1263 as penance for a dispute with the Bishop of Durham, and after his death Dervorguilla made it a permanent endowment.

Balliol was initially a college for poor scholars; in thanks, three requiem Masses were said each year for the family. In 2013, the college celebrated its 750th anniversary. One of the oldest Oxford colleges, in 1979 it admitted female students.

'Scatter my Ashes'

Cremation and having one's ashes scattered is a request found often in modern wills. However, it was far more unusual in 1943 when Beatrix Potter asked Tom Storey, her farm manager, to scatter her ashes and to keep secret the precise location in the Lake District where he carried out her wishes.

Other famous women have requested the same. Princess Margaret in 2002 and actress Diana Rigg in 2020 both preferred to be cremated. Anne Seymour Damer (1748–1828), who first broke with convention by becoming a sculptor, did so again in her funeral plans, requesting to be buried with items such as her sculptor's apron and tools, and also the ashes of her favourite dog. In 1960, Countess Edwina Mountbatten requested a burial at sea. Dorothy Levitt, a famous racing driver who died in 1922, asked to be buried in a field by the sea. Barbara Cartland (d. 2000), writer of romantic fiction, was buried in the grounds of her home at Camfield Place, Hertfordshire, saying she would rather be there than in the churchyard 'with all those sinners'!

With My Bow and Arrow
Erna Simon (*née* Seimert), born in 1894, and Ingo Simon were both keen archers who began collecting bows and arrows from Britain and elsewhere around the world. This grew into a vast collection of some 4,000 bows, arrows and assorted paraphernalia. Erna, who won the women's individual event at the 1937 World Archery Championships, gave half of the collection to the Museum of Manchester in the late 1940s. The rest was bequeathed to the museum in 1973, when she died.

All the Archbishop's Books
During the seventeenth century, York Minster's library held just one hundred books. However, a bequest by Archbishop Tobias Matthew's widow Frances vastly expanded the collection to more than 3,000 books. Frances Matthew (*c.* 1550–1629) was buried in the lady chapel, close by her husband's tomb. Perhaps in recognition of such generosity, she has her own fine monument.

Be Certain I am Dead!
Elizabeth de Burgh, Lady of Clare and founder of Clare College in Cambridge, made her will in 1355, five years before she died. In it, she was clear about a certain stipulation: 'I will that my body be not buried for fifteen days after my decease.'

She Changed History
Lyn Macdonald was fascinated by the stories told by the soldiers from the First World War. Just as well, because without her efforts to interview and collect more than six hundred stories we would

not appreciate the sacrifice and bravery of so many ordinary soldiers. Until then, most war historians, the majority of them male, focused on military strategy and leading figures rather than events on the ground, eyewitness accounts and the fine detail of life for the troops.

As a journalist. Lyn first travelled with the 'Old Comrades', visiting the battlefields in the early 1970s. Realising that as the old soldiers died their stories would be lost, she began her interviews in the best spirit of oral history, though she never liked this description. Her book *They Called It Passchendaele*, published in 1978, was a bestseller. It changed the way historians wrote about war, fostering a recognition that ordinary soldiers had their own powerful and important stories to tell. Lyn died in 2021, aged ninety-one, leaving her interview tapes to the Imperial War Museum.

Mothers and Sons
Barbara Hepworth (d. 1975), one of the twentieth century's pioneer sculptors and one of few women in a male world, decided to cut her son Simon out of her will after he sold a sculpture she had given him. Author Muriel Spark (d. 2006) also cut her son out of her will. Robin was her only child, but for the last decade of her life she would not speak to him. She had left his father when Robin was young, and her parents in Edinburgh raised him. Muriel became a Catholic while Robin was drawn closer to the family's Jewish roots.

Which Is Better, to Bequeath or to Give?
Queen Adelaide bequeathed a bracelet to her sister-in-law Princess Mary. The following year, Princess Mary gave the diamond bracelet to their niece Queen Victoria, saying she preferred to give rather than bequeath.

With a Trace of Malice
When Maggie Greville (see chapter 10) died in the 1940s, she left nothing to her friend Beverley Nichols. The playwright's error had

occurred back in 1931, when he refused her request to stand as MP at a crucial by-election against Duff Cooper.

Nanny and the Tractor
Minnie Barnes was nanny to Frances Campbell Preston (*née* Grenfell), lady-in-waiting to the Queen Mother, and her sister Laura. Always a saver, Minnie left the two women all her savings. This was such a generous sum that it enabled Frances to buy a tractor for her son's fish farm.

Only Women May Inherit
Miss Jane Parminter, together with her sister Elizabeth, their cousin Mary and a friend, set off in 1784 on an extensive tour which included France, Switzerland and Italy and the Alps. The Grand Tour was usually the preserve of the first sons of wealthy families rather than ladies. A typical example from 1790 was when Jane Austen's brother Edward (Knight), adopted by a rich couple, visited Dresden and Rome. A Grand Tour usually involved an itinerary of visits to the best cities in fashionable Europe as well ancient Roman and Greek sites.

Just a few miles from Exmouth you will find a charming house with a high roof which was originally thatched. This is A La Ronde, a sixteen-sided house inspired by a church in Ravenna in the north of Italy. When the Parminter ladies returned home with 'curiosities' from their travels, they commissioned the house as a place to store everything. There was also a delightful garden filled with rare and tropical plants. When Jane died in 1811, she left the house to her cousin Mary. Neither were married. In 1849, Mary left the house to unmarried women in the family, with the proviso that the bequest would be cancelled if anyone should marry after inheriting.

For some 200 years the house descended (almost always) according to a female principle of inheritance. Since 1991, A La Ronde and all the treasures within, including a shell gallery, belong to the National Trust after a public appeal raised the money to buy the house.

Other Wills

Only to the Deserving Poor

Many charitable gifts were given through the ages to those who were 'deserving'; in other words, those who were respectable folk in terms of morals, religion and honesty. This was the case in the Bedfordshire village of Aspley Guise in the early 1800s when Elizabeth Hervey left £600 for the two parishes of Holcote and Salford. The poor would receive six loaves of bread each week, and ready-made clothes such as waistcoats as well as blankets – but only if they attended church.

Similarly rigid views continued into the twentieth century. Work was so scarce in Lincoln in the 1920s that each winter morning men waited by the roadside to see if local employers and farmers would choose them for any task. Those who were not selected that day had no money for food, clothes or coal for their family. Local chapels and churches did offer charity, but, as a wife named Alice Ellen put it to her granddaughter many years later, this was only for those who attended that particular chapel or church – 'the deserving poor'.

Alice Ellen and her husband had five young children to feed and keep warm that winter when so little work was available. Fortunately, as regular chapel folk in Waddington they were 'deserving'. At the same time, her family (in Leiston, Suffolk) and his (in Boxmoor, Hemel Hempstead) shared what little they had. There was a small but steady flow of precious food parcels, home baking and warm clothes.

The Founding of Harvard University

Katherine Rogers (1584–1635) lived in a world to which early death was a frequent visitor. She was born and grew up in Stratford-upon-Avon, one of eleven daughters, around the time when William Shakespeare and his family lived there. Her father, a wealthy alderman, was one of three butchers in the town, also making money trading corn and cattle. So great was his fortune that by 1596 he had built one of the finest houses in Stratford-upon-Avon, now called Harvard House, after his grandson John.

In 1605, Katherine married the widower Robert Harvard, who was a butcher like her father. Robert lived in London, and some speculate that William Shakespeare might have been the matchmaker between the families. Certainly Shakespeare and Robert Harvard both lived in Southwark, London, at this time. Robert's shop near London Bridge was close by the Globe Theatre; they attended the same church and would have certainly known one another.

Some years later, Robert died from the plague. Within five weeks, Katherine lost not only her husband but four of their children as well. Two boys, John (b. 1607) and Thomas, were still alive when Katherine remarried to the cooper John Elletson. When Elletson died, Katherine inherited the lease of The Queen's Head on Southwark High Street, a valuable property. Richard Yarwood, a grocer and executor to Robert's will, soon became Katherine's third husband. Hers is the all too familiar story of women's lives in Tudor times, a series of marriages and children or stepchildren unlikely to reach adulthood. Plague and other deadly diseases were never far away.

When Katherine died in 1635, she left The Queen's Head to her sons. In a smaller bequest, she left to 'my loving friend Mr Moreton and Minister of Saint Saviours ... three pounds and my paire of silver haffed knyves'. Katherine, like many women of her class, was illiterate and made her mark rather than signing her will, though she might have been able to read. Her sons also received tenements in Barking near the Tower of London together with money.[4]

The following year, seeking religious freedom, the puritan John Harvard emigrated to Boston in the New World with his wife Ann, taking his large collection of 400 books. He was part of a large exodus later known as 'the Great Migration' when around 20,000 people went to America. Boston was only founded in 1630, so this truly was a New World.

It was to be a brief American life for John Harvard. He died in 1638, leaving a nuncupative (spoken) will. His books and half his estate (worth £779) were left to a newly founded school, and the rest went to his wife, who would marry again. The school

Other Wills

acknowledged such generosity by changing its name to Harvard College, which may well be familiar to readers.

Off with His Head!
Accused of plotting against James I, Sir Walter Raleigh was executed in 1618. This was a tragic end for such a brave man, who had been a writer, explorer, adventurer, poet, spy, sailor and even a pirate upon occasion. He led early expeditions to America, naming Virginia for the virgin Queen Elizabeth I, and in 1588 was one of England's heroes in the defeat of the Spanish Armada.

While Sir Walter was executed in the Tower of London, his wife Bess waited outside in a mourning carriage. Eventually his head was brought to her. She had it embalmed and for the rest of her life kept it in a red velvet bag. In 1647, it was passed to their son Carew. Family tradition says that when Lady Raleigh's young grandsons Walter and Carew died, they were buried with Sir Walter's head in St Mary's Church, West Horsley.

Off with His Head! 2
Sir Thomas More wrote *Utopia*, a book about an imaginary paradise – a world we have talked about and imagined ever since. He was also Lord Chancellor, and a friend of Henry VIII until he refused to accept the king's marriage to Anne Boleyn. Sir Thomas would not renounce his Catholic faith and was executed for treason in 1535. He could not accept Henry instead of the Pope as Head of the Church of England.

Sir Thomas's head, boiled and tarred, was placed at one end of London Bridge, which then was the only crossing over the Thames. These bloody, pickled heads were a grim reminder of the fate of anyone daring to disobey the king. Meg (Margaret) Roper, Sir Thomas's daughter, rescued his head. One account says the head was buried with her when she died, but another says it was left to her eldest daughter, Elizabeth, in 1544 and buried with her in the Roper family vault at St Dunstan's in Canterbury.

WHAT YOU MAY NOT KNOW ABOUT WILLS

A will is not legal unless it is signed by the testator and witnessed by two people. Queen Anne had not signed two wills found among her papers after her death, while Jane Austen also overlooked this detail. Later, two friends had to swear an oath that they recognised Jane's writing.

Will power ... In earlier centuries wills were most likely made by wealthier people. In the early 1900s, for example, only around one person in ten made a will.

The longest will is generally considered to be that written by Frederica Evelyn Stilwell Cook, who died in 1925 aged sixty-eight. Her will was handwritten in 1919 and extends to 1,066 pages (and more than 90,000 words). Buried in Richmond, London, she did not wish her age recorded on her tombstone, her diaries were to be burnt and her wedding ring was to be buried with her. More of an inventory than a will, the list includes buckles, furs, umbrella and parasol handles, and considerable amounts of lace and jewels. Venetian, Brussels, Maltese and Buckinghamshire lace were all carefully noted.

If you die intestate (without a will) in Cornwall, or without any next of kin, then the Duchy of Cornwall inherits under the law of *bona vacantia* or vacant goods. The duchy was created in 1337 to ensure an independent income for the monarch's eldest son, the Prince of Wales. Over a six-year period ending in 2012, £1 million came from unclaimed estates. Since 1975, a charity has distributed this money among various good causes for the South-West and Cornwall. Similar rules apply in the Duchy of Lancaster, with the same kind of charities helping to distribute the funds.

Royal wills have been 'sealed' since the early 1900s, meaning they are kept secret for ninety years. Princess Diana's will was not held to this rule, as she was no longer a royal (losing HRH status) after her divorce from Charles. The wills of Queen Elizabeth II, the Queen Mother, Princess Margaret in 2002 and the Duke of Windsor in 1972 were all sealed. When Prince Philip died in 2021, the High Court ruled that such secrecy was observed to maintain the 'dignity' of the royal family. To go to such lengths makes you wonder what secrets will one day be revealed...

The tradition of sealed wills began in 1911 with the express intention of avoiding scandal when Queen Mary applied to the High Court asking for her brother's will to be sealed. Prince Frank (Francis) of Teck died suddenly, leaving valuable family jewels known as the Cambridge emeralds to his married mistress Ellen (Nellie), Countess of Kilmorey. If made public, this terrible indiscretion on his part would have created a dreadful scandal around the royal family and so all was discreetly hushed up. Queen Mary also decided to buy back the family jewels at an eye-watering cost of £10,000.

The countess kept an emerald brooch from the set, and it was later worn by her daughter-in-law. Another heirloom, a pair of cufflinks engraved 'F. T.' for Francis of Teck, now belong to her great-grandson. As for the Cambridge emeralds, they were reset and worn by Queen Mary at her coronation in 1911 and during the state visit to India that same year. These days they are part of the Royal Collection.

GLOSSARY OF COMMON TERMS USED IN WILLS

Annuity: A sum of money paid to someone each year for the rest of their life.

Beneficiary: The person (or organisation/charity, etc.) who will receive assets from the deceased's will. A sole (or main) beneficiary inherits all – or almost all – of the estate.

Bequest (or legacy): A gift given in the will to an individual, charity or organisation

Chattels: The assets (belongings) of a person other than land. Jewellery, furniture, books and clothes can all be chattel or moveable property, but money cannot.

Codicil: An additional clause (or document) to an existing will. There may be more than one codicil and usually these are made closer to the time of death.

***Compos mentis*:** A Latin term meaning 'of sound mind', i.e. having the mental capacity to make a will. If somebody is not *compos mentis*, the will is invalid. This is why many wills begin with the phrase, 'Being of sound mind and body…'

Glossary of Common Terms Used in Wills

Entailing: Stipulating that inheritance (of a property, estate or title) is limited to certain individuals, usually to male heirs.

Estate: The property or assets of the deceased.

Executor: The person or people appointed to carry out the wishes of the deceased. This was a key role in royal wills. Joan of Kent, widow of the Black Prince, appointed sixteen executors for her will in 1385, including the Bishop of London and Bishop of Winchester. Wills in earlier centuries often saw money left for executors. Margaret, Duchess of Norfolk, who died in 1490, left a 'cup of gold' to her chief executor. Margaret Paston a few years before in 1484 appointed her son John executor, and a copy of her will plus all the notes made by John is now one of the treasures of the British Library. A female executor is an executrix.

A literary executor often holds considerable power, for example Jane Austen's sister Cassandra, who unfortunately destroyed many of Jane's letters. Queen Victoria appointed her daughter Beatrice as her literary executrix, and she spent years editing her mother's journals. When each one was finished she destroyed the original, meaning we have no idea what was changed or omitted. However, we now know that some of the letters between her parents included intimate marital details. Princess Beatrice borrowed some from the Royal Archives, later informing her nephew George VI that she had destroyed them. He replied, 'I thought you would, so I had photostat copies made before you saw them.'

Inheritance Tax: The tax paid on the deceased's estate including the current value of a house. Also known as Death Duties. In 1894, an estate duty tax (the first inheritance tax) was introduced to pay off the government's national debt of some £4 million. What a minuscule sum it seems compared to the current amount of £2.437 trillion.

In the late nineteenth and early twentieth century, inheritance tax crippled many aristocratic families. In 1938, the 9th Duke of Devonshire paid half a million while the 13th Duke of Bedford in 1953 had to either pay £4.5 million or lose Woburn Abbey. At Castle Howard, the death of a father and two sons in quick succession meant a crippling triple set of death duties. Petworth, another grand stately home (with its magnificent art collection), was given to the National Trust in lieu of inheritance tax. Hardwick Hall was another that in 1956 became part of the National Trust.

The starting level has not been raised since 2009, and will not change until 2028. Combined with increases in house prices, this means inheritance tax now applies to much of the middle class, rather than only to the wealthiest elite. It provides an impressive revenue: the amount raised in 2021 was £6.1 billion.

Intestate: If somebody has no will they are intestate. This happened to the singer Amy Winehouse, who died in 2011 aged twenty-seven. Her estate when valued for probate was nearly £3 million.

Inventory: A list of the property of the deceased person. From 1529 this was required for anyone with goods and chattels worth more than £5 and it was continued until 1782. The lists were so precise that even the cost of the clothes worn by the deceased and money in their pockets was included. No item was too small to be valued, and in the seventeenth-century inventories of individuals from St Helen's in Lancashire we find sieves, old pans and a smoothing iron: 'Earthen pottes worth ten pence owned by Jane Baxter, and for Margaret Houghton one ladder worth three pence and six pence for two sives [sic]. Elizabeth Garrnet of Bold was appraised on 28 November 1684 and owned two little old pannes and one smoothing iron, each was estimated to be worth six pence.'[1]

Glossary of Common Terms Used in Wills

Nuncupative will: A spoken will, often made by shortly before death, can be legally binding if witnesses who are present then sign a written document. Queen Charlotte dictated her will in 1818, as Queen Katherine Parr did in 1548. Another spoken will came in 1676 from Elizabeth Bee of Rugeley, Staffordshire, who declared, 'All that I have I give to George Bee my Sonne.'

Probate: The stage at which the will is 'proved' in court to become legal and valid. Often items such as jewellery are valued for probate purposes. Until January 1858, wills were proved in church courts including York and Canterbury (Wales and Scotland were dealt with separately). A will is not always written and prepared by lawyers, such as with the money given to establish the Luton and Dunstable Hospital in the early 1920s and 1930s just before the National Health Service was founded. This legacy, from Dunstable grocer Arthur Buckingham, was most appropriately written on a brown sugar bag. Donations from other wealthy locals and a public appeal by Luton's mayor raised £100,000. The hospital opened in 1939 and was considered to be the latest in modern medicine with six wards, 170 beds and a single telephone.

Proved: See 'Probate'. Often a will includes the date submitted for probate and the later date when it is 'proved' or settled. In earlier centuries it might take years before probate was granted, while more recently Covid-19 has led to long waiting times.

Testator: The person making a will. Testatrix is used for women.

Trust: Assets are given to trustees to use for the benefit of others (beneficiaries). Trusts set up for grandchildren or to help with the costs of children's education have been popular since Victorian times. A trust may continue until the beneficiary reaches a certain age, such as eighteen, twenty-one or even older. These days there is a limit to how long a trust can last, decided in the aftermath of a bizarre will in 1797 by Peter Thellusson. He decided to skip three generations before his money was distributed, but the ensuing legal challenges were long, convoluted and extremely expensive. The dispute is thought to have inspired Charles Dickens to write *Bleak House*. Eventually Peter's great-grandson Charles inherited all in 1858, including Brodsworth Hall, which Peter's great-granddaughter Pamela Williams (d. 1994) gave to English Heritage.

Appendix 1

THE WOMAN WHO STOLE OUR KING! WALLIS, DUCHESS OF WINDSOR AND HER JEWELS

> Hark the Herald Angels Sing,
> Mrs Simpson's pinched our King

A new version of 'Hark the Herald Angels Sing' was one of the popular carols at Christmas 1936. Though it begins traditionally, it is the second line that brought it bang up to date. It refers to American divorcée Mrs Wallis Simpson (*née* Warfield) and the fact that she had caught the eye of the new king, Edward VIII. He decided to give up his throne so he that could marry her, and their love affair became one of the most romantic stories of the twentieth century.

The words of the carol summed up the nation's feeling over the abdication crisis, when Edward VIII announced on the radio that he could not rule without the woman he loved by his side. A few people thought the king should be able to marry as he wished. But for many people, including most of the political establishment as well as the royal family, she was unacceptable as queen. Not only was she once divorced but she was in the process of obtaining a second divorce, clashing with all the strict moral codes and conventions of the 1930s.

Penalties for divorce applied at all levels of society. Even when the Duke of Marlborough divorced, the king asked him to resign as Lord Lieutenant. The broadcaster Joan Bakewell recalls that in the 1930s her mother would not speak to divorced women. Agatha Christie (b. 1890) as a divorcee could not present her daughter as a debutante at court. In 1931, before her court presentation, Mrs Simpson had to submit divorce papers proving she was the innocent party in the first divorce. In the early 1950s, at the Queen's coronation, more than one divorced duke enquired of the Lord Chamberlain whether they were allowed to attend.

The Early Years

The divorce hearing between Wallis and her second husband Ernest Simpson was held not in London but at Ipswich Assizes, well away from the press and public. The regional newspapers, however, were not so easily distracted, though the reporting was discreet. The *Liverpool Echo*, for instance, reported the *decree nisi* on the same day it was granted. Admittedly it was a short article buried deep inside the paper on page 12, squeezed between the results of the Newmarket horse races and 'late commercial news'. Still, anyone and everyone with London society or royal connections would know about Wallis Simpson and why she might be divorcing her second husband.

Divorce was still rare because of the legal difficulties and the social stigma. Any king of England was also Head of the Church of England, which staunchly opposed the divorce. Edward therefore had to choose either to rule or to marry Mrs Simpson. The Prime Minister, Stanley Baldwin, also informed him that the government could not condone the marriage.

The majority of the public had been kept in the dark, and when news of the relationship finally broke at the end of 1936 it came as a great shock to most. The British papers had all agreed to remain silent on the topic and those 'in the know' had to read the French and American press instead. Abroad, the story was being reported, followed (and photographed) with great interest.

There had been other mistresses, but this affair was different. At one of Edward's first engagements as king this was clear, as Wallis

Simpson attended without her husband, who until then had typically gone with her. As Prince of Wales, Edward had expected Wallis to be invited to any event he attended and was furious with Lady Londonderry on one occasion when she did not invite Wallis. In August 1935, Wallis and Edward were in Biarritz taking a cruise around the Mediterranean. They were also photographed together while skiing in Austria.

At Belvedere Fort, rooms were allocated for Mrs Simpson's use for her weekend visits. The fort was Edward's beloved house in Windsor Great Park, which he remodelled after seeing sophisticated homes in Long Island on his American tour. The interior and gardens together with swimming pool reflected the latest 1930s American style so much admired by the duke.

Mrs Simpson was always fashionable and glamorous, with that certain *je ne sais quoi*. Her wedding trousseau would include clothes and accessories by Chanel and eighteen items from Elsa Schiaparelli's 1937 collection. By 1934 she had already become a loyal customer of Cartier's London shop regardless of the expense or even the continued financial insecurity of her husband. At certain times she would send the Cartier bills to Ernest at his London office, the idea being that he would be too preoccupied by work demands to question the extravagance.[1]

Freda Dudley Ward, one of Edward's previous mistresses, had received Boucheron jewels, which perhaps explains why Wallis preferred Cartier.[1] Some of the jewellery Mrs Simpson received from him included royal family pieces. One item mentioned after the Ednam Lodge burglary some ten years later was a long pearl necklace which once belonged to Queen Alexandra. Estimated to be worth £5,000, it was, together with other items, recovered the following morning with the duchess's jewellery case. The stolen goods amounted to a value of roughly £20,000, but the thief escaped.

One gift from Edward was a Cartier engagement ring with an immense emerald (19.77 carats) bought at the dazzling cost of £10,000. By contrast, a Cartier tiara bought by his brother

George VI for his wife Elizabeth to celebrate their twentieth wedding anniversary had cost £835. Even this had been expensive at the time, but compared to the engagement ring it sounds positively cheap.² To put the cost in some kind of perspective, though from a few years later, on the outbreak of war civil servants were moved en masse from London to Colwyn Bay, Wales. To hire a room in a house cost £1 1s (a guinea), which inevitably led to their local nickname as 'guinea pigs'.

Even in the early years of their affair, the money spent on Wallis's jewels is simply breathtaking. In 1937, for example, the bills of two Paris jewellers came to £7,000.¹ One extravagant and most unusual piece for Wallis's fortieth birthday was a platinum necklace set with diamonds and an asymmetrical tassel with five rows of rubies. Designed by Van Cleef & Arpels, it was inscribed, 'My Wallis from her David 19.VI.36.' David was Edward's name among family and friends.

1936 and a Royal Crisis

The Abdication Crisis was quickly over in 1936, the year of three kings. After George V died, Edward VIII was proclaimed but never crowned. Then his younger brother became George VI. The news broke during October, and all was done and dusted by mid-December. The abdication document was signed at Fort Belvedere, with a financial settlement to buy out Edward's interest in Balmoral and Sandringham at more than £300,000 (around £10 million today), together with an annuity of £25,000. Only later did George VI discover that his brother, who pleaded poverty during those discussions, had already received £1 million from his Duchy of Cornwall revenues.

There was resentment on both sides. Edward felt badly treated by his family, claiming he had hardly enough money to survive. This partly explains why he was tempted in the early 1950s to write his memoirs, for which he was offered a fee of £500,000. The book was a bestseller and serialised by the *Daily Express*. There was no real resolution to the dispute between the brothers, who were once such devoted friends. Edward could not keep his beloved Fort Belvedere, and soon after the abdication its contents were delivered to him in the south of France. Many years later, when James Pope-Hennessy visited the Windsors in France, the duke said his mother Queen Mary always refused to discuss the abdication.[3] Mother and son did not meet again until 1945, nearly nine years after the crisis.[4]

The coronation planned for May 1937 went ahead, albeit with Edward's younger brother George VI being the man who was crowned. It was too late to stop the production of countless souvenirs, including a modern-looking half-pint mug in pale cream. Edward's head is the open top of the mug. His face, in profile, is on the side of the mug – and for many years it was the toothbrush holder for at least one irreverent family. He looks every inch a handsome and proud king of England. Instead, however, he went with Wallis into exile while the couple awaited her divorce. Lawyers said they must live apart, Edward in Austria and Wallis in France, until the divorce went through. Otherwise, it might be compromised and the decree declared invalid. The divorce arrived in June, the month after George's coronation.

The French government later generously offered the couple a home in Paris. For the wedding, in the spirit of *entente cordiale*, a number of souvenir First Day Covers were published to commemorate the wedding. Needless to say, few if any celebrations were held in England.

A Wedding in France

Designed by Mainbocher, Mrs Simpson's wedding dress was a pale blue called 'Wallis blue'. Slim-fitting and elegant, with a bodice buttoned to the neck and long sleeves, it was worn with a halo hat which together with the gloves and shoes matched the colour of the dress. Many American department stores quickly commissioned their own copies of the dress. In 1950, she gave the dress to the Metropolitan Museum in New York; by then the glorious blue had faded into cream.

The new Duchess of Windsor was not given the title of HRH – Her Royal Highness – nor did anyone from the royal family attend the wedding, creating only more coolness. The wedding was a quiet but happy affair, with fewer than twenty guests for the ceremony and an evening dinner. A villa hired near Biarritz was taken on a ten-year lease and the Windsors began to enjoy their new life. In spring 1938, one of the trickiest questions of etiquette was whether or not ladies should curtsey to the duchess. It was required when greeting an HRH, but of course Wallis was not afforded this title.[4]

The War Years and After

The Windsors expected to return to England, but except for the duration of the Second World War, when the duke was Governor of the Bahamas, France would be their home. In Paris a grand villa in the Bois de Boulogne was given to the couple at a peppercorn rent by the nation, and the duke was granted tax-free status. The Windsors' dinner parties, lunches and weekend stays were famous. The duchess was a thoughtful hostess and the couple were both popular.

Their friends became known as the 'Windsor Circle'. In effect, they became Paris royalty. They were seen at every important event, such as the 1958 concert by Maria Callas. The duchess often dressed in Dior and Givenchy, receiving the ultimate compliment from Christian Dior as he invented a dark purple-blue especially to match the colour of her eyes.

The gifts of expensive jewels from the duke continued, and even their pet pugs ate from solid silver bowls. Extended trips to America, evening parties, dancing, nightclubs, lunch, weekend guests, playing bridge and canasta – this was exactly how the duke and duchess wished to spend their time. Portofino in Italy was one of the places they loved visiting. To an outsider such an existence seems lacking in purpose, but then, as now, many enjoyed such a life.

Though each of them published an autobiography, and the duke kept an immense number of books, neither was bookish. There were certain exceptions, such as at Christmas 1945 when copies of the bestseller *In Pursuit of Love* were sent to all their friends as presents, evidently amusing author Nancy Mitford, who suddenly found herself famous. (The book sold an astounding 200,000 copies that first year.)

New York was an annual highlight, Apartment 28 at the exclusive Waldorf Astoria being their home from home every year from 1940 to 1960. In 1957, when their royal suite was needed for the state visit of the duke's niece Queen Elizabeth, the hotel excelled itself in diplomacy. A special suite on the same floor was created and set aside for the Windsors. The duchess insisted the rooms were decorated in her favourite blue colour with matching re-upholstered armchairs. Even the cushions had portraits of their beloved pugs stitched in needlepoint.

When in France the duke loved to play golf (invariably he used the long French lunchtime when the golf course was almost empty) and enjoyed gardening at their weekend retreat. The duchess probably was happiest in Paris (or on trips to New York) as she preferred haute couture clothes, hats and handbags, gloves and of course designer shoes such as those handmade by Salvatore Ferragamo. Always, always, *très élégante*. As her friend Diana Mosley said, it was an indoor rather than an outdoor hunting, shooting and fishing life. 'The Duchess never wore gumboots.' Simply unthinkable. Wallis was always conscious of fashion, eager to be the most stylish woman in the room. The duke was also a fashion icon, and by a strange quirk of fate his expensive Savile Row suits gained a new lease of life when they were auctioned in Paris and bought by Charlie Watts, drummer of the Rolling Stones. The checked suit and a pink suit were his favourites and in the modern photos they are just as eye-catching as they must have been when worn by the duke.

Le Moulin, a Weekend Retreat

The duchess once admitted, 'I adore to shop.' She took French lessons though the duke never would, preferring to speak Spanish or German. Le Moulin, a converted eighteenth-century mill near Versailles, became their weekend house. It was the only house they ever owned outright. The garden was so large it could absorb the duke's passion for creating an English garden, designed by Russell Page and worked by five gardeners. It took three years to complete the renovations and repairs necessary to make the house their own and to build the guest accommodation.

Their weekend journey was a short drive out from Paris and made in grand style. The staff would drive ahead to get the house ready for guests. Later, the duke would drive his Chevrolet while the duchess drove a striking blue Cadillac. It was friends rather than family that occupied their lives as there were no children or stepchildren. Visits to England were few and far between.

Quite early, by the end of the 1930s, both Prime Minister Neville Chamberlain and King George VI were considering reconciliation. The duke's younger brother the Duke of Gloucester and his wife stopped in Paris on their way back from Kenya to meet the Windsors. Dinner at a smart restaurant was to be the sounding board, but when the talks were reported by the British press the public response was almost entirely negative. The idea was quickly abandoned. Alice, Duchess of Gloucester later recalled how upsetting it was to receive so many critical letters from the public.

Diamonds and Pearls

Many of the jewels Wallis received were special commissions from the duke. He was closely involved with their design, spending hours discussing the details. Often these were dramatic statement jewels which could not fail to impress, though some considered them too showy to be in good taste. In any case, they made a bold statement: I can afford the very best jewellery. Fashions in jewellery move on just as they do in clothing, and some were reset or refashioned, as with the Cartier emerald engagement ring in 1958.

The duchess's favourite stones were sapphires and rubies, and she also collected yellow and canary diamonds. Whether some were family heirlooms from Edward's grandma Alexandra is unclear. Certainly, the duke was her favourite grandson and she had wished to leave jewels for his wife when he did marry.[3] Michael Nash's suggestion is that he received uncut stones rather than actual jewellery, and these were used for some items.

According to Michael Nash, Queen Alexandra (d. 1925) did not make a will because she distrusted lawyers, making it virtually impossible to prove or disprove which jewels belonged to whom.[3] Suzy Menkes in *The Royal Jewels* featured the Wallis Collection and in doing so expressed the view that the duchess should leave her jewels to the royal family,[2] thereby making amends for the past. Instead, there was an auction.

Surely if the duke wished for the jewels to be given to the royal family this would have been mentioned in his will. He must have considered the ultimate fate of the jewels. His will was sealed in 1972, so we do not know what he wrote.[3] The will was 'unsealed' in 2017 for the Royal Archive, but this was only done to establish who owned copyright of his letters for the hugely popular Netflix drama *The Crown*.

The duchess lived on in Paris for another fourteen years, but truly this was a miserable shadowland for her. She experienced a long and steady decline in her health, suffering strokes and eventually dementia. By the end of her life she was a recluse, bedridden and surrounded not by friends or family but by doctors and nurses, a few loyal servants and her dragon of a French lawyer.

Wallis, Duchess of Windsor was nearly ninety when she died in 1986. After a Paris ceremony with full honours, her coffin was brought to England. Queen Elizabeth, the Queen Mother, Prince Charles and Princess Diana, and Prime Minister Margaret Thatcher attended the funeral. It was a simple ceremony at St George's Chapel in Windsor Castle. The duchess did not wish for a funeral address, so with a final blessing by the Archbishop of Canterbury her coffin was taken to Frogmore, where the duke was buried. This resting place was just a few miles from Belvedere Fort, where they had first lived together in the 1930s.

Sale of the Century

It was the duchess's fearsome lawyer, Suzanne Blum, who organised the sale of the jewellery, declaring it was in the will. However, in his book *Royal Wills*, expert Michael Nash[3] is less than certain that the duchess did make a will. There was considerable media debate at the time about whether any jewels were royal heirlooms until Buckingham Palace issued a statement to say such jewels, together with ceremonial Garter robes and decorations, had been returned after the duke's death.

An auction was held by Sotheby's in April 1987, French law requiring that it take place within twelve months of the death of the duchess. A large red and white tent pitched outside the exclusive Beau Rivage Hotel in Geneva was the site of a two-day sale. It was quite a jamboree, with 1,000 wealthy bidders present and a further 600 in New York. The jewels had been kept in Morocco leather boxes stamped with the duchess's monogram. So great was their value that the pre-sale inventory took place inside the Banque de France, where the jewels were stored.[5]

Even in the early days, when forced to flee England during the Abdication Crisis, Mrs Simpson's jewellery was worth £100,000. Lord Brownlow had been asked to take Mrs Simpson to a secret destination in the south of France and began the journey in Edward's Buick. Only on reaching Dieppe did he discover that all the jewels were with them – an added responsibility on what became a nightmare journey as they were accompanied only by a single Scotland Yard detective and Edward's chauffeur for a two-day drive across France. It became a desperate struggle to avoid the pursuing reporters and photographers.[6]

The press was not just pursuing but waiting up ahead as well, a crowd lay in ambush at the villa gates in hopes of taking a photo of Mrs Simpson as she arrived at their destination. The term *paparazzi* was yet to be invented to describe a determined pack of chasing photographers, but it was very much in evidence here as they all hoped to capture and publish *the* photo of Wallis Simpson.

At the Geneva auction, the highest price paid for a single piece was nearly £2 million for a 31-carat diamond ring. Actress Elizabeth Taylor, a friend of the Windsors, bought a diamond brooch she had long admired, designed in the shape of the Prince of Wales's heraldic badge of *fleurs-de-lys*. Also on sale were the panther bracelet made by Cartier for the Windsors' twentieth wedding anniversary, a wildly ostentatious flamingo brooch, Queen Mary's pearl necklace (which came from the Russian royal family) and the duchess's large emerald engagement ring. Many years later, in 2010, the magnificent onyx-and-diamond panther bracelet sold for a far higher price of £4,521,250, making it the most expensive Cartier piece at that time.

The auction raised the immense sum of £31 million, six times what had been expected. The money was mostly given to the Pasteur Institute for Research, a world leader in AIDS research, which announced it was the largest sum it had ever received. There were other charity bequests, but the Pasteur Institute was the main beneficiary. The donation included a proviso that the money should not contribute, either directly or indirectly, to vivisection. The duchess's private papers went to her secretary, Johanna Schutz, while some valuable Louis XVI furniture, paintings and porcelain were destined for the Palace of Versailles.[7]

The American Duchess

For many Britons of the 1930s, Wallis Simpson was the woman who stole our king. Though their romance proved to be lifelong, public opinion was always against her. A letter to Queen Elizabeth (later the Queen Mother) from her friend Maggie Greville included a joke about a new hat called 'the Wallis – because it was shady, with no crown'.

Later the duchess became known as the 'American Duchess'. But was she really the villain of the story? Perhaps we should consider her own humorous words, which are today painted on the living room wall at their weekend retreat, Le Moulin (The

Mill): 'I may not be the miller's daughter but I've certainly been through the mill.'

Now, some ninety years later ... déjà vu. Here we are again, watching another American duchess creating similar controversy after marrying Prince Harry. Harry and Meghan's romance and fairy-tale wedding, then the birth of a son, was rapidly followed by a decision to leave royal life. First came a move to Canada and then, just ahead of the Covid-19 lockdown of 2020, there was a move to California and the arrival of a second child. Almost all of it has unfolded in the harsh public spotlight. Some called it Megxit, a Brexit-related epithet that puts responsibility for the move on Megan. And like the Duke of Windsor, Prince Harry has released a memoir (with a reported advance of $20 million) and has fallen out with his brother, who was once his best friend. At the time of writing, it remains unclear whether or not the queen's death in 2022 can heal this family quarrel and usher in a reunion.

We must wait to see if history is any kinder to the Duchess of Sussex than it was to Wallis, Duchess of Windsor.

Appendix 2

NORTHAMPTON WILLS: WOMEN'S VOICES FROM THE FIFTEENTH CENTURY

A coverlet of grene with rede lyons and whyte ... my best scarlet kyrtyll [petticoat] and my best blewe gown furrid ... a great brass pott ...

Joan Getyn, widow, 6 May, 1503[1]

Every will tells a story, and those from fifteenth-century Northampton highlight pious concerns, devotion to the church, gifts of clothes and household goods – all the typical bequests made by women at this time. Most of the early wills in this collection were written in Latin by scribes. Apart from three wives, most of the wills belong to widows. Sometimes, we find some directions as to burial. Joan Ball, who had been married twice, asked in her will to be buried beside her first husband. Meanwhile, Ricardina Mose in her will writes about a 'natural daughter', a phrase used then for an illegitimate child.

Northampton was a small, bustling town during the fifteenth century, with many of the same trades found in large cities such as York and London. Merchants and butchers, dyers and weavers, tanners, bakers and shoemakers are among the occupations we discover in the wills. There were the essential brewers, too. Life seems to have been comfortable enough for some, with feather beds mentioned in some wills, but still many poorer families lived cheek by jowl with well-off neighbours.

In the wills we find several sums of money that illustrate local traditions. For instance, the high altar of a church might receive twelve pence (over in a village in East Norfolk it was six pence). While an executor might receive anything between three and twenty shillings for their efforts in making sure the will was honoured.

Evident in the wills is the significant role played by women, who almost always are named as executrix by husbands. Sometimes when a father left money to sons and daughters the girls received an equal share, which might be five marks (a mark was 13s 4d) or more. A daughter might receive as much as 100 shillings.

Jewellery is only mentioned in sixteen wills, illustrating how little was owned. Northampton was essentially a working town, and bequests are far more concerned with devotion and piety. Rosaries and rosary beads of coral, jet or amber were popular bequests for a daughter, goddaughter or granddaughter. Even a single bead might be handed down.

Nine churches within the town are mentioned as well as various religious establishments close by including St John's Hospital, the Cluniac Delapré Abbey and Convent, and the Augustinian St James's Abbey. Another Cluniac site was St Andrew's Priory. Joan Ball left four pence to each of the nuns at Delapré Abbey, which was built in 1145. Possibly she had a sister, aunt, niece or cousin living there as a nun.

Cloth is often mentioned in the wills, and in some even the varieties bequeathed are noted. This is not so surprising when one considers that Northampton was closely involved in the wool trade. The town was well known for the skill of its dyers and had a guild of weavers. Indeed, the work done in Northampton was of such superior quality that it is thought cloth was sent from London to be dyed there. The wills mention velvet and worsted; wool, tapestry and silk; painted cloth and linen; diaper, which was linen woven with a diamond pattern and used for towels and table linen; coarse cloth including russet, lawn, hemp and frieze; flax and musterdelevers.

The last mentioned, musterdelevers, is from the town of Montivilliers in Normandy. A mixed grey woollen cloth, it was hardwearing, practical and useful for cloaks, jackets or gowns. Sometimes the colour of gowns mentioned provides us with an idea of what was popular. Black, used of course for mourning, was the most expensive dye to produce and therefore clearly signalled that the wearer was wealthy. Other colours indicate a brighter, deeper spectrum of colours than we might have imagined, with blue and crimson, green and rose, mulberry and russet, scarlet and tawny, violet, and a red known as sangwyn.

In most cases men leave one or two items of clothing, and the same is generally true of women. One assumes that if possible much would be dispersed before someone died, with the rest being covered in the will. One exception is Lady Isabel Peche (d. 1479), a wealthy widow who kept her own chapel. Her will includes expensive silk gowns that were furred, as well as two gowns for her servants:

> ... to Alice Torey, my servant, my black gown. Item I bequeath to Alice Johnson, also my servant, my green gown lined with buckram [a stiff cotton cloth] with black velvet around the collar ...

Trimmed with Fur

Furs were fashionable, used to trim cloaks and dresses. Not only were they warm during cold winters but they were objects of conspicuous wealth; someone with a fur-trimmed gown was clearly well off. One can imagine pieces of fur were rarely discarded but transferred to decorate new clothes. Furs mentioned include black bouge (sheepskin) and lambskin on a black gown, given by Agnes Clerke to her sister Joan Bennett. Others are squirrel, otter and polecat, pine marten, fox and beaver. In Cornish wills from between 1342 and 1540, similar types of fur are mentioned: marten, bouge, polecat, squirrel, and miniver or white fur.[2] Rabbit fur was also used; Henry VII ordered black rabbit fur from Norfolk as a luxurious way to line his nightgowns.

In medieval times there were things called sumptuary laws that restricted which social classes could wear certain colours and styles of clothing, and also the type of fur they could use. However, those lower down the social scale with sufficient income were often as keen to wear the same expensive clothes and furs as the nobility. Citizen's wives and daughters in the City of London were known to show off the same luxury clothes and fine jewels as the ladies at court. Trade might make a family extremely prosperous, and a successful merchant (or lord mayor) could even achieve a better income than a nobleman. Sylvia Thrupp's review highlights such evidence from merchant wills, which include large and varied amounts of rich clothes and jewels mentioned as bequests.[3]

Below are extracts from some Northampton wills from the period discussed.

I Bequeath My Soul to God Almighty: Joan Ball of Northampton, 1473

In the name of God Amen the 7th day of February 1473 I Joan Ball, wife of Simon Ball of Northampton, brasier [a worker in brass], in sound mind and good memory make my testament in this wise. First, I bequeath my soul to Almighty God, to the Blessed Mary His Mother and all the saints of the court of heaven, my body to be buried in the chapel of the fraternity of Corpus Christi in the church of All Saints, Northampton, next to the grave of William Wellys, mercer [merchant], my late husband.

Item I bequeath to the fraternity of the said chapel 6s 8d. Item I bequeath to the high altar of the said church 3s 4d. Item I bequeath to the fraternity of St George in the same church 12d. Item I bequeath to the fraternity of the Holy Cross in the same church 12d. Item I bequeath to the fraternity of St John the Baptist in the same church 12d. Item I bequeath to the fabric of the church of St Michael in the town of Northampton 3s 4d. Item I bequeath to the fraternity of St Thomas the Martyr of the almshouse near to the south gate of Northampton twenty ells [a length of cloth of 45 inches] of linen cloth. Item I bequeath to each order of mendicant brothers in the town of Northampton 20d. Item I bequeath to the Abbess of the monastery of Delapré near Northampton 12d and each nun of the said house 4d. Item I bequeath to one suitable chaplain to celebrate in the church of All Saints in the town of Northampton for the health of my soul and the souls of the said William Wellys and Simon Ball and Alice, former wife of the said Simon, my husband, and the souls of our parents and the souls of all the faithful departed £20 of good and legal English money. Item I bequeath to John, my son, 20 marks of good and legal English money. Item I bequeath to Joan, my daughter, ten pounds of legal money ...

Joan Ball, wife of Simon Ball, brasier, 7 February, 1473, proved 23 March, 1473 in the church of the Hospital of St John, Northampton

Clothes and Household Stuff

... I bequeath to Joan Dyve, my natural daughter, one gown of crimson dye furred. Item I bequeath to the said Joan another gown of blue colour furred and another gown of russet furred with 'le blak shankys' [fur from the lower legs of animals].

Item I bequeath to the same Joan Dyve, my daughter, one feather[bed] and one mattress. Item I give and bequeath to the said Joan Dyve, my daughter, two covers, one white and the other green and two pairs of blankets and four pairs of sheets, one bolster and four pillows, one large money box, one chest ... I bequeath to the same one rosary of jet and a pater noster [lord's prayer] of silver and gilt.

Item I bequeath to the same Joan Dyve one large brass pot and one large brass dish bound with iron...

Ricardina Mose, wife of Robert Mose, 12 January 1473

... Item I bequeath to Margaret Knyghton and the use of her children one three gallon brass pot and one four gallon pan. Item I bequeath to Emma Clerke one bed, that is to say one mattress, one pair of sheets and one coverlet and two pillows ...

Em[...] Whyte, widow, 1 August 1491

A Woman's Will

... to the same Thomas my son six silver spoons, my best bowl and ewer of laten [an alloy of metal resembling brass] and one bed cover of green colour. Item, I bequeath to Agnes Sheparde, my daughter, six of my best sheep and one three gallon brass bowl and my best vessel called in English a great brass pan, one pair of best sheets, one cloth and towel of diaper, which vessel, bowl, sheets, cloth and towel are in the care of the said William Bull, my son ...

Alice Bull, widow, 19 November 1494

Item I bequeath [to the wife] of my sayd brother my beste gown of vyolet ingreyn furred ...

Alice Wynge, wife of William Wynge, 4 September 1495

... Item I bequeath to Agnes, the wife of Thomas Hancock, my gown of blue colour ornamented with silver and gold and gilt and one set of coral rosary beads with gold and silver. Item I bequeath to Agnes Byrde, my cousin, one set of round jet rosary beads with silver, one girdle [belt] ornamented with silver, one brass pot holding four gallons, one other brass pot holding one gallon, one brass pot holding 18 gallons, one basin with a metal ewer, one hallying [wall hanging of fabric] painted with pictures of the saints, namely St John the Baptist, St Christopher and John the Evangelist ...

Margaret Hancock, widow, 20 August 1480

... Item I bequeath to Agnes my dowghter a cowcher [mattress] one of the best and a bolster to the same a peyre [pair] of shets [sheets] a peyre of blankets a coverlet of grene with rede lyons and whyte [with red lions and white] ... a pleyne tabull cloth [plain table cloth] ... my best scarlet kyrtyll [kirtle or petticoat] and my best blewe gown furrid [furred] ... a great brass pott ...

Joan Getyn, widow, 6 May 1503

Appendix 3

THE WILL OF LADY MARGARET BEAUFORT

Lady Margaret Beaufort (1443–1509), mother of Henry VII and grandmother of Henry VIII, founded two Cambridge colleges. Both Christ's (founded 1505) and St John's (founded 1511) acknowledge Lady Margaret as founder, and both used her coat of arms, crest and motto. The work at St John's had not yet begun when Lady Margaret died in 1509, and she left a codicil to her will ensuring the executors would continue to establish the college. A portrait of Margaret, painted shortly after her death, can still be found at St John's. We see a striking, determined-looking woman with strong features, dressed plainly in a nun's black clothes with a white headdress covering her hair. Shown in pious prayer, she is nonetheless beside a richly covered altar and an expensive illuminated manuscript.

The original purpose for priests at colleges was to pray for the founder and their family, alongside educating new Catholic priests. Both colleges prospered, and by 1545 St John's had 152 fellows and scholars. Christ's, meanwhile, previously known as God's House, was moved to a new site in 1505. A sumptuous new gatehouse was built, proclaiming itself Lady Margaret's most generous gift. It still stands today, displaying her coat of arms and her statue above.

Margaret also encouraged her son Henry VII to complete King's College Chapel, which had been started before the Tudor dynasty by Henry VI, and so the heraldic symbols of the Tudor rose and the Beaufort white greyhound were added to the chapel. On the gatehouse at Christ's and at St John's a watchful eye can still spot the Beaufort yales (mythical creatures that look like antelopes).

A Pious Life

Lady Margaret lived a most pious, devout life, taking a vow of chastity in 1499 with the permission of her fourth husband, Thomas Stanley, Earl of Derby. Her day began at five o'clock when she said prayers with one of her gentlewomen. A book of hours is mentioned in her will which now belongs to St John's College. Given to Lady Anne Shirley on her wedding to Sir Ralph Vernon, a member of Lady Margaret's household, it includes the words, 'My good Lady Shirley ... to pray for me.' Margaret's French books, including Froissart's *Chronicles*, were left to her grandson Henry VIII, and her passion for reading perhaps explains why Lady Margaret owned two pairs of gold-rimmed spectacles that are recorded in the inventory of her possessions after her death.

Her collection of over fifty religious books was bequeathed to Christ's College, though we know she also owned less devout texts including Chaucer's *Canterbury Tales*. Peter Coss highlights the existence of pious women's reading circles, noting Lady Margaret's commission to Wynkyn de Worde in 1494 to print *Scale of Perfection* by the mystic Walter Hilton. The book was presented jointly with her daughter-in-law Queen Elizabeth to Mary Roos, lady-in-waiting to both women.[1]

As well as financial support to the colleges, Margaret's piety was expressed by her role as the main patron for the rebuilding of Great St Mary's, Cambridge's university church in Market Square.

Black Velvet and Ermine

After her son became king, Lady Margaret divided her time between her estates in the Midlands and court, where her

London household boasted as many as two hundred retainers. The inventory of her belongings when she died reveals a sumptuous wardrobe including seven black velvet dresses; some were trimmed with ermine, the most expensive fur, which was only worn by royalty.[2]

Lady Margaret's will refers to her as a princess, and clearly this is how she regarded herself through her own royal descent and her marriage to Edmund Tudor, half-brother of Henry VI. Some of her later letters are signed 'Margaret R' (for *Regina* or queen). Her own royal descent came from her grandfather John Beaufort, who was the eldest child of John of Gaunt, son of Edward III.

Assuming her son Henry VII would survive her, he was named as main executor of the will. However, he died in April 1509, a few months before his mother, with Henry VIII crowned between the two deaths. Lady Margaret's income was estimated to be £3,000 each year as well as around £15,000 in goods. This was a vast fortune when compared to the £800 John Spencer spent the year before to buy Althorp House and its estate of 13,000 acres in Northampton.

Lady Margaret wished to be buried in Westminster Abbey, the most important monastery in London. Fortunately, she did not know nor could have ever imagined that her grandson Henry VIII would banish the Catholic faith, breaking with the Pope and a thousand years of history to drive England forward as a Protestant country. Thereafter, there was a rapid seesaw over religion as Henry's son Edward VI avidly continued with the Protestant faith while his successor Mary I favoured a Catholic revival. Only through the long reign of Elizabeth I did England enter into a sustained period as a Protestant country.

Lady Margaret's main residence at Collyweston, Northamptonshire later belonged to her great-granddaughter Elizabeth I (who only visited once, during a progress of 1566). Apart from a tithe barn, little has survived of Collyweston, though we know it had a grand chapel with a choir of nineteen children and twenty-four men. Demolished in 1640, all that remain are traces of the garden terraces, the boundary of the park and the site of the fishponds, which were an essential source of fresh fish for any large household.

Queen Elizabeth's School in Wimborne was also founded by Lady Margaret. Her mother and father were buried at Wimborne Minster, and a chantry was established there to say Masses for his soul forever. In Margaret's elaborate will, the priest was requested to 'teach Grammar freely to all' and lands were allocated to cover the expense. In 1563, her great-granddaughter Elizabeth I confirmed the arrangements for a school to be known as Queen Elizabeth's School.

To the Ryngers of the Bells

Lady Margaret made detailed provision in her will for the long journey south, nearly 100 miles in all, for her burial at Westminster Abbey:

> We bequeath to the curate of ev'y church where our body shall reste at nyght 3 shillings 4 pence. And to the wardens and parishners of ev'ry such church to the'use of the same church 10 shillings in money and 2 torches. And to the ryngers of the bells of ev'ry suche church 3 shillings 4 pence.

In the event, it was hardly any procession at all as she died in London after attending Henry VIII's coronation. With impeccable timing, she died a day after her grandson's eighteenth birthday. One of her illuminated prayer books and a travelling chest can be seen at the abbey among the exhibits in the Queen's Diamond Jubilee Galleries.

Below are some extracts from her will:

> In the name of ALMIGHTY GOD, Amen. We Margarete Countess of Richmond and Derby, Moder [mother] to the most excellent Prince King Henry the VIIth, by the grace of GOD King of England and of France, and Lorde of Irelande, our most dear Son, have

The Will of Lady Margaret Beaufort

called to our remembrance the unstabilnesse of this transitory worlde, and that every creature here lyving is mortall, and the tyme and place of deth to every creature uncerteyn. And also calling to our remembrance the great rewards of eternal life that every Christen creature in stedfast faith of holy church shall save for their goode deeds done by theym in their present life, We therefore being of hole and goode mynde, etc., the VI day of Juyn, the yere of our LORD GOD a thousand five hundredth and eight, and in the XXIII yere of the reigne of our saide most dere son the King, make, ordeyn [ordain], and declare, our testament and last will, in manner and form following, that is to saye, First, we gif and bequeath our soule to Almighty God, to our blissed Lady Seynt Mary the Virgin, and to all the holy company in heven. And our body to be buried in the monastery of Seynt Peter of Westminster ... And to the bells ryngars the tyme of our enerment [interment], 16 shillings 8 pence ...

Item, we will that our executors geve [give] to every of our household servants 8 pence for every day, for their costs, to bringe them fro' Westminster unto the place where our household shall be kepte aftir our decesse [decease] for the space of a quarter of a yere [year] ...

And also to cont [count] and pay to every of our household servants, bothe man and woman, their wages for oon [one] halfe yere next after our decesse, as well to them that will departe within the quarter aftir our decesse, as to theym that will tarry and bide togider [together] in household during all the same quarter ...

We make and ordeyn our executors Richard Bishop of Wynchester, John Bishop of Rochester, my Lord Herbert the King's Chamberlayn, Sir Thomas Lovell, Tresuror of the King's household, Sir Henry Marney Chauncellar of the Duchie of Lancaster, Sir John Seynt John our Chamberlain (and Lady Margaret's step-brother), Henry Horneby our Chauncellor, Sir Hugh Asshton Comptroller of our household ...

... by reason thereof have founded and established in the same place a college, called Crist's college, of a maister, 12 scolers [scholars] felowes, and 47 scolers disciples there, to be perpetually founden and brough up in lernyng, virtue, and connying according to such statuts and ordynaunces and we have made and shall make for the same ...

Be it remembered, That it was also the last will of the saide Princesse to dissolve the hospital of Seynt John in Cambridgge, and to alter and to founde thereof a college of seculer persones; that is to say, a maister and fifty feolers and divers servants; and newe to bielde [build] the said college and sufficiently to endowe the same, with londs [lands] and tenements, aftir the maner and forme of other colleges in Cambridge; and to furnysshe the same, as well in the chapel, library, pantre, and kechen, with books and all other things necessary for the same. And to the performance whereof, the saide Princesse willed, among other things that hir executors should take the yflues, revenues, and profits of hir londs and tenements put in feoffament in the counties of Devonshire, Somersettshire, and Northamptonshire, etc ...

Also the said Princesse willed, that saide manor of Malton, in the shire of Cambrige, whiche belongeth to the said Crist's College should be sufficiently bielded and repayred, at hir coste and charge soo that the said maister and scolers may resort thidder, and there to tary in tyme of contagiouse seknes [sickness] at Cambrige, and exercise their learning and studies ...

Also the said Princesse willed, that all hir plate, juells, vestments, aulterclothes, books, hangyngs, and other necessarys belonging to hir chapel in the tyme of hir decesse, and not otherwise bequeathed, should be divided between hir said colleges of Criste and Seynt John, by the discrecion of hir executors ...[3]

NOTES

Introduction
1. Fraser, Antonia, *The Weaker Vessel: Woman's Lot in Seventeenth Century England* (Weidenfeld & Nicolson, 1984).
2. As found in the Lakenheath Anglo-Saxon burials, Suffolk, BBC Two, *Meet the Ancestors*, first broadcast 1999.
3. Fell, Christine, Clark, Cecily and Williams, Elizabeth, *Women in Anglo-Saxon England and the Impact of 1066* (British Museum, 1984); Whitelock, Dorothy (ed.), *Anglo-Saxon Wills* (Cambridge University Press, 1930).
4. Northamptonshire Archives and Heritage, Archdeaconry Court of Northampton Wills, Administrations and Inventories, and accounts. Mary Vickers, Spinster, 1631, Duston, nuncupative, Second Series Will and Inventory, Book, Box K, folio/page 23. With permission.
5. Hine, Reginald L., *Relics of an Un-common Attorney* (London: J. M. Dent & Sons, 1945).

1 In the Beginning with the Anglo-Saxons and Slaves
1. Whitelock, Dorothy, *Anglo-Saxon Wills* (Cambridge University Press, 1930) with permission; Telford, Lydia, *Women in Medieval England* (Amberley, 2018).

2. Parts of All Saints Church at Wing, Buckinghamshire are a rare Saxon survival from the seventh century and originally named for St Birinus, first Bishop of Dorchester; Saxon churches exist at Brixworth, Northamptonshire and Bradford-on-Avon.
3. St Edmundsbury Charters dated 1000–1002, S 1486 (stedmundsburychronicle.co.uk); Aethelflaed's will dated 1000 or 1002.
4. Tollerton, Linda, *Wills and Will-making in Anglo-Saxon England* (York Medieval Press, 2011).
5. Loyn, H. R., *Anglo Saxon England and the Norman Conquest* (Routledge, 1991, 2nd edn); Lester-Makin, Alexandra, *The Lost Art of the Anglo-Saxon World: The Sacred and the Secular Power of Embroidery* (Oxbow Books, 2019).
6. Pitts, M. W., New Causewayed Enclosure near Oxford, *British Archaeology Journal*, 145 (2015).
7. Owen-Crocker, Gale R., *Dress in Anglo-Saxon England* (Boydell, 2010 edn). Lecture given at Sutton Hoo, *Anglo-Saxon Woman, Women, Womanhood* (June 2018); *Digging Up Britain*, BBC 4 Programme (2016).
8. Emma died in Winchester and is buried at the Old Minster alongside King Canute. See O'Brien, Harriet, *Queen Emma and the Vikings: The Woman Who Shaped the Events of 1066* (Bloomsbury, 2005).
9. Wood, Michael, *The Essay: Anglo-Saxon Portraits – Wynflaed* (BBC Radio 3, 2013).
10. Whitelock, Dorothy (ed.), *The Will of Aethelgifu, A 10th Century Anglo-Saxon Manuscript* (Oxford University Press, 1968); Hagen, Ann, Aethelgifu's Will, *The Bedfordshire Magazine*, 25 (1995), pp. 102-105.
11. The will was sold at Sotheby's in London in 1969, bought by the Scheide Library, Princeton University.
12. British Library's 2019 exhibition, *Anglo-Saxon Kingdoms: Art, Word, War*.

13. Reproduced in *St Albans Abbey Newsletter*, 7 June 1993.
14. Stenton, Frank, *Anglo-Saxon England* (Oxford University Press, 1943); Mitchell, Barbara, Anglo-Saxon Double Monasteries, *History Today*, 45 (10) (1995).
15. Cooper, Kate, *Band of Angels: The Forgotten World of Early Christian Women* (London: Atlantic Books, 2014); Yorke, Barbara, *Nunneries and the Anglo-Saxon Royal Houses* (Bloomsbury, 2003).
16. Ellison, Clare, *St Hilda of Whitby* (The Catholic Printing Company of Farnworth, 1964).
17. Stenton, Doris Mary, *The English Woman in History* (London: George Allen & Unwin, 1957).
18. Lapidge, Michael, Blair, John, Keynes, Simon and Scragg, Donald (eds), *The Wiley Blackwell Encyclopaedia of Anglo-Saxon England* (Wiley and Sons, 2014, 2nd edn).
19. Hagen, Ann, Aethelgifu's Will. *The Bedfordshire Magazine* (1995), vol 25, pp102–105.
20. Sawyer Charter no. 1482, The Will of Abba the Reeve. (https://esawyer.lib.cam.ac.uk/charter/1482.html)

2 Wives, Widows and a Thief Called Cutpurse Moll

1. Power, Eileen, *Medieval English Nunneries: c. 1275 to 1535* (Cambridge University Press, 1922).
2. Oliva, Marilyn, *The Convent and the Community in Late Medieval England: Female Monasteries in the Diocese of Norwich, 1350-1540* (Boydell and Brewer, 1998). For the Countess of Devon see note 8.
3. Nicolas, Nicholas Harris, *Testamenta Vetusta: Being Illustrations from Wills, of Manners, Customs etc. As Well as the Descents and Professions of Many Distinguished Families from the Reign of Henry the Second to the Accession of Queen Elizabeth Volume 1* (Nichols & Sons, 1826).
4. Reynolds, Philip L., and Witte, John (eds), *To Have and to Hold: Marrying and its Documentation in Western Christendom 400-1600* (Cambridge University Press, 2007); Rollo-Koster, J. and

Reyerson, K. L. (eds), *For the Salvation of my Soul: Women and Wills in Medieval and Early Modern France* (St Andrews Studies in French History and Culture, No 5. Centre for French History and Culture of the University of St Andrews, 2012)

5. Edwards, Dorothy, *et al.* (eds), *Early Northampton Wills*; St Faith's Hexton Guidebook (Mrs Ashley Cooper), Hertfordshire.
6. Lepine, David and Orme, Nicholas (eds), *Death and Memory in Medieval Exeter* (Devon and Cornwall Record Society, 2003); Amor, Nicholas R., *Late Medieval Ipswich: Trade and Industry* (Boydell and Brewer, 2011).
7. French, Katherine, *The Good Women of the Parish: Gender and Religion after the Black Death* (Pennsylvania: Penn Press, 2008).
8. Nicolas, Nicholas Harris, *Testamenta Vetusta*.
9. Falvey, Heather (ed.), *Pre-Reformation Wills from Rickmansworth Parish (1409-1539)* (Rickmansworth Historical Society, 2021); Barron, Caroline and Sutton, Anne F. (eds), *Medieval London Widows, 1300-1500* (Hambledon Press, 1994); Barker, Jessica, *Stone Fidelity: Marriage and Emotion in Medieval Tomb Sculpture* (Boydell and Brewer, 2020); Howse, Christopher, Head and Shoulders above a Stone Coverlet, *The Daily Telegraph*, 4 July 2020; Roskell, J. S., Clark, L. and Rawcliffe, C. (eds), *The History of Parliament: the House of Commons 1386-1421*.
10. Staples, Kate Kelsey, *Daughters of London: Inheriting Opportunity in the Late Middle Ages* (Brill, 2011).
11. Glanville, Philippa and Faulds Goldsborough, Jennifer, *Women Silversmiths, 1685-1845: Works from the Collection of the National Museum of Women in the Arts* (Thames & Hudson, 1990).
12. Nankervis, Nan, Zennor Women in Wills 1600-1750 in Lomax, Pam, *Women of West Cornwall 1600-1945* (Penwith Local History Group, 2016).
13. Davies, Clifford Stephen Lloyd, A Woman in the Public Sphere: Dorothy Wadham and the Foundation of Wadham College, *The English Historical Review*, 118 (478) (2003).

14. Harding, Vanessa, *The Dead and the Living in Paris and London, 1500-1670* (Cambridge University Press, 2007).
15. Carroll, William C., *Fat King, Lean Beggar: Representations of Poverty in the Age of Shakespeare* (New York: Cornell University Press, 1996).
16. Freeman, Arthur, *Elizabeth's Misfits* (New York: Garland Publishing, 1978); *Mary Frith or Cutpurse Moll, the Roaring Girl*, East End Women's Museum, London (published online 2016).
17. Bence-Jones, Mark, *The Cavaliers* (Constable, 1976).
18. Akkerman, Nadine, *Invisible Agents: Women and Espionage in Seventeenth-century Britain* (Oxford University Press, 2018).
19. Childs, Jessie, *God's Traitors: Terror and Faith in Elizabethan England* (London: The Bodley Head, 2014).
20. Howse, Christopher, How the Rookwoods Survived Notoriety, *The Daily Telegraph*, 7 January 2017.
21. Fraser, Antonia, *The Gunpowder Plot: Terror and Faith in 1605* (Weidenfeld & Nicolson, 1996).
22. P5/1588/19 with permission from Wiltshire Wills and Ancestry (www.wshc.org.uk).
23. University of Cambridge, *Curious Objects* (Cambridge University Library, 2016).

3 Witches Historic and Modern

1. Leslie, Ellen, Historic Houses – What's Lurking in your Walls?, *Country Life*, 10 January 2012.
2. Swann, June, Shoes Concealed in Buildings, *Costume*, 30 (1996).
3. Walker, Simon, *The Witches of Hertfordshire* (Stroud: Tempus Publishing, 2004).
4. Lipscomb, Suzannah, *Witchcraft* (Ladybird Books, 2018).
5. Brooks, Libby, Campaign for Memorial to Scotland's Tortured and Executed 'Witches', *The Guardian*, 30 October 2019.
6. A Brief History of Boughton (https://chesterwalls.info/boughton.html).

7. Barber, Jill, *Jane Wenham of Walkern, 1712* (https://www.hertsmemories.org.uk/content/herts-history/towns-and-villages/walkern/jane-wenham-of-walkern-1712)
8. Norah, Lofts, *Domestic Life in England* (Weidenfeld & Nicolson, 1976).
9. Munby, Lionel M., *The Common People Are Not Nothing: Conflict in Religion and Politics in Hertfordshire, 1575 to 1780* (Hertfordshire Publications, 1995).
10. McAleavy, Tony, *The Witches of 17th Century Malmesbury* (Athelstan Museum, 2015).

4 *The Extreme Danger of Dying in Childbirth*

1. White, Jerry, *London in the Eighteenth Century: A Great and Monstrous Thing* (The Bodley Head, 2012); Sim, Alison, *The Tudor Housewife* (Sutton Publishing, 1996); Furtado, Peter, *Restoration England* (Shire Publications, 2010).
2. Newton, Diana and Lumby, Jonathan, *The Grosvenors of Eaton: The Dukes of Westminster and their Forebears* (Chester: Jennet Publications, 2002); Wellcome Collection, London MS 632; Hearn, Karen, A Fatal Fertility? Elizabeth and Jacobean Pregnancy Portraits, *Costume*, 34 (2000); Hearn, Karen, *Portraying Pregnancy* (London: Paul Holberton, 2020) – based on a 2020 exhibition at the Foundling Hospital, London: *Portraying Pregnancy: From Holbein to Social Media*.
3. Loades, David, *Chronicles of the Tudor Kings* (Worthing: Bramley Books, 1996); Obituary for Nafis Sadik, *The Times*, 6 September 2022.
4. Victoria and Albert Museum, Renaissance Childbirth (vam.ac.uk)
5. Nash, Michael L., *Royal Wills in Britain from 1509 to 2008* (Palgrave Macmillan, 2017); Stone, J. M., *The History of Mary I, Queen of England* (London: Sands & Co., 1901).
6. Foreman, Amanda, *Georgiana, Duchess of Devonshire* (London: Random House, 2001).

7. Hattersley, Roy, *The Devonshires: The Story of a Family and a Nation* (London: Vintage, 2014); Chapman, Caroline and Dormer, Jane, *Elizabeth & Georgiana: The Duke of Devonshire and His Two Duchesses* (John Murray, 2002); LeFanu, William, (ed.), *Betsy Sheridan's Journal: Letters from Sheridan's Sister* (Oxford University Press, 1986).
8. Bell, Patricia (ed.), *Bedfordshire Wills 1484-1533* (Bedfordshire Historical Record Society, 1997).
9. French, Katherine, The Material Culture of Childbirth in Late Medieval London and its Suburbs, *Journal of Women's History*, 28 (2) (2016).
10. Weir, Alison, *The Six Wives of Henry VIII* (London: Vintage Books, 2007).

5 Fewer Wills and Far Less to Leave

1. Lang, Sheila and McGregor, Margaret, *Tudor Wills Proved in Bristol 1546-1603* (Bristol Record Society, 1993).
2. Allen, Marion E., *Wills of the Archdeaconry of Suffolk 1625-1626* (Boydell Press, 1995).
3. Clay, J. W. (ed.), *North Country Wills: Being Abstracts of wills Relating to the Counties of York, Nottingham, Northumberland, Cumberland, and Westmorland, at Somerset House & Lambeth Palace* (Durham: Surtees Society, 1912); Letters to the Editor, *Country Life*, 9 October 2019.
4. French, Katherine L., *The Good Women of the Parish: Gender and Religion after the Black Death* (University of Pennsylvania Press, 2008).
5. Jones, Jeanne, *Family Life in Shakespeare's England* (Sutton Publishing, 1996); Wyatt, Peter (ed.), *The Uffculme Wills and Inventories: 16th to 18th Centuries* (Devon and Cornwall Record Society, 1997).
6. Higgs, Laquita M., *Godliness and Governance in Tudor Colchester* (University of Michigan Press, 1998).

7. Adams, Beverly (ed.), *Lifestyle and Culture in Hertford... Wills and Inventories 1660-1725* (Hertfordshire Record Society, 1997).
8. Reiber DeWindt, Anne and DeWindt, Edwin Brezette, *Ramsey: The Lives of an English Fenland Town, 1200-1600* (Catholic University of America, 2006).
9. Flood, Susan, *St Albans Wills 1471-1500* (Hertfordshire Record Society, 1993).
10. Nankervis, Nan, *Zennor Women in Wills*.
11. Barker, Harriet, *Family and Business During the Industrial Revolution* (Oxford University Press, 2017); Erickson, Amy Louise, Using Probate Accounts in Evans, Nesta, Arkell, Tom and Goose, Nigel (eds), *When Death Do Us Part: Understanding and Interpreting the Probate Records of Early Modern England* (Local Population Studies, 2000); Munby, Lionel M., *Life and Death in Kings Langley: Wills and Inventories 1498-1659* (Kings Langley Local History and Museums Society, 1981); Cliffe, John Trevor, *The World of the Country House in the Seventeenth Century* (Yale University Press, 1995).
12. Black, Jeremy, *A History of the British Isles* (Palgrave Macmillan, 2012, 3rd edn); Presland, Mary (ed.), *Axelltrees to Winnowsheets: The Wills and Inventories of Forty-eight Women who lived in the Area now within the St Helens Borough Boundary, 1625-1698* (St Helens Association for Research into Local History, 2011); Honigmann, E. A. J. and Brock, Susan (eds), *Playhouse Wills, 1558-1642: An Edition of Wills by Shakespeare and his Contemporaries in the London Theatre* (Manchester University Press, 1993).
13. Hine, Reginald, *Relics of an Un-common Attorney*; Hughes, Clair, *Hats* (Bloomsbury, 2017).
14. Bell, Patricia (ed.), *Bedfordshire Wills*.
15. Orme, Nicholas (ed.), *Cornish Wills 1342-1540* (Devon and Cornwall Record Society, 2007).
16. Nicolas, Nicholas Harris, *Testamenta Vetusta*.

17. Norton, Elizabeth, A*nne of Cleves: Henry VIII's Discarded Bride* (Amberley, 2010); Courtauld, Simon, *Lady of Spain: A Life of Jane Dormer, Duchess of Feria* (Cricklade: Anthony Eyre, 2021).
18. Bennett, Judith and Whittick, Christopher, Philippa Russell and the Wills of London's Late Medieval Singlewomen, *The London Journal*, 32 (3) (2007); Evans, Vivienne, *Dunstable in Transition 1550-1700* (Dunstable: The Book Castle, 1998).
19. James, Susan E., *Women's Voices in Tudor Wills, 1485-1603* (Farnham: Ashgate Publishing, 2015); Spicksley, Judith (ed.), *The Business and Household Accounts of Joyce Jeffreys Spinster of Hereford, 1638-1648* (Oxford University Press, 2012); Spufford, Margaret, *Contrasting Communities: English Villages in the Sixteenth and Seventeenth Centuries* (Cambridge University Press, 1974).
20. George, Edwin and Stella, *Bristol Probate Inventories 1657-1689* (Bristol Record Society, 2005).
21. Record of an English Village 1375-1854 – Earls Colne, Essex. (https://wwwe.lib.cam.ac.uk/earls_colne/intro/index.htm); ERO D/ABR9/210.
22. Dyer, James, *The Stopsley Book* (The Book Castle, 1998); Gordon, Sheila, Slater, Mary and Slater, Michael, *The Giggleswick Wills Project 1390-1702*; Giggleswick Wills and Inventories - Yorkshire Dales Community Archives; Warwickshire County Record Office CR1391/2/2; Starr, Burgis Pratt, *A History of the Starr Family of New England, from the Ancestor, Dr Comfort Starr of Ashford, County of Kent, England, who Emigrated to Boston, Mass, in 1635* (Case, Lockwood and Brainard, 1879); Monger, George P., *Marriage Customs of the World* (ABC-CLIO, 2013)

6 A Green Parrot, Two Grandsons and Sutton Hoo

1. Bell, Patricia (ed.), *Bedfordshire Wills*.
2. Cooper, Tarnya and Eade, Jane, *Elizabeth I and Her People* (National Portrait Gallery, 2013); National Archives, PROB

11/37/342; Medici, Catherine, More Than a Wife and Mother: Jane Dudley, the Woman Who Bequeathed a Parrot and Served Five Queens in Levin, Carole (ed.), *Scholars and Poets Talk About Queens* (Palgrave, 2015).
3. Forster, Margaret E., *Churchill's Grandmama: Frances, Duchess of Marlborough* (The History Press, 2010).
4. Field, Ophelia, *The Favourite: Sarah, Duchess of Marlborough* (London: Hodder and Stoughton, 2002).
5. Sitwell, Edith, *English Women* (Glasgow: W. Collins, 1942), chapter on Sarah Jennings, Duchess of Marlborough.
6. Kishlansky, Mark, Why the Richest Woman in Britain Changed Her Will 26 Times, *London Review of Books*, 24 (22) (2002).
7. Williams, Gareth, *Treasures from Sutton Hoo* (British Museum, reprinted 2019); Gerrish, Oliver, *Edith Pretty of Sutton Hoo: The True Story* (YouTube Video, 28 January 2021).
8. Lapidge, Michael, *et al. The Wiley Blackwell Encyclopedia of Anglo-Saxon England.*
9. Ruffoni, Kirsten, *Viking Age Queens: The Example of Oseberg* (LAP LAMBERT Academic Publishing, 2013).
10. Care Evans, Angela, In Debt to the Amateurs: The Photographs of Miss Lack ARPS and Miss Wagstaff ARPS, *The Newsletter of the Sutton Hoo Society*, 30 (1999).

7 A Castle in Norfolk and Feather Beds

1. Edwards, Dorothy, *et al.* (eds), *Early Northampton Wills*. With permission.
2. Weir, Alison, *Queen Isabella: She-Wolf of France, Queen of England* (Pimlico Books, 2006).
3. Mallialieu, Hugh, This Woman's Work, *Country Life*, 1 May 2019.
4. Hilton, Lisa, *Queens Consort: England's Medieval Queens* (Weidenfeld & Nicolson, 2008).

5. Roskell, J. S., Clark, L. and Rawcliffe, C. (eds), *The History of Parliament: the House of Commons 1386-1421*; Wade Labarge, Margaret, *Medieval Travellers: The Rich and the Restless* (London: Hamish Hamilton, 1982).
6. David Thomas suggested Anne was either mentally incapacitated or a simple, loyal, domestic soul. Thomas, David, *Shakespeare in the Public Records* (London: Her Majesty's Stationery Office, 1985); Woods, Michael, *In Search of Shakespeare* (BBC Books, 2003).
7. Alsford, Stephen (ed.), Last will and testament of a merchant's widow, *Florilegium urbanum* (http://users.trytel.com/~tristan/towns///florilegium/lifecycle/lcdth17.html)
8. Bell, Patricia (ed.), *Bedfordshire Wills*.
9. Hiskey, Christine, *A to Z Through the Archives of Holkham Hall* (Coke Estates, 2012).

8 Jane Austen and the Regency Era

1. Bridge, Mark, Top of the Pox: London's Sin City Past, *The Times*, 6 July 2020.
2. The Gadbury Sisters, *The Secret History of My Family* (BBC 2, 2016); Mary Reibey (Molly Haydock) letter to her aunt Penelope Hope, Sydney, 8 October 1792, Mitchell Library, State Library of New South Wales, Australia; Walsh, G. P., Reibey, Mary (1777-1855), *Australian Dictionary of Biography* (National Centre of Biography, Australian National University, 1967); Thistlethwaite, Rupert, *History of Cadhay Manor and its Occupants – Ottery St Mary, Devon* (Privately published, 2012).
3. Silverman, Laura, The Grand British Mansion Saved by a Deported Cross-dressing Horse Thief, *The Daily Telegraph*, 21 April 2019.
4. Wilson, Margaret, *Almost Another Sister* (Kent Arts and Libraries, 1990).
5. Mallalieu, Huon, Grotesque and Distinguished, *Country Life*, 2 December 2020; Chater, Kathy, *How to Trace your Family*

Tree in England, Ireland, Scotland and Wales (London: Hermes House, 2003).
6. Baker, Kenneth, *George IV, A Life in Caricature* (Thames & Hudson, 2005); Mallalieu, Huon, Queen of Hearts, *Country Life*, 2 August 2017; Scarisbrick, Diana, *Diamond Jewelry: 700 Years of Glory and Glamour* (Thames & Hudson, 2019).
7. Kramer, Ann, *Sussex Women* (Snake River Press, 2007), chapter on Maria Anne Fitzherbert.
8. Plowden, Alison, *Caroline and Charlotte: Regency Scandals 1795-1821* (Sutton Publishing, 2005).

9 Actors and Miss Burdett-Coutts, the Wealthiest Woman in England

1. Parker, Derek, *Nell Gwyn* (Sutton Publishing, 2001).
2. Perry, Sarah, Roach, Joseph and West, Shearer, The First Actresses: Nell Gwyn to Sarah Siddons, *National Portrait Gallery Exhibition Guide* (2011).
3. Hodder, John and Lucas, John, *Hertfordshire: A Portrait in Colour* (Wimborne: Dovecote Press, 1993); TNA: PROB 11/389 Will of Nell Gwyn, dated 9 July 1687. Includes codicil dated 18 October 1687. Proved 7 December 1687.
4. Taylor, Richard, *Secrets of the National Archives*, chapters The King's Mistress and The King's Wife (London: Ebury Press, 2014).
5. Nash, Michael L., *Royal Wills in Britain*.
6. Tomlinson, Sophie, *Women on Stage in Stuart Drama* (Cambridge University Press, 2005).
7. Baron-Wilson, Cornwell Margaret, *Memoirs of Harriot, Duchess of St Albans* (H. Colburn, 1839)
8. Healey, Edna, *Lady Unknown: The Life of Angela Burdett-Coutts* (Bloomsbury, 1978).
9. Anon, Putting Poverty on the Map, *The Oldie,* December 2019; Wallace, Tim, Royal Family found to Live Longer than their Subjects, *The Daily Telegraph*, 27 December 2021.

10. Corbett, Sue (ed.), *The Times Great Women's Lives: A Celebration in Obituaries* (The History Press, 2014); Howse, Christopher, The Abbey Hoodwinked over Heiress's Dead Body, *The Daily Telegraph*, 27 June 2020, reporting an earlier article by Dr Julian Litten in the *Westminster Abbey Review*.

10 *The Tale of Peter Rabbit* and the National Trust; Votes for Women

1. Taylor, Judy, *Beatrix Potter: Artist, Storyteller and Countrywoman* (Frederick Warne, 1986, republished 2011).
2. Mrs Greville's will published in *The Times*, 8 January 1943; Evans, Siân, *Mrs Ronnie: The Society Hostess who Collected Kings* (National Trust Books, 2013); Champ, Gemma, *Jubilee: Anatomy of A Tiara* (Sotheby's, 2022).

11 *Emily Tinne's Wardrobe and Emily Green, a Servant*

1. Howse, Christopher, Tons of Horse Manure and Whale Oil till 11pm: review of *Oxford Street: The Survey of London Vol 53* edited by Andrew Saint, The *Sunday Telegraph*, 24 May 2020.
2. Rushton, Pauline, *Mrs Tinne's Wardrobe: A Liverpool Lady's Clothes 1900–1940* (The Bluecoat Press, 2006).

12 *1,000 Years of Women's Lives and Women's Wills*

1. Atterbury, Paul and Allum, Marc, *Antiques Roadshow: 40 Years of Great Finds* (William Collins, 2017); Zook, Melinda S., *Challenging Orthodoxies: The Social and Cultural Worlds of Early Modern Women* (Routledge, 2014).
2. Wilkinson, Louise J., *Women in Thirteenth-century Lincolnshire* (London: Royal Historical Society, 2015); Alberge, Dalya, Revealed: How Women Bankrolled Rival to 17th Century Globe Theatre, *The Observer*, 11 December

2022. Theatre shares are also mentioned in some wills included in Playhouse Wills, see chapter 5 note 12; Filbee, Marjorie, *A Woman's Place: An Illustrated History of Women at Home from the Roman Villa to the Victorian Town House* (Ebury Press, 1980).
3. Orme, Nicholas (ed.), *Cornish Wills*; Walkley, Christina, *Welcome Sweet Babe: A Book of Christenings* (Peter Owen, 1987).
4. Bell, Patricia (ed.), *Bedfordshire Wills 1531-1539*.
5. Casson, Catherine, Casson, Mark, Lee, John and Phillips, Katie, *Compassionate Capitalism: Business and Community in Medieval England* (Bristol University Press, 2020); Allen, Marion E., *Wills of the Archdeaconry of Suffolk 1625-1626* (Boydell Press, 1995).
6. Matthews, John Hobson (ed.), *Cardiff Records: Volume 3 Wills 1702-1717* (Cardiff, 1901). British History Online: www.british-history.ac.uk/cardiff-records/vol3.
7. Erickson, Amy Louise, *Women and Property: In Early Modern England* (Routledge and Kegan Paul, 1993), Table 12.1; Barraud, Enid Mary, *Barraud, The Story of a Family* (London: The Research Publishing Company, 1967).
8. de Courcy, Anne, *Society's Queen: The Life of Edith, Marchioness of Londonderry* (Phoenix, 1992); Hughes, Emma, The Right Trousers, *Country Life*, 3 March 2021; *Guidebook to the Castle and Garden of Mey* (Nick McCann Associates, 2017); Goodall, John, The Castle of Mey: Inside the Queen Mother's Beloved Home in Scotland, *Country Life*, 3 February 2019.
9. Till death do us part? Divorce in medieval England, *The National Archives Blog*; E 135/7/1 by Claire Kennan.
10. Miles, Rosalind, *Who Cooked the Last Supper?* (Three Rivers Press, 2001); Briggs, Asa, *Victorian Things* (Penguin, 1988).
11. Isba, Anne, *The Excellent Mrs Fry: Unlikely Heroine* (Bloomsbury, 2010); The Rajah Quilt at the National Gallery of Australia (nga.gov.au).

12. Midgley, Clare, *Women Against Slavery: The British Campaigns 1780-1870* (Routledge, 1995); *Free Thinking: Women and Slavery* (BBC Radio 3, 13 January 2021); Huxley, Anthony, *A Vision of Eden: The Life and Work of Marianne North* (Royal Botanic Gardens, 2000).
13. Mallalieu, Huon, Grotesque and Distinguished, *Country Life*, 2 December 2020.
14. Wright, Tim, The Formidable Lady behind the Queen's brooch, *The Daily Telegraph*, 17 June 2021.
15. Obituary of Gladys Eva, *The Times*, 7 May 2021.
16. Connolly, Cressida, *The Rare and the Beautiful – The Lives of the Garmans* (Fourth Estate, 2004).

13 Other Wills: Molly the Bruiser, Chasing Butterflies and Harvard University

1. *St Albans Abbey Guidelines* (7th edn, June 1993), Dorothy Whitelock's translation by Jane Kelsall.
2. Bennett, Judith M. and Mazo Karras, Ruth, *The Oxford Handbook of Women and Gender in Medieval Europe* (Oxford University Press, 2013).
3. P5/1799/27, with permission from Wiltshire Wills Project (wshc.org.uk).
4. Prerogative Court of Canterbury, 1635, PROB 11/168.

Glossary of Terms

1. Presland, Mary (ed.), *Axelltrees to Winnowsheets*.

Appendix 1: The Woman Who Stole Our King! Wallis, Duchess of Windsor and Her Jewels

1. Cartier Brickell, Francesca, *The Cartiers: The Untold Story of the Family Behind the Jewellery Empire* (Ballantine Books, 2019).
2. Munn, Geoffrey C., *Tiaras: A History of Splendour 1800-2000* (ACC Art Books, 2001); Menkes, Suzy, *The Royal Jewels* (Grafton Books, 1986).

3. Nash, Michael L., *Royal Wills in Britain.*
4. Pope Hennessy, James, and Vickers, Hugo (ed.), *The Quest for Queen Mary* (Hodder and Stoughton, 2018); de Courcy, Anne, *Chanel's Riviera: Life, Love and the Struggle for Survival on the Côte d'Azur, 1930-1944* (Weidenfeld & Nicolson, 2019); Zeigler, Philip, *King Edward VIII* (HarperCollins, 1990).
5. Fury, Alexander, A King's Ransom, *Financial Times,* 27 June 2020.
6. Sebba, Anne, *That Woman: The Life of Wallis Simpson, Duchess of Windsor* (Weidenfeld & Nicolson, 2011).
7. Menkes, Suzy, *The Windsor Style* (Grafton Books, 1987).

Appendix 2: Northampton Wills: Women's Voices from the Fifteenth Century

1. Edwards, Dorothy, Forrest, Margaret, Minchinton, Jacqueline, Shaw, Michael, Tyndall, Beryl and Wallis, Patience (eds), *Early Northampton Wills* (Northamptonshire Record Society, 2005). With permission.
2. Orme, Nicholas (ed.), *Cornish Wills.*
3. Thrupp, Sylvia L., *The Merchant Class of Medieval London, 1300-1500* (University of Michigan Press, 1989).

Appendix 3: The Will of Lady Margaret Beaufort

1. Coss, Peter, *The Lady in Medieval England 1000-1500* (Sutton Publishing, 1998).
2. Nicolas, Nicholas Harris, *Testamenta Vetusta.*
3. Gough, Richard and Nichols, John, *A Collection of All the Wills now known to be Extant, of the Kings and Queens of England, Princes and Princesses of Wales, and Every Branch of the Blood Royal, from the Reign of William the Conqueror, to that of Henry the Seventh Exclusive* (London: J. Nichols, 1780); Jones, Michael K. and Underwood, Malcolm G., *The King's Mother: Lady Margaret Beaufort, Countess of Richmond and Derby* (Cambridge University Press, 1992).

BIBLIOGRAPHY

Aitken, Rhona, *The Memsahib's Cookbook: Recipes from the Days of the Raj* (London: Piatkus, 1989).

Allison, Julia, *Midwifery from the Tudors to the Twenty-First Century: History, Politics and Safe Practice in England* (Routledge, 2020).

Allwood, Rosamond, Axell, Vicky, Boyce, Lucienne, Campbell, Jill, Jones, Margaret, Miller, Kate and Ward, Jo (Editors: Bethany Barnett-Sanders and Emma Lenton) *Suffrage Stories: Tales from Knebworth, Stevenage, Hitchin and Letchworth* (Stevenage Museum, 2019).

Andrews, Maggie and Lomas, Janis, *The History of Women in 100 Objects* (Cheltenham: History Press, 2018).

Anstee, Margaret, *Never Learn to Type: A Woman at the United Nations* (Chichester: John Wiley, 2003).

Arman, Joanna, *The Warrior Queen: The Life and Legend of Aethelflaed, Daughter of Alfred the Great* (Amberley, 2017).

Atkinson, Diane, *Rise Up Women! The Remarkable Lives of the Suffragettes* (London: Bloomsbury, 2018).

Austen-Leigh, James Edward, *A Memoir of Jane Austen by her Nephew* (Bentley 1870, republished by The Folio Society, 1989).

Bailey, Brian, *Almshouses* (London: Robert Hale, 1988).

Barron, Caroline, Post-Black Death: A 'Golden Age' for Medieval Women? *History Extra*, 2 February 2016.

Bell, Susan Groag. Medieval Women Book Owners: Arbiters of Lay Piety and Ambassadors of Culture. (1982) in *Signs*, 7, number 4.

Bennett, Judith M. and Mazo Karras, Ruth (eds), *The Oxford Handbook of Women and Gender in Medieval Europe* (Oxford University Press, 2013).

Bennett, Sue, *Five Centuries of Women and Gardens* (London: National Portrait Gallery, 2000)

Birkett, Dea, *Off the Beaten Track: Three Centuries of Women Travellers* (London: National Portrait Gallery Publications, 2004).

Black, Maggie and Le Faye, Deirdre, *The Jane Austen Cookbook* (British Museum, 1995).

Boase, Tessa, *The Housekeeper's Tale: The Women who Really ran the English Country House* (London: Aurum Press, 2014).

Borman, Tracy, *Witches, James I and the English Witch-Hunts* (London: Jonathan Cape, 2013).

Bostridge, Mark, *Florence Nightingale: The Woman and her Legend* (Viking, 2008).

Brand, Emily, *The Georgian Bawdyhouse* (London: Shire Books, 2012).

Broderick, Marian, *Bold, Brilliant and Bad: Irish Women from History*. (Dublin: The O'Brien Press, 2018).

Burman, Barbara and Fennetaux, Ariane, *The Pocket: The Hidden History of Women's Lives 1660-1900* (New Haven: Yale University Press, 2020).

Cartwright-Hignett, Elizabeth, *Lili at Aynhoe: Victorian Life in an English Country House* (London: Barrie & Jenkins, 1989).

Castor, Helen, *She-Wolves: The Women who Ruled England before Elizabeth* (London: Faber and Faber, 2011).

Chandler, Michael and the Duchess of Norfolk, *Historical Women of Norfolk* (Stroud: Amberley Publishing, 2016).

Churchill, Sarah, *A true copy of the last will and testament of Her Grace Sarah, late duchess dowager of Marlborough: with the codicil thereto annexed.* (London: M. Cooper, 1744).

Clark, Alice, *Working Life of Women in the Seventeenth Century* (London: Routledge and Kegan Paul, 1982 first published 1919).

Bibliography

Clark, Nicola, *Gender, Family and Politics: The Howard Women 1485-1558* (Oxford University Press, 2018).

Clayton, Mary, *The Cult of the Virgin Mary in Anglo-Saxon England* (Cambridge University Press, 2010).

Cooper, Kate, *Band of Angels: The Forgotten World of Early Christian Women* (London: Atlantic Books, 2013).

Cooper, Suzanne Fagence, *The Victorian Woman* (V&A Publications, 2001).

Cope, Phil, *Holy Wells: Cornwall* (Brigend: Seren Books, 2010).

Culme, John and Rayner, Nicholas, *The Jewels of the Duchess of Windsor* (New York: Rizzoli International Publications, 1991).

Davies, Jennifer, *The Victorian Kitchen* (London: BBC Books with Guild Publishing, 1989).

Davies, Lucy, Something to Remember Me By, *The Telegraph Magazine*, 1 January 2022.

Davies, Val, *State Beds and Throne Canopies* (London: Archetype Books, 2003).

De Hamel, Christopher, *A History of Illuminated Manuscripts* (London: Phaidon Press, 1986).

de La Haye, Amy, *A Family of Fashion: The Messels, Six Generations of Dress* (London: Philip Wilson, 2005).

Dillinger, Johannes, *The Routledge History of Witchcraft* (Routledge, 2019).

Docray-Miller, Mary, *The Books and the Life of Judith of Flanders* (Abingdon: Routledge, 2015).

Dolan, Brian, *Ladies of the Grand Tour: British Women in Pursuit of Enlightenment and Adventure in Eighteenth-Century Europe* (HarperCollins, 2001).

Duffy, Eamon, Holy Maydens, Holy Wyfes: The Cult of Women Saints in Fifteenth- and Sixteenth-century England, *Studies in Church History*, 27 (1990).

Duncan, Sophie and Lennon, Rachael, *Women and Power: The Struggle for Suffrage* (National Trust, 2018).

Duncan-Jones, Katherine, *Ungentle Shakespeare: Scenes from His Life* (London: Arden Shakespeare, 2001).

Ebrey, Helen, *Myddle: The Life and Times of a Shropshire Farmworker's Daughter in the 1920s* (Ludlow: Merlin Unwin Books, 2016).

Eckstein, Eve and Firkins, June, *Hat Pins* (Shire Books, 1992).

Edwards, Amelia, *A Thousand Miles up the Nile* (Gettysburg: Big Byte Books, 2016). First published in 1877, it was a bestseller.

Evans, Angela Care, *The Sutton Hoo Ship Burial* (London: British Museum, 1986).

Evans, Siân, *Ghosts: Spooky Stories and Eerie Encounters from the National Trust* (Swindon: National Trust, 2006).

Evans, Siân, *Maiden Voyages: Women and the Golden Age of Transatlantic Travel* (London: Two Roads, 2021).

Fiddick, Jane and Hamilton, Caroline, *Our Dollshouses* (Hudson's Media, 2015).

Flanders, Judith, *The Victorian House: Domestic Life from Childbirth to Deathbed* (HarperCollins, 2003).

Fletcher, Anthony, *Growing up in England: The Experience of Childhood 1600-1914* (Yale University Press, 2008).

Fraser, Flora and Berkeley, Maud, *Maud, The Illustrated Diary of a Victorian Woman* (San Francisco: Chronicle Books, 1987).

Freeman, Charles, *Luton and the Hat Industry* (Borough of Luton Museum and Art Gallery, 1976).

Fury, Alexander, A King's Ransom in The Art of Fashion, Issue 12 Jewellery Special, *FT Weekend*, Summer 2020.

Gee, Loveday Lewes, *Women, Art and Patronage from Henry III to Edward III: 1216-1377* (Boydell, 2002)

Gehrer, Julienne (ed.), *Martha Lloyd's Household Book* (Oxford: Bodleian Library, 2021).

Gere, Charlotte; Rodoe, Judy; Tait, Hugh and Wilson, Timothy, *The Art of the Jeweller: Catalogue of the Hull Grundy Gift to the British Museum* (British Museum, 1984).

Goodacre, Julian, *The Scottish Witch-hunt in Context* (Manchester University Press, 2002).

Goodman, Anthony, *Joan, the Fair Maid of Kent* (Woodbridge: Boydell Press, 2007).

Bibliography

Gosling, Lucinda, *Debutantes and the London Season* (Shire Books, 2013).

Green, Charles, *Sutton Hoo: The Excavation of a Royal Ship Burial* (Brecon: Merlin Press, 1963).

Green, Dennis H., *Women Readers in the Middle Ages* (Cambridge University Press, 2007).

Hanawalt, Barbara A., *The Ties that Bound: Peasant Families in Medieval England* (Oxford University Press, 1989).

Hanawalt, Barbara, *The Wealth of Wives: Women, Law and Economy in Late Medieval London* (Oxford University Press, 2007).

Harris, Barbara Jean, *English Aristocratic Women 1450-1550: Marriage and Family, Property and Careers* (Oxford University Press, 2002).

Harris, Barbara, *Sisterhood, Friendship and the Power of English Aristocratic Women, 1450-1550* in Daybell James (ed.), *Women and Politics in Early Modern England* (Ashgate, 2004).

Harris, Carol, *Women at War 1939-1945* (Andover: Pitkin Publishing, 2013).

Harrison, Rosina, *Rose: My Life in Service* (London: Futura, 1977).

Harrower-Grey, Annie, *Scotland's Hidden Harlots and Heroines: Women's Role in Scottish Society from 1690-1969* (Barnsley: Pen and Sword, 2014).

Haste, Cate and Booth, Cherie, *The Goldfish Bowl: Married to the Prime Minister* (Vintage, 2005).

Heyer, Georgette, *The Spanish Bride* (London: William Heinemann, 1940).

Hickman, Katie, *She-Merchants, Buccaneers and Gentlewomen: British Women in India* (Virago, 2019).

Hickman, Peggy, *A Jane Austen Household Book* (Exeter: David and Charles, 1977).

Hill, Bridget, *Women Alone: Spinsters in England, 1660-1850* (Yale University Press, 2001).

Hindley, Geoffrey, *The Anglo-Saxons: The Beginnings of the English Nation* (London: Robinson, 2006).

Hodgson, Barbara, *No Place for a Lady: Tales of Adventurous Women Travelers* (Berkeley, California: Ten Speed Press, 2002).

Holdsworth, Angela, *Out of the Doll's House: The Story of Women in the Twentieth Century* (BBC Books, 1988).

Holland, Tom, *Aethelflaed: England's Forgotten Founder* (London: Ladybird, 2019).

Horwood, Catherine, *Gardening Women: Their Stories from 1600 to the Present* (Virago, 2010).

Houlbrooke, Ralph A., *The English Family 1450-1700* (London: Longman, 1984).

Housego, Molly and Storey, Neil R., *The Women's Suffrage Movement* (Oxford: Shire Publications, 2012).

Howe, Elizabeth, *The First English Actresses: Women and Drama 1660-1700.* (Cambridge University Press, 1992).

Howell, Georgina, *Daughter of the Desert: The Remarkable Life of Gertrude Bell* (London: Macmillan, 2006).

Hughes-Hallett, Penelope (ed.), *The Illustrated Letters of Jane Austen (My Dear Cassandra)* (London: Collins and Brown, 1990).

Humphrey, Carol, *Sampled Lives: Samplers from the Fitzwilliam Museum* (Cambridge: Fitzwilliam Museum, 2017).

Hutton, Ronald, *The Witch: A History of Fear, from Ancient Times to the Present* (Yale University Press, 2017).

Jacobs, Flora Gill, *A History of Doll Houses: Four Centuries of the Domestic World in Miniature* (London: Cassel & Co, 1954)

Jones, Peter Murray and Olsan, Lea T., Performative Rituals for Conception and Childbirth in England, 900-1500, *Bulletin of the History of Medicine*, 89 (2015).

Kelly, Matthew, *The Women who saved the English Countryside* (chapter on Beatrix Potter) (Yale University Press, 2022).

Kolsky, Rachel, *Women's London: A Tour Guide to Great Lives, Guidebook to the Women who Shaped London through the Centuries and the Legacy they Left Behind; Scientists, Suffragettes and Pioneers* (IMM Lifestyle Books, 2018).

Kramer, Ann, *Sussex Women* (Chapter on Marianne North) (Lewes: Snake River Press, 2007).

Lacey, Robert, *The Lady of the Mercians*, chapter in *Great Tales from English History* (London: Little, Brown, 2003).

Larman, Alexander, Wallis and Edward: Inside the Love Affair that Rocked the Royal Family, *The Telegraph Magazine*, 27 June 2020.

Le Faye, Deirdre and Gehrer, Julienne, *Martha Lloyd's Household Book: The Original Manuscript from Jane Austen's Kitchen* (Bodleian Library, 2021).

Le Faye, Deirdre (ed.), *Jane Austen's Letters* (Oxford University Press, 2011).

Legget, Jane, *Local Heroines: A Travel Guidebook to Women's History in Great Britain* (London: Thorsons, 1988).

Leneman, Leah, *The Scottish Suffragettes* (Edinburgh: National Museum of Scotland, 2000).

Lester-Makin, Alexandra, *The Lost Art of the Anglo-Saxon World: The Sacred and the Secular Power of Embroidery* (Oxford: Oxbow Books, 2019).

Lethbridge, Lucy, *Servants: A Downstairs View of Twentieth Century England* (Bloomsbury, 2013).

Levey, Santina M. and Thornton, Peter K., *Of Household Stuff: The 1601 Inventories of Bess of Hardwick* (National Trust, 2001).

Licence, Amy, *Cecily Neville: Mother of Kings* (Amberley, 2014).

Linnane, Fergus, *Madams: Bawds and Brothel-Keepers of London* (History Press, 2005).

Lister, Anne and Whitbread, Helena *The Secret Diaries of Miss Anne Lister* (London: Virago Modern Classics, 2010 Volume 1, 2020 Volume 2).

Livingstone, Natalie, *The Mistresses of Cliveden: Three Centuries of Scandal, Power and Intrigue in an English Stately Home* (London: Hutchinson, 2015).

Lowe, Nicola A., Women's Devotional Bequests of Textiles in the Late Medieval English Parish Church 1350-1550, *Gender & History*, Vol 22, No 2 (August, 2010).

Lummis, Trevor and Marsh, Jan, *The Woman's Domain: Women and the English Country House* (Viking, 1990).

MacMillan, Margaret, *Women of the Raj: The Mothers, Wives and Daughters of the British Empire in India* (London: Thames & Hudson, 1988).

Maids and Mistresses: Celebrating 300 Years of Women and the Yorkshire Country House, 2004. (Yorkshire Country House Partnership (ychp.org.uk))

Martin, Joanna (ed.), *A Governess in the Age of Jane Austen: The Journals and Letters of Agnes Porter* (London: Hambledon Press, 1998).

Marwick, Arthur, *Women at War 1914-1918* (London: Fontana, 1977).

May, Trevor, *The Victorian Domestic Servant* (Shire Publications, 2002).

Mayor, Elizabeth, *A Year with the Ladies of Llangollen* (Penguin, 1986).

McCarthy, Helen, *Women of the World: The Rise of the Female Diplomat* (Bloomsbury, 2014).

McCash, June Hall, *The Cultural Patronage of Medieval Women* (University of Georgia Press, 1995).

McGurk, Patrick and Rosenthal, Jane, The Anglo-Saxon Gospel Books of Judith, Countess of Flanders: Their Text, Make-up and Function, *Anglo-Saxon England*, 24, p251-308 (1995).

McLeod, Kirsty, *Wives of Downing Street* (HarperCollins, 1976).

Mendelson, Sara and Crawford, Patricia, *Women in Early Modern England* (Oxford: Clarendon Press, 1998).

Miles, Lambert, Death and Memory: Clothing Bequests in English Wills 1650-1830 *Costume* 48(1) p46-59 (2014).

Modert, Jo, *Jane Austen's Manuscript Letters in Facsimile* (Southern Illinois University Press, 1990).

Morrell, Jemima, *Miss Jemima's Swiss Journal* (London: Putnam, 1962).

Morris, Christopher (ed.), *The Illustrated Journeys of Celia Fiennes 1685-c1712* (Sutton Publishing, 1995).

Morrison, Susan S., *Women Pilgrims in Late Medieval England* (Routledge, 2000).

Mosley, Diana, *The Duchess of Windsor* (London: Sidgwick & Jackson, 1980) reissued London, 2003.

Moyle, Anwyn and McDonald, John F., *Her Ladyship's Girl: A Maid's Life in London* (London: Simon & Schuster, 2014).

Musson, Jeremy, *Up and Down Stairs: The History of the Country House Servant* (John Murray, 2009).

National Portrait Gallery, *100 Pioneering Women* (National Portrait Gallery, 2018).

Nicholson, Mavis, *What Did you Do in the War Mummy?* (Bridgend: Seren, 2010).

Nixon, Kirsteen, *The World of Florence Nightingale* (Pitkin Publishing, 2011).

North, Marianne, *Recollections of a Happy Life* (Cambridge University Press, 2011).

Norton, Elizabeth, *The Lives of Tudor Women* (London: Head of Zeus, 2016).

O'Brien, Rosemary, *Gertrude Bell: The Arabian Diaries, 1913-1914* (Syracuse University Press, 2000).

Olusoga, David, The Treasury's Tweet Shows Slavery is Still Misunderstood, *The Guardian*, 13 February 2018.

Orton, Diana, *Made of Gold: Biography of Angela Burdett-Coutts* (London: H. Hamilton, 1979).

Oxley, Deborah, *Convict Maids: The Forced Migration of Women to Australia* (Cambridge University Press, 1996).

Page, F. C. G., *Following the Drum: Women in Wellington's Wars* (London: Andre Deutsch, 1986).

Partner, Robert Bell, *The Rajah Quilt* (National Gallery of Australia, 2016).

Pasternak, Anna, *Untitled: The Real Wallis Simpson, Duchess of Windsor* (London: William Collins, 2019).

Paul, Joanne, *The House of Dudley* (London: Michael Joseph, 2022).

Plowden, Alison, *The Case of Eliza Armstrong: A Child of 13 Bought for £5* (BBC Books, 1974)

Plowden, Alison, *Women All on Fire: The Women of the English Civil War* (Sutton Publishing, 1998).

Prichard, Sue, *Quilts 1700-2010: Hidden Histories, Untold Stories* (London: V&A Publications, 2012).

Probert, Rebecca (ed.), *Catherine Exley's Diary: The Life and Times of an Army Wife in the Peninsular War* (Kenilworth: Brandram 2014).

Purnell, Sonia, *Grand Dame of Downing Street* (London: Aurum Press, 2015).

Rae, Janet, *The Quilts of the British Isles* (London: Deirdre McDonald Books, 1996).

Rappaport, Helen, *In Search of Mary Seacole: The Making of a Cultural Icon* (Simon & Schuster, 2022).

Rappaport, Helen, *No Place for Ladies: The Untold Story of Women in the Crimean War* (London: Aurum Press, 2007).

Rose, Lionel, *Massacre of the Innocents: Infanticide in Great Britain 1800-1939* (Routledge, 2017).

Rosenthal, Joel T., *Margaret Paston's Piety* (London: Palgrave Macmillan, 2010).

Rosenthal, Joel, T., Aristocratic Cultural Patronage and Book Bequests, 1350-1500, *Bulletin of John Rylands Library* (1981), Volume 64, Issue 2.

Salih, Sara (ed.), *The Wonderful Adventure of Mrs Seacole in Many Lands* (Penguin Classics, 2005; first published as an autobiography in 1857).

Scott, James, *The Women who Shaped Modern Art in Britain* (London: Unicorn, 2021).

Sebba, Anne, *Samplers: Five Centuries of a Gentle Craft* (London: Weidenfeld & Nicolson, 1979).

Self, Jonathan and Hardy, Joanna, Sozzani, Franca and Judah, Hettie, *Emerald: Twenty-One Centuries of Jewelled Opulence and Power* (Thames & Hudson, 2013).

Shutte, Valerie, Royal Tudor Women as Patrons and Curators, *Early Modern Women* Vol 9 No 1 (2014).

Sim, Alison, *The Tudor Housewife* (Stroud: Sutton Publishing, 1996).

Simon, Linda, *Lost Girls: The Invention of the Flapper* (London: Reaktion Books, 2017).

Sinclair, Joseph, *A Soldier of the Seventy-first: From De la Plata to Waterloo 1806-1815* (London: Frontline Books, 2010).

Skelcher, Mary and Durrant, Chris, *Edith Pretty: From Socialite to Sutton Hoo* (Leiston Press, 2006).

Slack, Sue, *Cambridge Women and The Struggle for The Vote* (Amberley, 2018).

Smith, Kathryn A., *Three Women and Their Books of Hours* (British Library, University of Toronto Press, 2003).

Sneddon, Andrew, *Witchcraft and Magic in Ireland* (Palgrave, 2015).

Spence, Jon, *A Century of Wills from Jane Austen's Family 1705-1806* (Jane Austen Society of Australia, 2001).

Spufford, Margaret, *Contrasting Communities: English Villages in the Sixteenth and Seventeenth Centuries* (Cambridge University Press, 1974).

St Hill Davies, Elizabeth and Dodwell, Fiona, *Hidden from History: Women in Stevenage 188-1988.* (Stevenage Borough Council, 1988).

Stafford, Pauline, *Queen Emma and Queen Edith: Queenship and Women's Power in Eleventh-century England.* (Oxford: Blackwells, 1997).

Stamp, Agnes, Women and the War, *Country Life*, 6 February, 2014 and Aslet Clive, Women and the War, *Country Life*, 29 January, 2014.

Stone, Lawrence, *The Family, Sex and Marriage in England, 1500-1800* (New York: Harper and Row, 1977).

Storey, Neil R. and Housego, Molly, *The Women's Land Army* (Shire Publications, 2012).

Strasdin, Kate, *The Dress Diary of Mrs Anne Sykes: Secrets from a Victorian Woman's Wardrobe* (London: Chatto & Windus, 2023)

Strickland, Agnes and Strickland, Elisabeth, *Lives of the Queens of England from the Norman Conquest* (Philadelphia: Lea and Blanchard, 1844) 3 Volumes.

Stuart, Dorothy M., *The English Abigail* (Macmillan, 1946).

Tallis, Nicola, *Uncrowned Queen: The Fateful Life of Margaret Beaufort, Tudor Matriarch* (London: Michael O'Mara, 2019).

Taylor, Ina, *Victorian Sisters: The Remarkable Macdonald Women and the Great Men they Inspired* (Much Wenlock: Ellingham Press, 2006).

Theophano, Janet, *Eat my Words: Reading Women's Lives through the Cookbooks they Wrote* (Palgrave Macmillan, 2003).

Thomas, Keith, Witchcraft and Society, in Owens, W. R. (ed.), *Seventeenth Century England: A Changing Culture* Vol 2 (Milton Keynes: Open University, 1980).

Tomalin, Claire, *Jane Austen: A Life* (London: Penguin, 2012).

Trollope, Joanna, *Britannia's Daughters: Women of the British Empire* (Pimlico, 1983).

Underhill, Francis, *For Her Good Estate: The Life of Elizabeth de Burgh* (London: Palgrave Macmillan, 2000)

Venning, Annabel, *Following the Drum: The Lives of Army Wives and Daughters Past and Present* (London: Headline Review, 2005).

Waller, Maureen, *The History of the English Marriage: Tales of Love, Money and Adultery* (London: John Murray, 2010).

Warburton, P. Richard and Warburton, Elizabeth, *The Story of Britain's First Female Ambassador: Dame Anne Warburton* (Kindle Direct Publishing: 2018).

Ward, Jennifer, *Women in England in the Middle Ages* (Bloomsbury, 2006).

Ward, Jennifer, *Women of the English Nobility and Gentry, 1066-1500* (Manchester University Press, 1995).

Warner, Kathryn, *Isabella of France: The Rebel Queen* (Amberley, 2017).

Waters, Thomas, *Cursed Britain: A History of Witchcraft and Black Magic in Modern Times* (Yale University Press, 2019).

Waterson, Merlin, *The Servants' Hall: A Domestic History of Erddig* (Routledge, 1980).

Whittell, Giles, *Spitfire Women of World War II* (London: HarperCollins, 2008).

Williams, Gareth, *Treasures from Sutton Hoo* (British Museum, 2011).

Wilson, Deborah, *Women, Marriage and Property in Wealthy Landed Families in Ireland 1750-1850*. (Manchester University Press, 2013).

Windsor, HRH The Duke of, *A King's Story, The Memoirs of HRH the Duke of Windsor* (London: Cassell, 1951).

Windsor, The Duchess of, *The Heart has Its Reasons: The Memoirs of the Duchess of Windsor* (Michael Joseph, 1956), republished by Sphere Publications, 1980.

Winn, James Anderson, *Queen Anne: Patroness of Arts* (Oxford University Press, 2014).

Wood-Legh, Kathleen, *Perpetual Chantries in Britain* (Cambridge University Press, 1965).

Woods, Michael, *The Story of England* (London: Viking, 2010).

Wyld, Helen, *Embroidered Stories: Scottish Samplers* (Edinburgh: NMSE Publishing Ltd, 2018).

Wynn, Stephen and Wynn, Tanya, *Women in the Great War* (Pen and Sword, 2017).

Other Sources

British History Online (british-history.ac.uk).

Country Life.

Desert Island Discs, BBC Radio 4: Rachael Heyhoe-Flint, Dame Margot Fonteyn, Sybil Hathaway Dame of Sark and Rose Harrison.

Great Lives, BBC Radio 4: Jane Austen, Aethelflaed Queen of Mercia, Queen Elizabeth I, Queen Katherine Parr, Enid Blyton, Elizabeth Frink, Gertrude Jekyll, Queen Emma, Mary Kingsley, Octavia Hill, Bess of Hardwick, Dorothy Sayers, Vera Brittain, Dame Rose Heilbron, Jayaben Desai, Millicent Fawcett, Florence Nightingale and Sylvia Pankhurst.

In Our Time, BBC Radio 4: Mary Wollstonecraft, Boudicca, Suffragism, Dorothy Hodgkin, Medieval Pilgrimage, Dorothy Sayers, Mary Queen of Scots, Jane Austen, Christina Rossetti and Caroline Herschel.

National Archives Currency Converter (nationalarchives.gov.uk).

Oxford Dictionary of National Biography.
Saxon charters and wills, The Electronic Sawyer (https://esawyer.lib.cam.ac.uk/).
Unsung Heroines, BBC Radio 4 Extra: Caroline Norton.
You're Dead to Me, BBC Radio 4: Boudicca, Mary Shelley and Eleanor of Aquitaine.

Researching your Own Family History and Family Wills

Barratt, Nick, *Who Do You Think You Are? Encyclopedia of Genealogy: The Definitive Reference Guide to Tracing your Family History* (BBC Books, 2008).
Clarke, Tristram, *Tracing your Scottish Ancestors* (Berlinn Books, 2012).
Ingham, Mary, *Tracing your Service Women Ancestors* (Pen & Sword Books, 2012).
Raymond, Stuart A., *The Wills of our Ancestors: A Guide for Family & Local Historians* (Pen and Sword, 2012).
Reader's Digest, *Explore your Family's Past: Trace your Roots and Create a Family Tree* (Reader's Digest, 2000).
Rowlands, John and Rowlands, Sheila, *Welsh Family History: A Guide to Research* (Genealogical Publishing Company, 2009).
Wagner, Henry, North, Dorothy, *Huguenot Wills and Administrations in England and Ireland, 1617-1849* (Huguenot Society of Great Britain and Ireland, 2007).

The Government's probate website has copies of wills registered after 1858 which can be searched by surname and year of death. It is of course a particular advantage in such searches to have an unusual surname; if your search includes the Smiths, Browns or Greens it is almost impossible. See *Find a will* (probatesearch.service.gov.uk). See also Local Wills, noted below – there are many more county and town collections. In most centuries people of higher rank (who usually had more to leave or property in two or more dioceses) would use the Prerogative Court of Canterbury, the church court, to prove the will. Until 1858 all wills were proved by the church courts. These are held by the National Archives.

Local Wills

Bricket Wood Society, *All My Worldly Goods: An Insight into Family Life from Wills and Inventories 1447-1742* (1991)

Buller, Philip and Buller, Barbara, *Sarratt Wills and Inventories 1435-1832* (Philip and Barbara Buller, 1982)

Emmison, F. G. (ed.), *Essex Wills, Volume 2 1565-1571* (New England Historic Genealogical Society, 1983)

Ford, Judith, *A Study of Wills and Will-making in the Period 1500-1533 with Special Reference to the Copy Wills in the Probate Registers of the Archdeacon of Bedford 1489-1533*, PhD Thesis (Open University, 1992)

Halifax Probate Group (eds.), *'People all full of Business': The Inhabitants of Halifax from Probate Records 1688-1700* (Workers' Educational Association, 2018).

Johnston, J. A., *Probate Inventories of Lincoln Citizens 1661-1714* (Lincoln Record Society, 1991)

Vann, Richard T. Wills and the Family in an English Town: Banbury, 1550-1800, *Journal of Family History*, Winter 1979

Wrightson, Keith, *Ralph Tailor's Summer: A Scrivener, His City and The Plague* (Yale University Press, 2011)

Probate material, wills and inventories for various counties and areas including seventeenth-century Exmoor, see Victoria County History at victoriacountyhistory.ac.uk.

INDEX

Aethelflaed, Queen of the Mercians 24
Aethelgifu 14, 16, 20, 22-3, 25, 196
almshouses 8, 31, 38, 244
Anglo-Saxon wills 9, 14-28 passim, 99
Anglo-Saxon female saints 24, 31-2
Actors, actresses and acting 63, 70, 116-128 passim, 146
Austen, Jane 8, 13, 57, 77, 99, 103-115

Baillie, Lady Olive 165-6
Balliol College, Oxford 10, 215
Beaufort, Lady Margaret 10, 33-4, 74, 248-253
beds 50, 83, 99, 101-2, 118, 120, 246
  featherbeds 71, 94, 99-100, 102, 245
body snatchers 7

Boer War, the 125, 146-7
books (as bequests) 7, 15, 37, 44, 51, 58, 107, 126, 128, 130, 170, 200, 207, 213-14, 216-17, 220
  illuminated manuscripts 33-4, 97, 129, 248, 251
  Gospel Books and prayer books 18-21, 33-4, 251
  Book of Hours 33-4, 249
bride carts 77-9
Burdett-Coutts, Angela 116-128

Catherine, Queen (Catherine of Aragon) 36, 59, 73, 121
Catholicism 10, 30, 37, 41-3, 53, 58-, 72, 82-4, 115, 118, 120, 175, 198, 202, 208, 210, 217, 221, 248, 250
chantry chapels 8, 31, 97, 205, 251
charity, charitable bequests 32, 38, 75, 125, 130, 148-150, 154, 192, 223-4, 219, 239

Index

Charles II 116-17, 119-20, 208
Charlotte, Princess (daughter of George IV, the Prince Regent) 63-4, 77
Charlotte, Queen 108-9, 227
Childbirth – see pregnancy/death in childbirth
childlessness 11, 32, 69, 135, 139, 185, 192, 199, 211-12, 236
Christ's College, Cambridge 10, 248-9
Civil Service, the 134, 162, 194
Civil War, English 14, 41, 48, 73, 156, 168-9, 204
convicts 175, 189
 transported 111, 113-14, 175
Clare College, Cambridge 30, 216
Cok, Christina 98-9
Crimean War, the 125, 149, 170-174
Cutpurse Moll (Mary Frith / Mary Markham) 39-40

Devonshire, William, Duke of 60
Devonshire, Georgiana, Duchess of 59-61
Dervorguilla of Galloway 10, 215
Dissolution of the Monasteries 9-10, 14, 17, 142
dowry 8, 30, 75, 77-8, 95

education 10, 125, 129, 131, 142, 149, 161, 162-3, 181, 227
Elizabeth I 36, 42, 47, 52, 58, 67, 84, 221, 250-251
Elizabeth II 35, 77, 96, 139, 166, 192, 223
Elizabeth, The Queen Mother 45, 138, 163-5, 218, 223, 237, 239
embroidery / samplers 9, 16, 43, 54, 67, 99, 102-3, 107, 167
Emma of Normandy, Queen of England 17
Epstein, Lady Kathleen 194-5
Exley, Catherine 109-10

female virtue and modesty 8, 39, 55, 145, 150, 160, 161, 245
female friendship 60, 83, 87, 134-35
Fiennes, Celia 156, 168-70
First World War 44, 85, 92, 105, 110, 128, 131, 137, 147, 183-5, 213, 216
founding of colleges and bequests to 10, 36-8, 154, 162, 219, 216

Garman Ryan Art Collection Walsall 194
Girton College, Cambridge 134, 161-3

godchildren 35, 72, 154
grandchildren 71, 100, 123, 130, 149, 156, 227
Green, Emily 141, 143, 145-50
Greville, Margaret (Mrs Ronnie) 137-40, 217, 239
Gwyn, Nell 116-18

Harvard University 67, 219-21
Henry VIII 17, 34, 36, 62, 72, 81-2, 99, 116, 121, 154, 221, 247-50
Hull Grundy, Anne 143

infant mortality 52-3 *and see* pregnancy / death in childbirth
Ireland 26, 49, 85, 161-2, 202, 250
Isabella of France, Queen of England 57, 94-8, 166

jewellery, bequests of 15, 26, 31, 33, 57-8, 104, 109, 115, 138-40, 144, 170, 191, 212, 223, 237-8, 242, 244
  mourning jewellery 77, 106
Judith of Flanders, Countess of Northumbria 18-19, 33

Landmark Trust, the 11, 137, 206
Leeds Castle 97, 164, 166

livestock, bequests of 7, 25, 28, 35, 68, 196, 246

Marlborough, Sarah, Duchess of 57, 86, 88
marriage 17, 33-4, 40, 52, 55-7, 59, 61-3, 67-8, 71, 73, 79, 85, 95, 101, 114, 123, 126, 138, 163, 185, 191, 197, 220-21, 230, 250
  arranged / diplomatic marriage 17-18, 94-5, 115
  marriage contracts 30, 95-6
  marriage gift / settlement 20, 24, 75, 78, 88 *and see* dowry
  remarriage 15, 30, 33, 68, 112, 220
Mary I, Queen 36, 52, 58-9, 66, 250
Mary II, Queen 199
Mary, Queen of Scots 57-8, 200, 210
Mass, Catholic 23, 31-2, 43, 72, 75, 215, 251
memento mori 77
Mey, Castle 164
mothers, unmarried, stigma attached to 124-5, 185, 197

National Gallery, the 201, 212
National Trust, the 10-11, 85, 135-9, 203, 210, 218, 226
Nightingale, Florence 54, 125-6, 149, 170-74

Index

North, Marianne 12, 179
Northampton, medieval wills 70, 241-46
Northumberland, Jane, Duchess of 81, 83
nuns 20-21, 24, 27, 29, 32, 42-3, 71, 209, 214, 242, 245, 248

Parliament 43, 58, 96, 132-4, 167, 175-6, 204, 212
   House of Commons 132-4, 173, 199
Peacock, Elizabeth 49-50
piety 17-18, 21-2, 29, 31, 82, 154, 241-2, 248-9
pilgrimage / pilgrims 18, 25, 73, 100
Potter, Beatrix (Beatrix Heelis) 11, 136-7, 202, 215
Pretty, Edith 90, 92
prayers and bequests, for the salvation of the soul 9, 21-2, 25, 27, 30-32, 43, 46, 50, 68, 72, 75, 99, 115, 197, 205
pregnancy / death in childbirth 52-64
pregnancy portraits 55-6
pregnancy wills 57-8, 200
Protestantism 10, 30, 41, 43, 72, 84, 114, 118, 120, 198, 202, 249
purgatory 10, 22, 43

quilts and coverlets 35, 99, 101-3, 107, 175

recipes and recipe books 7, 34, 46, 49, 105, 107, 200
Reformation, the, and Dissolution of the Monasteries 9-10, 14, 17, 20, 24, 43, 53, 167, 206
Reibey, Mary (Molly Haydock) 112-13
Rogers, Katherine (Katherine Harvard) 219
Russell, Philippa 74-6
Ryan, Sally 195

Scotland 47, 49, 57-8, 62, 97, 132, 137, 147-8, 162, 181-2, 192, 198, 201, 204, 208, 215, 227-8
St John's College, Cambridge 248
Seacole, Mary 173-4
Second World War 44, 47, 85, 130, 168, 183, 185, 197, 200, 234
Siddons, Sarah 121
slaves and slavery 14-27, 111, 176-9, 188, 197
   Ladies anti-slavery associations 177-8
   slave markets 23
spinning and weaving 9, 15-16, 20, 48, 70

spinsters 9, 35, 66-7, 78, 120, 135, 155, 188, 218
Suffragettes 181-2, 186-8
Suffragists 181
superstition 46, 51, 53
Sutton Hoo, Anglo-Saxon ship burial 12, 88-93

tapestries 7, 9, 15, 21, 99, 242
Tinne, Emily 141-7, 149
Trigg, Anne 7, 13

university education for women 131, 161-3, 180

Valiente, Doreen 44-5
Vane-Tempest, Frances Anne 85
Victoria and Albert Museum 102, 166, 178
Victoria, Queen 53, 57, 61, 109, 126, 149-50, 157-8, 171, 181, 206-7, 211, 217
virtue 8, 29, 32, 39, 75, 145, 150, 153, 252
Votes for Women campaign 161, 178, 181, 186-7
Representation of the People Act 1928 189

Wadham, Dame Dorothy 36-8
Wadham College, Oxford 36-8
Wales 10, 33, 67, 71, 73, 114, 121, 158, 174, 181, 184, 202, 209, 213, 223, 227, 231-2, 239
Wallace Art Collection 212
Wenham, Jane 48-50
Westminster Abbey 31, 33, 53, 58-9, 81, 127-8, 131, 173, 187, 249-50
widows 9-10, 14-15, 22, 24, 30-44, 48, 62, 65-9, 71, 80, 95, 98, 100-102, 114-15, 134, 152, 154, 156, 164, 173, 179, 184-5, 197, 199, 209, 211, 216, 214, 220, 225, 241, 243, 245-6
 inheritance 68
 thirds 30
Windsor, Duke of 166, 223-7, 239-40
Windsor, Wallis, Duchess of 229-240
witches / witchcraft 44-51
 East Anglia Witch hunt 48
 tax raised for witchcraft trials 48
wives
 husband's permission to write a will 16, 27, 57, 67
 role of, to produce son and heir 55, 58, 73, 94
 appointed by husband as executrix 36, 40, 69-70, 173, 209, 242
Wynflaed 14, 19-22